Sam's
BEST SHOT

James Best lives in Sydney with his wife, Benison, and three sons. His youngest son, Sam, was diagnosed with autism spectrum disorder, aged three, in 2004. James has been a general practitioner for over twenty years, and his medical practice has a special focus on children with disabilities. In the years since Sam's diagnosis, he has become an advocate for people with autism, presenting regularly at seminars and conferences. His articles on autism and parenting have been published in the medical and mainstream press and he has contributed to guidelines for doctors on the management of autism.

Dr James Best

Sam's
BEST SHOT

A father and son's life-changing journey through autism, adolescence and Africa

ALLEN&UNWIN
SYDNEY·MELBOURNE·AUCKLAND·LONDON

First published in 2017

Allen & Unwin
83 Alexander Street
Crows Nest NSW 2065
Australia
Phone: (61 2) 8425 0100
Email: info@allenandunwin.com
Web: www.allenandunwin.com

Cataloguing-in-Publication details are available
from the National Library of Australia
www.trove.nla.gov.au

ISBN 978 1 76011 314 8

Map by MAPgraphics
Set in 11/17.25 pt Centennial Light by Bookhouse, Sydney
Printed and bound in Australia by Griffin Press

10 9 8 7 6 5 4 3 2 1

Dedicated to my son, Samuel Thomas Best

A young man braver than Harry Potter

Contents

Prologue   xi

1   Passengers only beyond this point   1
2   Hell for leather   5
3   Training wheels off   19
4   The Baz Bus   29
5   Tension in the Transkei   39
6   The Mountain Kingdom   52
7   Thinking outside the square   62
8   I don't want to be normal   68
9   Lion country   78
10 Sand safari   89
11 Namboobia   100
12 Easy eights   119
13 Marshmallows and googols   130
14 Zim   140
15 The dementor at the falls   149
16 Jungle Junction   163
17 Two *wazungu*   171
18 Mr Friendly   181

19 Mushroom-Farm style   189
20 The lake of stars   199
21 Ten out of ten   212
22 The Shire   225
23 Zomba   233
24 Bordering on the ridiculous   240
25 Expect the unexpected   252
26 Swings and roundabouts   260
27 Fever!   272
28 The greatest waterfall of the Nile   280
29 Let's get lost   291
30 Playing Quidditch   300
31 Prayers and chickens   310
32 The Africa of dreams   325
33 When September ends   337
34 Rolling with the punches   346
35 Life lessons   359
36 Sam in charge   366
37 Zanzibar   377
38 A boy to a person   386
39 Life skills   391

Epilogue   397
Acknowledgements   401
Resources   403

'If a man can keep alert and imaginative, an error is a possibility, a chance at something new; to him, wandering and wondering are part of the same process, and he is most mistaken, most in error, whenever he quits exploring.'

WILLIAM LEAST-HEAT MOON, *BLUE HIGHWAYS*

'In my experience, the best thing parents and educators can do for a child with autism is to get the child out into the world—with the appropriate supports. Of course that's true of all children, not just those with autism: the children who progress the most, who develop to their fullest potential, are those who are exposed to a variety of experiences.'

BARRY M. PRIZANT, PHD,
UNIQUELY HUMAN: A DIFFERENT WAY OF SEEING AUTISM

'. . . in a society that seems to expect all our children be high achievers it's easy to imagine that a disabled child might be harder to love. Instead I've found the reverse to be true. Watching our little fellow struggle and overcome all the challenges thrown his way has made him so much more precious in our eyes. We despair at his occasional setbacks and triumph at his successes. I will expect you will find the same and come to love your little person more than you could ever have imagined. Good luck on your journey.'

BENISON O'REILLY (SAM'S MOTHER),
THE AUSTRALIAN AUTISM HANDBOOK

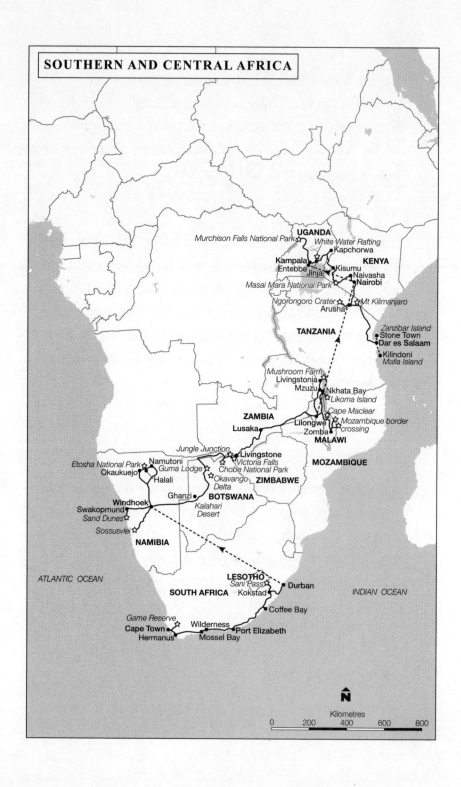

SOUTHERN AND CENTRAL AFRICA

UGANDA
Murchison Falls National Park ☆
White Water Rafting
Kapchorwa
KENYA
Kampala
Entebbe
Jinja
Kisumu
Naivasha
Nairobi
Masai Mara National Park
Ngorongoro Crater ☆
Arusha
☆ Mt Kilimanjaro
TANZANIA
Zanzibar Island
Stone Town
Dar es Salaam
Kilindoni
Mafia Island
Mushroom Farm
Livingstonia
Mzuzu
Nkhata Bay
Likoma Island
Cape Maclear
Mozambique border
crossing
ZAMBIA
Lilongwe
Zomba
Lusaka
MALAWI
Jungle Junction
MOZAMBIQUE
Etosha National Park
Namutoni
Guma Lodge
Livingstone
Victoria Falls
Chobe National Park
Okaukuejo
Halali
Okavango
Delta
ZIMBABWE
Windhoek
Ghanzi
BOTSWANA
Swakopmund
Sand Dunes ☆
Kalahari
Desert
Sossusvlei ☆
NAMIBIA
LESOTHO
Sani Pass
Durban
Game Reserve
SOUTH AFRICA
Kokstad
Coffee Bay
Cape Town
Wilderness
Hermanus
Mossel Bay
Port Elizabeth

ATLANTIC OCEAN

INDIAN OCEAN

N̂

Kilometres
0   200   400   600   800

Prologue

1985

It's the orange vinyl chairs I remember clearly. The rest blurs in my mind, receding into shadows that I want to shine a light on, but also don't.

My family were gathered in a quiet room off the side of the emergency department, my parents having taken a call from the police telling them to come to the hospital straightaway. Something to do with my seventeen-year-old brother, Matthew. Something serious.

A camping accident, a stupid accident.

We huddled, trembling together on the orange chairs, as the social worker quietly told us that he was gone. My mother and father fell against each other. The rest of us, the other five kids, gravitated towards them, a scrum of screaming, crying. There is one noise I can never erase from my memory: the low wounded animal moan that came from my mother.

It rained at the funeral. The whole school was there.

I always believed I should have prevented it, the accident. I should have helped. I had always helped Matthew. We were

Irish twins, born within a year of each other. He was a vulnerable, sensitive boy, and I was not. I was his protector, and I had failed him.

I cannot visit the grave. I never have.

2004

The paediatrician phoned me at my general practice surgery. I was between patients. I knew my wife, Benison, was taking our youngest son, three-year-old Sam, to see him today and was, as always, apprehensive about such visits.

He didn't beat around the bush. 'James, I think Sam is on the autism spectrum.'

My head swam. I felt sick.

'Why don't you come over and I'll have a chat with you and Benison together?' he continued calmly.

I stood up and tried to leave, but dizziness overcame me and I clutched at the doorframe. My colleague Jenny looked up from the adjacent consultation room. 'James, what's wrong?'

I told her and started to weep. 'Oh my God, Jenny, my child has a disability.'

I am still grateful for her perfect response. She sat me down and said, 'James, he is still your Sam. He hasn't changed today; he is still your lovely boy. You just get over there; I'll cover the rest of your patient list. We'll sort everything out at this end.'

In the car, thoughts and questions tumbled into each other like a pile-up on a freeway. I drove past the old brick stack on Corunna Road in Stanmore, its crimson and umber bricks rising like a minaret against the blue sky, its intensity and sharpness mirroring my feelings.

At Dr Rowell's surgery, Sam waded among the scattered toys on the waiting-room floor, lost in his own world. The door to Greg's room was open and I walked in. Benison sat upright, red-eyed, beseeching me to provide some sort of answer, some reassurance, but I had none. Greg showed me to a seat and started to tell us about our new future. Our education in autism had begun.

No one wakes up one morning, turns to their partner and says, 'Hey, let's have another child, one with a disability. That will make our lives more interesting.' Autism is one of those random twists of fate, a mixing of the wrong, or at least different, combination of genes. It's not uncommon though; at least one in every hundred people are on the autism spectrum, ranging from the intelligent but socially awkward geeks who populate high-tech industries to severely disabled people who may never speak and will need support throughout their lives.

Sam, it's transpired, is neither of these: he sits somewhere in the middle, but beyond that description defies categorisation. He is uniquely, unapologetically Sam.

He was our third son, born by caesarean section on 1 February 2001. Right from the word go he appeared 'different' to Benison: distant, and difficult to settle. Not worryingly different, but it was there. At his six-week baby check, she queried his poor eye contact with the paediatrician, concerned about developmental delay. Autism was not on our radar. How that would change over the years.

Between six and twelve months of age, Sam seemed to be okay, even friendly, social. We have photos from that time that show a friendly, smiling, engaged bub. We started making plans for a major home renovation.

Then, around his first birthday, the difference returned, although we didn't immediately notice. It sneaks up you, ambushes you. Photos from his first birthday celebration show him surrounded by his smiling big brothers but his own expression is blank and uncomprehending. He became a tearaway who, if not strapped into his stroller or mesmerised by a Wiggles video, would run and run and run. Toys held no appeal for him, except to scatter across the floor. He learnt a few words only to forget them.

One day, when we were living in our rental house, our own house half-demolished for renovations, I glanced at him in his high chair and the word 'autism' entered my mind for the first time. I shook my head and dismissed it.

After Sam's second birthday, Benison started him in swimming lessons. In a class alongside children the same age, his differences became impossible to ignore. It was more than disobedience: he didn't even seem to understand what the instructor was saying.

Another trip to Dr Greg, the paediatrician. This time Sam was diagnosed with global speech delay. Speech therapy commenced and Sam began attending a playgroup for kids with developmental problems. But it was like a bandaid for a gaping wound: what small progress he made in language was more than counteracted by his increasingly abnormal behaviours as he retreated into his own world.

Another year passed, until that fateful day in February 2004 when Dr Greg changed Sam's diagnosis to autism, and with it our lives.

A few days later we held a belated third birthday party for Sam. The invitations had been delivered weeks earlier and it was too late to cancel. As the children from his day care laughed and bantered, Sam sat in a corner repetitively brushing his face with the paper decorations for an hour—this was 'stimming', an autistic behaviour we would soon learn much about. Not engaging, not communicating, not socialising. Of course it was autism. As a doctor I felt incredibly stupid. I'd let denial cloud my judgement.

For months we struggled, grieving. Grieving for the loss of our parallel son Sam—the one who *didn't* have autism. All the other aspects of our lives didn't go away. There was work for both of us, school and sport for our two older boys, Matthew and Nicholas. We plodded on, trying to keep our heads above water, trying to manage Sam's increasingly challenging behaviours and everything else, trying to deal with this unwelcome stranger in our lives, autism spectrum disorder.

We were learning fast about autism. For Sam, it manifested as deficits in social skills, in communication skills, in coping with the sensory challenges the world throws at us: lights, sounds, touches, smells, tastes. It was screaming at the sound of hair dryers and vacuum cleaners, refusing most foods except bread and milk. It was repetitive behaviours, obsessive behaviours, tantrums, and just being weird, different to other kids. Sam, sitting in the corner, lining up his Thomas the Tank Engine trains.

In our darkest moments we wondered what the future held. Would he have friends? Would he ever have a job, a girlfriend, independence, any quality of life? Most of the autism literature of the time was relentlessly bleak, talking about institutions, profound disability, offering little or no hope. Would this be the life for our Sam? We were lost in a fog.

A few months later, Benison picked herself up and started to read, determined to find out all she could. She immersed herself in all of it: the useful, the relevant, the scientifically valid, and the other junk too. As a medical writer, she knew how to analyse and scrutinise, to question and to doubt.

Intensive early intervention, we discovered, was the answer. Otherwise known as bloody hard work and bucketloads of money. The version of intervention we chose was Applied Behavioural Analysis—at the time, in 2004, this was pretty much the only evidence-based game in town. For thirty hours a week, Sam worked on his social and communication deficits one on one with a therapist. If he sat still for two minutes in a chair, or completed a puzzle, he would be rewarded with a treat, such as a play with Dorothy the Dinosaur or Thomas train, or just a swing around in the air and a whoop. Thirty hours a week, week in, week out.

I was still carrying the guilt for failing my brother, but Sam was not lost forever, only missing, and I began to wonder if I could heal my own wounds by helping my son. For Benison, it became her mission, her passion. We became a team: Team Sam. And our therapists—young university undergrads, male and female—became our friends, our brothers and sisters in arms. Benison quit her job to effectively become the office manager of this new small business, with Sam's social and communication skills our stock in trade. She joked the neighbours would start gossiping about the stream of young men entering our house while I was at work. My medical practice changed: I became a family doctor focused on autism. Both Benison and I wrote books and articles, gave talks and presentations, became supporters of Autism Awareness Australia and lobbied for funding and research.

Sam learnt to sit still and complete puzzles and games, to hold a pencil, to spell simple words and know his days and months of the year. He began talking in short sentences. Our confidence grew hand in hand with Sam's development. In a soul-crushing day for us soon after his autism diagnosis, he'd undergone testing with a psychologist and been assessed as moderately to severely developmentally delayed. Twenty months later he was retested and had made leaps and bounds, his IQ now in the borderline normal range. As we'd always suspected, Sam had intelligence; we'd just had to learn how to reach past the autism and tap into it.

Yet along with this intelligence came a complete lack of street smarts and a fearlessness that was at times life-threatening. Children with autism frequently wander from care and come to grief; drownings, in particular, are frighteningly common. Twice, after only a moment's inattention on our part, Sam had escaped and wandered onto roads. On the second of these occasions, he'd climbed through an open window and followed our cat down the street, to be rescued by a stranger as he wandered across a nearby busy road.

His interest in cats led to another near miss. Benison had been in the kitchen when there was a knock on the door. It was our neighbour two doors down. In the space of five minutes, four-year-old Sam had placed a stepladder against our back fence, climbed up onto the neighbour's roof and then somehow jumped across a four-foot gap onto the adjacent neighbour's roof! No one was game to follow him and to this day we have no idea how he did it. Like the cat he was following, he somehow had nine lives.

As kindergarten approached we had to accept that Sam was still not ready for a mainstream schooling. Yes, he knew his numbers and letters and days of the week, but even in kindergarten you have to sit still and pay attention to the teacher and this was still way beyond Sam. Like so many kids on the spectrum, he was a mixed bag.

Meanwhile, newer approaches to autism that focused on relationship skills and social development had begun to emerge. While a solid evidence base was still developing, the theory and concepts of these approaches fitted in with mainstream ideas on child development, itself very well grounded in evidence.

We pursued one of these programs, Relationship Development Intervention, with Sam for a few years. It was parent-driven, rather than relying on paid therapists. We read, we studied, and we applied our new skills as parents and teachers.

One of the key principles behind these programs is that a core deficit of autism is an inability to cope with uncertainty. Individuals have trouble filtering out all the information that the world throws at them, and so will gravitate towards activities and situations that are predictable: computers, maths, lining up blocks. One plus one always equals two. If you hit the R button on the keyboard it always types R. This security of binary certainty was a warm blanket that kept confusion at bay. Because social interaction with other human beings is so unpredictable, this is what people on the spectrum withdraw from most.

Imagine landing on another planet where everyone else knows the lingo except you. That's what it's like having autism. Of course you're going to reach for safety, to go where you feel competent. Unfortunately, this withdrawal, while comfortable, is a double-edged sword: if you avoid your fellow human beings, you fall further behind in developing the communication and social skills required to negotiate our ever-changing world.

These new theories suggested the remedy was a gradual and controlled exposure to uncertainty and unpredictability. The terminology used in this emerging branch of psychology is 'exposure to a dynamic environment', rather than a static one: to expose your child to graduated doses of uncertainty and, if they coped okay, to reinforce their success by acknowledging it.

This took time. People on the autism spectrum often process information, especially when conveyed as speech, slower than the rest of us. In practice this meant, basically, that you had to slow down, and you had to shut up. The normal one- or two-second delay in response to a question like 'What is your name?' or 'How old are you?' in a small child could take five or ten seconds for someone on the spectrum.

For parents, this meant waiting. Lots of waiting. I remember the first car trip where I put this into action when Sam was aged five. Previously I would have opened the door, helped him up onto the seat and put on his seatbelt. But this day I just waited, standing next to the unlocked car, while Sam looked at the ground and toed lines in the gravel. Thirty seconds passed. Then he noticed we weren't moving and looked up at me. Without talking, I looked at the car door handle and then back at him. A light bulb switched on. He opened the door and climbed up onto the seat himself, even attempting the seatbelt. I've never opened a car door for him since. The importance of this lay not in the fact he learnt to get into the car by himself, but that he turned to me, his father, for guidance in how to learn a skill for himself. Finally, he was learning what humans have known for millennia—that you learn best from other people.

Throughout primary school, Sam's progress was like a game of snakes and ladders: a general upwards trajectory with some slips down along the way. While we tried to remain positive, there was no denying autism was often hard work. With Sam, the normal activities of childhood were all exercises in hyper-vigilance: on holidays, would he have a tantrum on the plane? During a trip to a shopping mall, would he disappear, forcing us to call security? At the beach, would he wander off and drown? When going to children's birthday parties, would he join in the games or hide in a bedroom? Visiting the park, would he push that little girl off the swing? Some days we'd arrive home pleasantly surprised. Other days . . . well, there was always alcohol. While our friends managed their children's or perhaps even their own disappointment at not making the cricket team or missing out on the ballet prize, we reframed our expectations to simply avoiding crises.

His 'stims' also proved resistant to intervention. Self-stimulatory behaviour is a repetitive action that's calming. All of us stim to a certain degree—chewing pencils, doodling, twirling our hair—but for people on the autism spectrum stims are a way of shutting out overwhelming sensory stimuli, as their nervous systems find it hard to filter out sounds, smells and certain lights. Sam especially likes colours and can line up or shuffle coloured pencils or cards for hours. Often he hums along. And unfortunately, unlike hair twirling or nail-biting, Sam's stims aren't subtle and just come across as odd.

Sam went to a private special-education school with small classes and a comfortable, supportive environment, where he thrived academically and the teachers grew fond of his quirky ways. Still, no school is perfect. Sam suffered subtle bullying from the more able kids—even among special-needs kids there is a pecking order—and he became increasingly anxious. After a McDonald's birthday party with his classmates, Benison arrived home distraught: a group of children at the party had deliberately frozen him out. As he wolfed down his burger, one little girl, herself on the autism spectrum, had called him disgusting and was forced by her mother to apologise. Sam, insulated by his lack of social awareness, missed the worst of it but his mother did not.

When he was about ten, his anxiety manifested itself as a strange tic: eye blinking combined with a stuttered 'tic, tic, tic'. We were gutted, fearing Tourette's syndrome. Tourette's can occur with autism but is more often linked to Attention Deficit Hyperactivity Disorder (ADHD), which is another common co-diagnosis with autism and which Sam also has. These connections make intuitive sense, all being neurological conditions, but our boy, with his obsessions and stims, provoked enough backward glances without adding tics to the mix.

Off we went to Dr Greg again, only for him to determine within a few minutes that Sam's apparently involuntary 'tic' was entirely within his control, in other words another stim. I felt equal parts relieved and embarrassed, but that's why doctors should never treat family members: it's impossible to be objective. A few sessions with a speech therapist and the problem was fixed. The anxiety, however, persisted. We started Sam on medication and took him to see a child psychologist to manage the worst of these stresses.

As high school approached, where he should go posed a new dilemma. We visited a special-needs high school only to be told by the principal that Sam was too bright to attend. A 'satellite' autism class in a public high school was an option but places were limited. The fact was there was no ideal place for Sam. With our options narrowing we wondered whether we should try mainstream schooling. Benison wasn't sure but I, being a glass-half-full sort of person, wanted to give it a go, so we enrolled him at De La Salle College, a mainstream Catholic boy's school in the inner Sydney suburb of Ashfield, which boasted a veritable mixing pot of cultures. With his colour-coded books and laminated timetable, scratchy grey woollen trousers and a backpack emblazoned with the school crest, he went off to high school in 2014.

In the first months, Benison felt physically ill with anxiety. How would Sam cope with the frequent bells and period changes, and a different teacher for every subject? He was less street-smart than the average six year old and was now at the mercy of over six hundred teenage boys. Every day she deposited him at the school gates, she said, was like letting go of him on a trapeze. Would he be rescued by other caring hands or fall crashing to the ground?

Most days, there were hands out to catch him. The wonderful learning support team helped Sam to navigate this confusing new environment. Guiding, redirecting, intervening when Sam needed help. Sam was eased into the school day gradually over the course of the first term: initially attending for two periods, then home for lunch, then staying for three periods, and then finally sticking out the whole day. It was exhausting for him and it was exhausting for us.

Unfortunately, the thing about autism is its unpredictability. A brilliant day, where Sam was switched on and engaged and compliant, could be followed the next by a spaced-out Sam, who shut out the world with stims, refusing to even open a schoolbook. He'd lie down on the ground in class and not get up, or simply abscond. On more than one occasion he was found wandering aimlessly in the playground when he should have been in class. In an early science lesson, he became terrified by a lit Bunsen burner and ran screaming from the lab. The 'old-school' teacher was not impressed. How could we explain to him that we'd taught our son—whose fearlessness as a young child had almost been fatal—the danger of fire a little too diligently?

The worst days were those when the school's phone number appeared on my mobile screen, the heart-sink call. Schools, we've found, rarely call with good news. Sam had 'lost it', had a meltdown, was uncontrollable. Could we please come and pick him up? Late one term, he swatted at a learning-support counsellor because she disagreed with him over whether a bear would beat a shark in a fight. These were the weighty topics that occupied Sam's mind. She wasn't hurt and took it in good humour but the school had no choice but to suspend him for a few days.

We naturally worried about bullying, but to our unending joy the boys responded to Sam's oddness and the inevitable class disruptions magnificently. They were patient, understanding and supportive. The teachers explained that the boys in his year had cocooned him. 'No one touches Sam,' they said. We cried when we were told.

There were teachers, too, who went the extra mile. A young maths teacher saw Sam's potential and took him aside for extra tuition. Sam thrived in maths that year.

Still, attempts by the school to get Sam to socialise were hitting a brick wall. At recess and lunchtime, he sat alone with his computer, ignoring the banter and games of handball, alone in his online world. Language, especially social language, had always been a problem for Sam, and as he grew the gap between him and his peers became more evident. He found conversation difficult. Sam could talk at length about the history of Disney films, but if you asked him about his weekend you'd likely be met with uncomprehending silence. While for most of us the best conversations are those that take us to new places, novelty was only confusing for Sam. He preferred predictability, conversations where you knew the answers because you'd had the same discussion over and over again. Would a bear beat a shark in a fight? Who was worse: Lord Voldemort or Hitler?

In class, he needed to be prompted to get his books out, to write notes, to listen. He couldn't buy his lunch at the tuckshop, make a phone call or catch a bus. Anxiety and avoidance were his default settings. Despite all our efforts, we wondered if we were mollycoddling him. Did we need to take away the guardrails, to push him further towards independence?

Sam was now approaching puberty. He was a combustible cocktail of hormones and childlike innocence. There were pimples, there was talk about girls, there was a deepening voice, and then there was more talk about girls. And while Sam matured, the scientific world was becoming increasingly aware of the importance of the teenage years to neurological development.

Adolescence is a time of huge physical changes, not least in the brain. Only in the very first years of life is the reshaping of our neural wiring more profound. It's for this reason adolescence has been described as a second infancy or a second spring. One such transformation in the brain is the formation of the covering, myelin, around the long thin extensions of neurones called axons. When a nerve grows this insulating cover, the electrical transmission down the axons increases in speed by up to one hundred times, making the neurones much more efficient. Myelination, which starts at the bottom and back of the brain and works its way up and forward, starts to reach the frontal cortex—where much of our social skills, our planning and our strategic thinking is based—during adolescence.

Neuronal growth also increases in early puberty, particularly in the number of connections between neurones, followed by a period of 'pruning', where less-used nerves, connections and pathways are cleared away. In *The Primal Teen, New York Times* science and health editor Barbara Strauch described the teenage brain as 'still very much a work in progress, a giant construction project. Millions of connections are being hooked up; millions more are swept away. Neurochemicals wash over the teenage brain, giving it a new paint job, a new look, a new chance at life.'

In mitigating the effects of autism, attention has traditionally been focused on intervening in the earliest childhood years, when the brain is inherently more plastic and able to be remodelled. This, it seemed, was the best opportunity to improve outcomes and scientific evidence largely backs this theory up. But then why not during adolescence as well?

Combining what we knew about autism, and what we knew about adolescence and neurobiology, it just made sense to Benison and me to seize this opportunity. We decided on a prolonged and intense exposure to uncertainty, to unpredictability, to a dynamic environment, in the form of an epic journey during the peak of adolescence, with the objective of expanding Sam's horizons and reducing his disability for the rest of his life.

That was the theory. We had no scientific evidence that it would work. Nobody has performed an intervention of this sort; well, not that we were aware of. Our plan was a punt, a stab in the dark, albeit one underpinned by scientific understanding.

Over time, we formulated what our intervention would actually look like. One of us would need to stop work and apply ourselves full throttle to this, just like in the early days. We both knew I was the logical choice.

We realised that I had already intuitively been taking on the role of Captain Uncertainty throughout his primary school years: taking Sam camping, or anywhere away from screens, away from the security they provided. Spontaneously, we would up and go on day trips here, there and everywhere. He was always on my hip. If I went somewhere that wasn't work, he came too. Exposure, exposure, exposure.

If Benison was the engineer, I was the mechanic, the grease monkey applying the theory in practice. I'd always played the role of the helper, even as a child with my brother Matthew, just eleven months younger than me. I had been his protector and his death had only magnified this impulse, known in psychology circles as a helping drive. Carl Jung wrote of a wounded healer that only a wounded physician could heal effectively. Perhaps that was me? It had been hard-wired, shaping my career as a family doctor. Now I was presented with a chance to direct my helping drive to my own son.

We wondered how long the intervention should be. I thought twelve months, similar to a gap year, but Benison knew we wouldn't last that long, we'd burn out; she's always been the sensible one. Anyway, we wouldn't be able to afford it. Sam's autism and early intervention had left us much less well off than we should have been at this stage of life. However we had been planning to sell the family home and downsize one day, given our older sons were seventeen and twenty years old. We decided to fast-track the plans and use some of the money from the downsizing to help fund the trip.

My work was an obstacle. I was a partner in a medical practice, and a prolonged absence would inevitably have an impact. After involved negotiation with my partners we eventually reached an agreement.

Where would we go? Sam and I had to get away so he couldn't constantly access the internet and it would have to be somewhere

where he would have to deal with novelty, unfamiliarity. Camping around Australia? The usual backpacker jaunt around Europe? No, if we were going to do this, we needed to do it properly. The developing world, we decided, would be better, but nothing too unsafe. In South America, language was a barrier, as it was in East Asia. India was a possibility, but . . . how about southern and eastern Africa? The classic overland route from Cape Town to Nairobi usually took around six to nine months. That Sam had a minor obsession with African animals, complaining bitterly that Australian native animals were boring in comparison, was the clincher. So, the decision was made: Africa, for a minimum of six months, and then we'd see how we go. The objective was twofold: to expose Sam to uncertainty and a dynamic environment, inherent in backpacking in the developing world, and to also use the time to work actively on his neuroplasticity by undertaking activities that required him to use multiple parts of the brain at once.

As disciples of science, Benison and I of course wanted to measure it. Soon we were speaking to leading autism researcher David Trembath at Griffith University in Brisbane. David's special interest is in novel approaches to autism, and particularly N=1 studies, where there is only one individual being studied. While studies of this type give limited information, their flexibility allows greater potential for new concepts to be explored. Sam was to become a pilot study, if you like.

David designed a study which required me to record videos of Sam on the road, which David's team would randomise and then study to see if a significant improvement could be measured over the trip.

We sold the house and set the ball in motion.

As word got out, it seemed everyone became interested. Reactions ranged from jealousy to 'What about lions/Ebola/crime/disease?' People started telling us it should be a blog, a book, a documentary. In time, it became all three. A patient of mine set up a blog for us. A book contract was signed with a publisher. Another patient told a documentary film company she'd previously worked with about our plans and the next thing we knew Benison, Sam and I were being filmed at length. On camera, the interviewers asked us some confronting questions.

'How do you know it will work?'

'How will you feel if it doesn't work?'

'How will this affect your relationship?'

Some of these questions we hadn't even asked ourselves. There was only one way we were going to find out.

CHAPTER 1

Passengers only beyond this point

Seven months, nine countries. Roughly a month in each, backpacking through South Africa, Namibia, Botswana, Malawi, Mozambique, Tanzania and Kenya, with quick transits to Lesotho and Zambia, and possibly Uganda. That was about as detailed as the plan got. Our trip was meant to be unpredictable, uncertain. I had booked one-way flights and accommodation for the first three nights in Cape Town, but after that it was up in the air.

Soon I started to doubt myself. I was planning to take my disabled teenager backpacking around Africa when I could barely look after myself travelling!

As departure day loomed I was also becoming increasingly stressed about the potential dangers involved in what we were doing. Could it end up being useless, or harmful, or even disastrous? I suspected Benison was worried too. Was I being too optimistic and glossing over real risks? Would I be putting Sam in harm's way? Was I doing this more for the kudos, more for myself, at the expense of my son? Was I simply kidding myself?

As part of planning for emergencies, Sam and I began practising making phone calls and role-playing how to find and approach appropriate people for help. I drafted an emergency letter for Sam to carry everywhere, which contained contact details in Australia as well as the Australian embassies and consulates in the countries we planned to visit.

We got Sam to practise finding the letter and presenting it to an imaginary passer-by. It read:

EMERGENCY LETTER—PLEASE HELP!

To whoever is receiving this letter,

The boy who is in possession of this letter is a fourteen-year-old Australian tourist by the name of **Samuel Best**. He has an **autism spectrum disorder**, which means he has difficulties with social skills and communication. He is meant to be travelling with his father, Dr James Best.

He has been instructed that if he is separated from his father for whatever reason, or his father should become incapacitated in any way, he should give this letter to a person who seems responsible or is in a position of power (eg. policeman, manager of hotel). Please, please assist him in any way you see fit—he will not be able to manage on his own. Any finances incurred by helping him will be reimbursed, and a healthy reward will be given for any assistance.

Watching Sam struggle to read the letter and effectively get the message across, I fretted further. I thought of a confused African on the receiving end of Sam's disjointed and at times mumbled delivery, struggling with his accent, perhaps not having the literacy or English skills to read the letter themself. While the letter was a good idea, it was anything but foolproof.

I had been thinking ahead with trepidation to the point where our long separation from the family would begin. In my mind's eye, it would be on a walkway at the airport underneath a sign that read ONLY PASSENGERS BEYOND THIS POINT. Sure enough, that was exactly how it transpired. We stood as a family unit in a tight circle.

I had an intense, tearful hug with Benison. 'You take care. I am so grateful to you for letting us do this,' I said. 'I love you so much.'

Tears were coming down her cheeks. 'Just stay safe,' Benison said. She hugged Sam with a bear-like grip and seemed reluctant to let him go. Eventually she did, rubbing his shoulders and patting his hair. 'I love you, my baby boy. You be good.'

'Yeah.' Sam was smiling but I could see his tension in the way he was shifting his weight from leg to leg, wringing his hands and scanning the terminal.

I hugged Matthew and Nicholas. Sam followed suit, on my prompt. 'Use arms, Sammy,' I instructed. He duly turned his usual lean-in-with-a-shoulder embrace into a more conventional hug for his two older brothers.

It was time for Sam and me to go. The two of us walked through the departures gate. The big adventure, the big experiment, the big gamble, had started.

Standing in the queue for customs, Sam began the first of several thousand attempts to terminate or shorten the trip. 'What do I say to not be allowed to go?' Sam asked.

'Don't you dare! This is not the place, Sam. These people are like police. You can get in big trouble,' I implored. He behaved himself at the counter. *Phew.*

Sam had flown before so he wasn't fazed by the flight ahead, but I could sense he was agitated. He continued to lobby hard to bring the return date forward. I continued to divert him with a 'We'll see,' which seemed to placate him better than a simple 'No' or ignoring him or changing the subject.

As his eyes flitted around the terminal and he paced around our seats in the gate waiting area, I wondered to myself what was going through his head. It had begun, we both knew it. I was scared. I wondered if he was terrified.

CHAPTER 2

Hell for leather

The flight to Cape Town was via Singapore and Johannesburg, taking twenty-two hours in total. Sam didn't like the fact that we stopped over in Singapore because he had read about its strict laws and was worried about being arrested. I assured him that this wasn't a concern in Changi airport. Sam and I both managed to grab six much-appreciated hours of sleep on the second leg, but we were feeling pretty ragged when we finally landed in Cape Town.

Flying with us was a cinematographer from the independent documentary company Heiress Films, who were filming our trip. The company specialises in human interest documentaries, often about health issues, and had been drawn to the novelty of what we were attempting. We had agreed to a participate because we felt the message of our journey was important. We did worry about the potential intrusiveness of the filming process, but weren't really sure what it was going to mean on a practical level.

Sam and I had met the cinematographer, Max, briefly a few days earlier when the filmmakers had filmed us packing and discussing the upcoming trip. He was in his early forties, a good-looking fellow with a sharp mind. Sam said he looked like Matthew Lewis, the actor who plays Neville Longbottom in the Harry Potter films. In the world according to Sam, everyone has to look like someone from the Harry Potter films, which were his latest and most intense obsession. Sam also dubbed him Fax. (Sam gives everyone he gets to know a nickname, usually based on rhyme or slight distortion of their actual name. Mine is Germs.)

Max would be travelling with us and filming us for the first ten days of our trip; documentary filmmaking is so prodigiously expensive that that's all Heiress Films could fund. He was very understanding with Sam. On the flight, Max asked lots of questions about how Sam thought and behaved, and also about the trip and its design and purpose. I'd grow to really appreciate his company, but I already knew from the brief taste of it at home that documentary filming is very intrusive. Set-ups, retakes, waiting, me being interviewed on camera, Sam being interviewed on camera, asking permission from people in shot and at film locations; it would all make for more work every day. We'd be living in a fishbowl.

Also, Max would be cramming as much activity as possible into the time he was with us. This had positives and negatives. It was great to have what amounted to a tour guide for the first part of our trip. And thanks to the film company there were some activities planned that we otherwise wouldn't have been able to afford. Finally, I hadn't backpacked in twenty-five years and wasn't up to speed with the modern travelling challenges of smart phones, internet access, travel websites and social media on the road since then, so it was very handy for an old bugger like me to have a savvy and experienced travel advisor on tap.

But the downside of fitting so much activity into the first week was that it would be exhausting for both Sam and me. We were already setting ourselves a very big challenge on a range of levels, and now from day one we were going to be going hell for leather. Sure enough, this would soon prove a problem.

At Cape Town airport, we were met by Liza, a local who had previously been involved with documentary making. Heiress Films had hired her to be our fixer—a film industry term for a local person employed to make things happen, using their local knowledge, when filming away from home, but which disconcertingly reminded me of The Cleaner in Quentin Tarantino's film *Reservoir Dogs*. Fortunately, Liza was nothing like Harvey Keitel's character, with her long hair loose around a kind face. She shepherded us to the airport Vodacom store and navigated us through the tedious process of organising local SIM cards, and data and prepaid data access for our phones and computers while Sam wrung his hands as he paced around the airport terminal. He has a distinctive 'bouncy' gait, a legacy of autism, whereby he springs and shifts on the balls of his feet, like a boxer in a prize fight. My anxiety in dealing with unfamiliar technology in a sleep-deprived and jetlagged fog, all the while keeping an eye on Sam, was palpable. On to the car-rental shop across the terminal: more paperwork, more stress, more filming. I had bribed Sam with about five chocolates by this point, so now the bouncing boy also had a chocolate-covered face and hands.

Our first drive in Africa was surprisingly easy. A motorway took us straight into the central business district of Cape Town. Traffic was light. Then Sam saw them: an entirely new set of road signs! And, wait for it: they were written in a different font than in Australia! No way!

Road signs had long been one of Sam's obsessions, since he was tiny. A prized fourth birthday present from some of his favourite therapists was a replica stop sign (which was also my personal favourite).

Sam had had myriad obsessions over the years. When he was in primary school it had been The Wiggles, Thomas the Tank Engine, Super Mario Bros and Windows operating systems. The last had been particularly challenging. He'd scoot past us into random offices to turn on their computers, or duck behind the counter in a supermarket and ask the confused shop assistant, 'Is that Window XP?'

For a while Sam had been fixated on the number five. At cafes, we'd have to wait for the number five table to become available, or Sam would swipe the number off the occupied table. One freezing winter day in Melbourne, Benison queued for an extra half-hour at a Ferris wheel at Luna Park because Sam refused to get in any other car than that marked five.

His obsessions and interests have become more sophisticated over the years, but he retains an affection for 'rare' signs, so it wasn't surprising that, faced with this anxiety-creating new environment, he latched on to this old favourite. He wiggled in his seat and flapped his hands. 'They have a one hundred and twenty on the motorway!'

We arrived at the hostel I had booked, and crashed—literally in Sam's case—into the room, flinging backpacks onto beds. The hostel was relaxed and well run; a warren of hallways and arches around a central courtyard where backpackers chilled on phones or iPads, drank beers around the pool table and swapped stories about travelling.

The challenge now was to stay awake throughout the afternoon and evening to get our discombobulated diurnal rhythms back into some sort of sync. I let Sam chill in the room, using the wi-fi to satiate his internet withdrawal syndrome. Google searches of Super Mario Bros and Emma Watson probably weren't typical of previous backpackers, but then this was Sam. Meanwhile, I sorted out our packs. The shampoo bottle had lost its lid in transit and leaked everywhere, which led to a few hours of cleaning and a fragrant backpack.

We were to get to know the staff quite well over the next few days. I found here—as I would subsequently discover everywhere we went—that people were fascinated by us and what we were doing. This wasn't something I'd expected.

I went for a stroll around the district to orientate myself. As soon as you walk out the door, you immediately look up as Cape Town's majestic Table Mountain towers above. The flat ridge at the top gives the mountain its name and cool moist air from two oceans—the Indian Ocean to the east and the South Atlantic to the west—sweeps up and condenses at the summit, leading to constantly swirling mist, its tablecloth.

Next to Table Mountain, facing out towards the South Atlantic Ocean, is another giant rocky outcrop, Lion's Head. Locals and tourists make the steep climb up the rock face to watch the sun set over the well-heeled coastal suburbs of the city. Five hundred years earlier, European sailors had traded with the local Khoisan herdsman for food on the slopes of Table Mountain and Lion's Head, as they replenished their ships in preparation for the ongoing journey to India and the Spice Islands.

The city itself, with bustling shopping strips, restaurants, cafes and pubs, was abuzz with chatter, traffic and music. The CBD and nearby Gardens district were sprinkled with open public spaces where children played near fountains and couples lay on the grass. Verandahs hovered over footpaths, and outdoor dining areas were full with people of all ethnicities. Cape Town appears smaller than it is as many of the sprawling suburbs, including the black townships, are hidden behind Table Mountain. The streets sweep up towards the mountains in all directions. I was reminded of San Francisco: acclivity, hum and multiculturalism.

As a newcomer to Africa, it was confronting to see the ubiquity of security. Razor wire, electric fences and security guards were everywhere. On the street corners, street dwellers hovered and occasionally approached looking for baksheesh. They were countered by men in fluoro jackets who shooed them away if the harassment became too intrusive. I was to learn from The Fixer that the men in jackets aren't official security guards but rather people who claim a small section of streetfront and survive on tips they receive from the people they protect in their patch. It was a delicately balanced ecosystem, with two species of predator and us as the game.

Late in the afternoon, Liza drove us over the ridge to Camps Bay and its wide white beaches. Her car—much loved, I'm sure, but past its prime—barely held the four of us and Max's large camera, and she flogged the clutch as we climbed over the ridge hoisted between Table Mountain and Lion's Head before hurtling around the curving road leading down the other side. Liza drives without fear for herself, her car or its contents.

Camps Bay sits under a line of towering cliffs that sweep south down towards the Cape of Good Hope. The sun was getting low, leading to what Max referred to as the magic hour for filming. As the sun approached the horizon, the arc of the waves flashed turquoise before they crashed forwards. Max filmed Sam and I talking and mucking around on the beach. Eventually the great orb touched the visible edge of the earth, distorted in its descent, and disappeared, heading for South America, leaving a cloudless sky.

'Sam, what do you want for dinner?' I asked.

'Pizza,' he snapped.

'How about fish and chips? Or perhaps pasta?' I suggested.

Sam shook his head. 'No. Pizza.'

'Can we try something different?'

'No.'

Pizza it was. Max knew an expat Aussie living locally so he'd asked her to join us for dinner. Jocelyn was a clinical psychologist who had married a Cape Town IT specialist, emigrated and had a couple of kids. She specialised in dealing with children and teenagers and their exposure to technology so the two of us clearly had a lot to talk about. She was also naturally interested in what we were doing and tried hard to connect with Sam.

Her children were younger than Sam, and wary of him as he fidgeted and bounced around in his chair, making odd noises to himself. Social situations where other children meet Sam and try to figure him out are always confronting. It would always underline his deficits to me. I felt a pang. Not at all their fault, but still the pain was there.

The next day Max and The Fixer wanted to start early. In the courtyard of the hostel, Max decided we could use a helping hand to carry his gear. He turned to a young bearded backpacker sitting behind him. 'You wouldn't be interested in coming up to Table Mountain with us today, would you? We're looking for someone to carry our camera gear. We'll pay you.'

The twenty-something young lad replied in a thick Scottish accent. 'Oh, why not? Yeah, sure.'

'Great, it's a deal,' Max said. 'We're gonna leave in about ten minutes.'

The young Scot shook Max's hand. 'I'm Rory, by the way.' I had never seen anyone employed by someone who didn't know their name, but this was to be a trip of firsts. We quickly found Rory to be a very clever and introspective fellow from Inverness. We unanimously decided to nickname him Sherpa.

Sam was confused. 'What's a sherpa?'

'Sherpas are people who live in the Himalayas and are good at climbing and carrying stuff up mountains.'

'Rory's a sherpa!' Sam exclaimed excitedly.

The Fixer arrived at the hostel and beckoned us out to the car. 'We should go now now.' We'd already discovered that in South Africa 'now' meant some time in the vaguely foreseeable future and 'now now' meant right then and there. We loaded the gear into the rental car and drove to the cable car station up on the ridge.

Sam is good with this sort of thing. He has been taught to deal with unusual travel experiences for most of his life. It's part of our parenting philosophy: dish up difference to him constantly and he will cope better and be more adaptive. Over the years, Benison and I have always kept him doing 'stuff', anything and everything different, but at the same time trying not to stress him too much. Make the jelly wobble on the plate, but not fall off.

So getting in a cable car heading up a very steep track was well within Sam's capability. Max, Sherpa, Sam and I ascended into the swirling mists of the tablecloth. At the top was a bustling collection of restaurants and tourist shops fronting the entrance to walkways around the top of the mountain. Waist-high fynbos shrubs covered the sandstone mountain top like afro hair. The mist swirled around us but right at the edge of the plateau it magically evaporated, allowing sweeping views across Cape Town to the Atlantic, with Robben Island sitting off the coast. Along the ridgeline, mist fell over the precipice like melting ice cream before disappearing.

A cold breeze ruffled our jackets. The cooler weather was ideal as today was to be our first crack at boxing. This was one of our pre-planned neuroplasticity exercises. Benison and I had selected a series of activities designed to increase the range of parts of the brain working in unison. Activities that involve multiple parts of the brain firing together increase the amount of traffic through the middle part of the brain that connects the left and right hemispheres. This neurological superhighway, the *corpus callosum*, is densely packed with neurones lying in parallel. Its name is Latin for hard body, because that's what the crowded structure feels like in the brain of a cadaver.

Corpus callosum traffic is reduced in autism. In a neurological sense, autism is thought to be not so much a lack of neurones as a lack of connectivity of the different parts of the brain. We theorised that if we exposed Sam to not only uncertainty and unpredictability but also to activities that required the use of multiple parts of the brain at once, it could lead to better brain connections and better outcomes. The activities we chose were boxing, chess, drawing, music, strategic card games and prolonged reciprocal conversations.

The boxing lesson went well enough. I had taken some boxing fitness classes at a local gym so I was familiar with the basics of positioning the hands and feet, and what a jab, cross, hook and uppercut were. The paediatric physiotherapist Sam had seen for motor delay issues in early childhood advised me that, from a neurological point of view, it would be better to get him to use his legs as well, to involve all four quadrants of the body, the left and right and the upper and lower body. So I threw some kicks in as well. It probably looked a bit odd, doing kickboxing amid tourists atop Table Mountain with a film crew recording our every action, but what the heck.

Soon The Fixer rejoined us and we cruised down the peninsula towards the Cape of Good Hope. The road there clings precariously to cliffs that plunge to the sea. In places the road has been cut *into* the cliffs. There was cliff wall to port, cliff plunge to starboard. Footage of this road featured in the Academy Award–winning documentary *Searching for Sugar Man*, and I remember watching the film and wondering where this amazing road was. Well, now we were on it, with me in the driver's seat.

Sam and I chatted, mostly about Harry Potter, and his crush, Hermione Granger, while Max sat in the boot of The Fixer's car with the back hatch open, filming our car as we drove along behind. I was worried I would run him over if he fell out.

Back at the hostel, Sam was having conversations with all the new people he was meeting. He was being pushed hard, and it was exhausting him. I knew it was good for him, but I also worried it might be too much. He was getting stroppy with me and flatly refusing to co-operate at times, especially in the evening, which was unusual. I wasn't giving him his usual Clonidine—a sedating medication prescribed by his paediatrician to regulate his sleep pattern, an approach commonly taken in autism—because I had realised he didn't need it. He was falling asleep early on his own, dog-tired from being pushed in areas that he found challenging, particularly dealing with people.

The next day we went on a safari. We'd all been looking forward to it. I had planned that Sam and I would go on a safari or two later in the trip, but Heiress Films wanted to get some footage as well so they'd offered to pay for this safari and I'd agreed. Now I wasn't sure how it'd go, with Sam so tired.

The three-hour drive north took us past vineyards and through rugged mountain terrain as we ascended up and onto the flatter Karoo district. The Karoo veld was carpeted with soft grasses and buttoned with koppies—small hillocks on the flats—where the hinge lines of the folded rock revealed both the age and the tortuous history of the landscape.

The occupants of the land revealed another tortuous history: white-owned grand farm estates contrasted with tin and trash townships. Sam noted the racial divide. 'Black people are poor in Africa,' he said.

Max and I tried to explain the history of apartheid and Nelson Mandela. Sam gave one of those thoughtful looks he does, looking to the side, and I wondered how much of what we had said had sunk in. Then he said, 'There are a lot of Africans in Africa.'

Well, there was no denying that.

Some poor townships were located near wineries, and locals holding what I we presumed to be stolen boxes of grapes would try to flag down cars to sell to them. How they got the grapes I don't know, because the vineyards in these areas were protected like Fort Knox, with huge electric fences, guards and razor wire everywhere. There were even road signs explicitly forbidding the sale of grapes on the roadside. Every now and then a truck or minivan would pull over and they would score a sale. There was tension in their manner and I wondered where my sympathies should lie: with people driven to desperate acts by poverty or with the farmers trying to protect their crops.

We arrived at the game reserve to witness the other end of the financial spectrum. It was a beautiful stone hotel full of rich and occasionally obnoxious Europeans and Americans. Children bombed into the pool, a fat German complained about his lunch, and Sam was freaked out by the peacock wandering between tables on the verandah. He'd been frightened of peacocks since one fanned his tail at him in an Australian wildlife park when he was little.

The documentary film company had organised a private truck for our safari. As our driver took us around the park we immediately started seeing buffaloes, hippos, rhinos, springboks, elands and, Sam's favourites, elephants and lions. Private game reserves occupy a grey ethical zone for me. They are by nature artificial, and the animals aren't really in their natural environment, particularly the more social animals. On the positive side they promote animal welfare and species protection. Kind of like a big zoo, but just for the wealthy.

The animals were amazing, but I was frustrated with Sam, who for the first half of the tour didn't seem to be paying much attention or even enjoying the experience. His interest in African animals was one of the principal reasons we had selected Africa as our destination. I could tell Max had noticed I was cranky. My fuse was short after the hectic last few days.

'Sam, pay attention will you!' I fumed. 'You're not even looking!'

Sam flapped his hands and licked his lips. Max watched thoughtfully.

Finally, as the truck entered the heavily fenced-off lion area, Sam, to my great relief, started to focus on the animals.

'What are the lions doing?'

'I can see lions!'

He laughed with delight, craning to see as the lions strolled up the road towards our now stationary vehicle. Our truck was soon surrounded by seven lions, some within two metres of us. We were quite elevated and they were probably very used to trucks, and hopefully well fed. Still, where the heck was the gun? Sam remained focused during a close encounter with two elephants soon afterwards. It turned into an amazing experience.

The three-hour drive home got us back to the hostel after dark. Sam was becoming very oppositional. I asked him to get off his Nintendo DS after dinner and he lost it. I threatened him with its confiscation and the situation spiralled. His behaviour worsened and my threatened consequences escalated. I was tired, and handled the situation poorly.

Shouting became screaming, grabbing became pushing, and finally he became violent. After Sam delivered a fairly effective klonk to my head with his DS I just had to get out of there. I went for a walk. We both had to calm down. My t-shirt was a bit torn, as was my soul. Second thoughts and self-doubt crept in, and then guilt. So much had been put on the line with this trip, and all I was doing was stressing my son out.

I was angry at myself. I should have known better than to escalate a situation with threats I knew I couldn't follow through on. Why was I pushing Sam so hard? What was the bloody point anyway? Was I really up to this? We were in Cape Town, for goodness sake. How was I going to cope when I was in the backblocks of Malawi and one of us got sick, or lost, or we were robbed?

When I got back to the room, Sam was looking sheepish as he sat on the bed. 'Hmm. I'm sorry, Dad.'

I sat across from him on the other bed and gently squeezed his knee. 'That's okay, mate. I shouldn't have yelled at you.'

He hung his head low. 'I'm sorry for hitting your head.'

'That's okay. You go to sleep,' I said.

Tomorrow was another day.

The next morning I arranged for Sam to have a conversation with the hostel manager. This was one of the types of interaction we were meant to film for the Griffith University study. Each week I was to make four short films of Sam: one of him checking out of accommodation, ordering a meal at a restaurant, giving a debrief of the trip to me, and having a general chat with a stranger.

His first video for the university study contained a gem. For the first time ever, I think, Sam made small talk. The hostel manager was trying to have a conversation with him about our stay and our plans. When there was a lull, Sam turned to her casually and asked, 'So, have you ever been to Australia?' What may have seemed insignificant to others was pure gold to me.

Hey, maybe this stuff was working? It lifted my spirits after the previous night's dramas.

CHAPTER 3

Training wheels off

The hectic days full of activities had really taken their toll on Sam and me, culminating in the confrontation over the Nintendo DS. Max understood my concern that Sam was becoming overwhelmed, so for a day we just chilled. We went for lunch in a cafe and hung around some public parks in the centre of Cape Town. In one, we came across giant chess set, so I seized the opportunity to teach Sam the rules of the game. His second neuroplasticity activity was underway.

Sam had seen chess played in the Harry Potter movies, so he agreed to learn. In the middle of a crowded park in the dappled sunshine under some sprawling figs, I showed him how the pieces were set up and what each piece could do in the game. With Max filming us, a few locals noticed and started watching,

The game commenced. I helped Sam decide which moves he should make and how the piece could be moved. He was needing a lot of support to stay on task. He was, however, picking up the concepts quickly and remained focused. A couple of scruffy old guys smelling of alcohol offered suggestions to Sam, which just ended up distracting him.

I made sure that Sam won the game so as to not prick his enthusiasm. It was all very tiring, running around the large board, explaining the rules and making the moves for both of us, keeping Sam's attention on the game and not the unsolicited advice from the sidelines, but we got there. Sam sported a big grin about 'winning' the game, and I was relieved we had made progress.

The following day, however, we were back in the thick of it, another jam-packed day. It was Easter Sunday so we were visiting a township church somewhere, I didn't know where, in Cape Town for mass and to hear the choir, followed up with a visit to a barbecue nearby. Liza had arranged for a second fixer with knowledge of the area we were to visit to drive us around; Donovan was an African with a soft voice and gentle nature.

The church took some finding but eventually Donovan got us there. Inside a nondescript building the congregation, dressed in their Sunday best, sat around a fifty-person choir, mostly female, all wearing purple velvet dresses with white trim and matching rimless hats. Altar boys and acolytes robed in scarlet assisted the minister, who was a large man with a booming deep voice and flowing white robes. He baptised a dozen or so babies, each gorgeous in white lace outfits, before the main service began.

South Africans tend to be strongly religious. Over eighty per cent of the population identifies as Christian, mostly Protestant, a legacy of European missionaries in centuries past. Most churches follow a combination of Christian teachings and African customs and traditions, including, of course, in their choice of music.

The singing started. The strength of the sound was physical, it lifted me off my seat. Max glanced across at me from behind the camera and tapped a fist to his chest, mouthing 'Wow'. Every member of the choir knew what was coming next and who was to sing which parts. Then they all dropped their heads and after a pause a tall woman in the third row lifted her chin and launched into a solo. I clutched Sam's hand as I felt the force of her voice. It was all in Xhosa so we couldn't understand a word but it didn't matter. In all my years I had never heard anything remotely close to the quality of her singing.

Unfortunately, Sam didn't like it. He found the singing too loud and I had to keep him from covering his ears with his hands so as not to cause offence. He was also bothered by the strong smell of incense, as an altar boy and girl continuously swung a censer while walking through the church.

His facial rash was further compounding his distress. Sam licks his lips when he's anxious, and eventually the continual exposure to saliva causes skin irritation. The rash is almost a barometer of his anxiety, although it can also be triggered by environmental conditions like cold weather or wind. His rash had started soon after we landed in Cape Town and had steadily worsened, despite my diligent application of Vaseline and a steroid cream. Apart from the discomfort, it also made him look weirder. The tall white boy with his hands on his ears, a red rash around his lips and unusual jerky movements was getting a few looks from the congregation, more of confusion than annoyance.

Soon the a capella became more rhythmic and the choir and congregation started to swing. I managed to get Sam to join in the clapping with a bribe: if he clapped one hundred times then we would leave. He did, and so then we did. The singing had been extraordinary but I wasn't sure if Sam had got much out of it. Once again, I started to wonder what the hell we were doing.

Donovan drove us to the barbecue restaurant. I didn't know what to expect. Was it going to be the four of us sitting around a table next a backyard Weber? The township seemed too busy and lively for anything that prosaic. I was right.

We parked and ambled up the street. Runty dogs sniffed garbage, plaster peeled off buildings painted with amateur advertising, footpaths were busy. Men wore flashy clothes, jewellery and sunglasses and women wore tight skirts and braided hair and talked loudly in Xhosa with its distinctive clicking sounds on mobile phones. Lots of noise, lots of action. On a corner wine tasting was offered from the top of a tin drum forming a makeshift table, vans and motorbikes honked as they zipped past, music pumped from somewhere and a man urinated on a wall.

It didn't feel threatening, but I was mindful to keep vigilant. Despite the obvious poverty, the mood was upbeat. It is said that the African concept of *ubuntu*—a sense of one's place within the human network, of what you can do to help others and where you belong—is strongly felt in the townships. It seemed that way to me.

We joined a queue that spilled from a shopfront onto the street. As we waited, Donovan filled us in on the South African barbecue tradition, called *braaivleis* (Afrikaans for 'roasted meat') or *braai* for short. More than a simple barbecue, it is an important social gathering with specific traditions and social norms, such as the cooking of the meat predominately being undertaken by men.

Hawkers worked the line, and I bought a hat that I would lose within a week. Half an hour later we reached the counter, which was piled high with raw meat. There was no other food on offer at all, just meat, meat, meat. I wasn't entirely sure what meat we were buying or how it had been prepared. Once again, we were both dealing with uncertainty. It was a good opportunity for Sam to practice ordering, so he did the talking and paid. We were directed around a corner and added our meat to a queue at the back of the shop where a large man, the *braai* master, was directing a staff of ten working on industrial-scale barbecues. Twenty minutes later we finally collected our cooked meat and, for a twenty-rand entry fee, about two Australian dollars, we got a stamp on the wrist and pushed our way into the throng in the large canvas-roofed eating area next door.

The place was pumping. The crowd was mainly African and coloured—the South African term for people of mixed African, European and Asian heritage—with a sprinkling of Europeans. African dance music blasted from the speakers, men playing bongo drums walked through the crowd for tips, and there was dancing, drinking and flirting aplenty. Once again, while a fascinating place, it was all too much for Sam. He complained about the noise and the smoke and the smells. He recoiled from the drummers when they spoke to him and was reluctant to eat anything beyond a simple sausage. He drew his knees up onto his chest as he sat on his plastic chair and covered his ears. We quickly ate our meat with our fingers and left.

While Donovan, Sam and I sat in the car waiting for Max, who had gone back to do some more filming by himself, a man approached. Donovan's African accent thickened to match our guest's as he leant through the passenger window. He wore a tight white t-shirt, a gold necklace and sunglasses and seemed to quickly clock something was going on with Sam as he chatted with Donovan, talking vaguely about needing 'some help'. I wondered why Donovan was putting up with him.

In an oily voice, he asked me, 'Where are you from, man?'

Donovan answered for us. 'They are from Australia.'

He looked at Sam, who was frowning as he stared out the window. 'Why are you so angry? You should smile and relax.'

Sam continued to ignore him.

'What is your name?' he asked.

I poked Sam gently and he turned and answered in a whisper.

The man continued to push, laughing and leaning further through the window, as Sam stared down the street. Eventually the talk of 'a need' crystallised into an amount: thirty rand. Donovan said he only had twenty for him and the cash passed hands. As he sauntered off, I asked Donovan why he had paid.

'I saw him coming. I was watching his body language and motion. He is used to hustling. I hand him twenty and I avoid a problem. Twenty is a small price to pay for safety. We look a bit unusual sitting in a car like this.' He paused for a while and then added, 'Anyway, he might need the money. It didn't cost me anything.'

'It cost you twenty,' I replied.

Donovan tilted his head. 'That is not much.'

'Isn't it encouraging him?'

'I suppose so, a bit.' Then he added, 'But he still might need it.'

Our last day in Cape Town was to be a more reflective and educational one, touring Robben Island. It was here that Nelson Mandela was imprisoned for eighteen years, along with an estimated twelve thousand political prisoners during the decades of the apartheid era.

I was pleasantly surprised to find how well Sam understood what had gone on. He has always been interested in crime and punishment, ever since these concepts were first seeded in his brain when he read about Toad being sent to prison for stealing a car in *The Wind in the Willows*. More recently, his very dominant obsession with Harry Potter meant he often referred to Azkaban prison and Sirius Black's escape from it. So the idea of being in custody was understood, but the example today was, of course, all too real.

During our discussion on the ferry to the island, I was able to get across to him that governments can behave unethically, that it can be okay to protest against the system, and people can go to gaol for the wrong reasons. He was able to understand what had happened during the apartheid era and the importance of Mandela and the truth and reconciliation process subsequent to his release.

As he looked into Mandela's cell, he said, 'The government was mean to him. They were a mean government.'

'Yes, they were Sam,' I replied.

'But he became president.'

'Yes, he did.'

'Did he punish them?'

'No, he wanted the country to be at peace, so he encouraged everyone to try to get along.'

He smiled and nodded, and thoughtfully stared at the small cell.

The island has been listed as a World Heritage site and it's not hard to see why. The guides are all ex-prisoners of the island and this brings a personal touch to what they're saying, which is incredibly moving. Our guide had been snatched, aged twenty, out of a meeting with forty-three like-minded friends and gaoled for five years. His description of the systems that operated inside the gaol and their effect on its intelligent and passionate young inmates was shocking and heartbreaking. Sam got it, and so did I.

As our group emerged from the dark prison corridors into the glare of the limestone courtyard, our guide took more questions.

'Did you know Mandela?' asked an American woman.

He nodded. 'Yes. I spoke with Madiba many times.'

'What was he like?'

He paused and smiled. 'He treated us like children at times. You need to understand we were political activists, and political activists have opinions on everything. Some of us didn't like being corrected by him.' He paused again. 'The other thing with Madiba was if you disagreed with him, he would not let you go until he could understand why you thought differently to him. He would be at you for days and days until either you convinced him you were right, or he convinced you. With me, I usually gave in and agreed with him.' He chuckled to himself. 'Maybe that is why he was such an effective leader. He hated not understanding another person's position.'

A bus took us over to the bleak quarry where the prisoners laboured all day every day, pointlessly breaking limestone rocks, purely to keep them busy. We went past a house where the Pan Africanist Congress leader Robert Sobukwe was held. In the early 1960s, The Prof was considered such a threat to the government that at the end of his three-year sentence for incitement a special law was passed, which contained what became known as the 'Sobukwe Clause', empowering the minister of justice to prolong the detention of any political prisoner indefinitely. The law was never applied to anyone else. Sobukwe was moved to Robben Island and kept in solitary confinement for six years. Even when he left prison he was banished to the dusty and remote small town of Galeshewe in the Northern Cape Province and kept under house arrest.

The next morning we left Cape Town, as well as our friends, both staff and guests, at the hostel. It was surprising how much we had bonded with them all in only a few days; a young man from Melbourne gave Sam a mini AFL football as a parting gift.

In my disorganised and flustered state getting bags onto the bus, I worried a daypack had been left behind. Max later said Sam had told me three times it was already on the bus, which I had ignored. Hearing this shook me. As the bus wound through Cape Town's suburbs I realised that I needed to listen, *properly* listen, to Sam, and value more what he had to say.

We were finally on the road, heading east on the Baz Bus, a backpacker bus that links the hostels along the coast. Our first stop was Hermanus, a quiet town on a rugged rocky coast. At lunchtime on our second day there, Max, Sam and I stumbled upon a small Indian eatery. Half restaurant, half Indian produce store, it had floor-to-ceiling shelves brimming with glass jars containing curry leaves, cinnamon sticks, cumin and seemingly every spice imaginable. The owner, Shareen, quizzed me about our travels. She was immediately fascinated by Sam. Some people just get him, and she was one of them. She glossed over his oddness, his overly loud speech when stressed, his clumsiness in spilling his drink on the table. She encouraged him in conversation, talking with him on his level about his interests. When he wandered towards the door, she quickly called him back before I could do the same. It was a balm for Sam and I to spend some time with someone who just *understood*, no explanation necessary.

Max parted ways with us the next morning. Our last encounter with him was as he filmed us departing on the bus, after a hurried goodbye in a roadside bus shelter in the middle of nowhere. All of a sudden, we were *really* on our own. It was a relief to have the stress of filming lift, and it also meant an end to the helter-skelter schedule.

I did, however, feel a rising anxiety about what lay ahead and a sudden pang of loneliness. I was going to miss Max. The training wheels were off. It was all up to me now. Or maybe, more importantly, it was all up to Sam.

CHAPTER 4

The Baz Bus

The next stop was Mossel Bay, a large town which sits at the western end of the 'garden route' of South Africa. This picturesque stretch of coast is backpacker heaven, all long wide beaches, rivers, lagoons and quaint villages. On the bus with us were twenty Europeans, mostly in their twenties, and the African driver. Our fellow travellers were curious about Sam and what we were doing.

Sitting next to Sam in the back seat of the bus was a twenty-year-old sports and language teacher from Hamburg who'd soon be volunteering as a teacher in Port Elizabeth for two months. We'd meet lots of expat volunteers and NGO workers on the South African backpacker circuit. He had a long conversation with Sam, which ranged over whether the teacher looked like Professor Lupin from the Harry Potter films (I didn't think so) to whether stomping hard on the ground scares lions away to a failed attempt to teach Sam how to count to ten in German. Maybe next time.

In a roadside cafe, Sam perched in a red vinyl booth with three backpackers hotly debating the relative merits of Harry Potter, *The Lord of the Rings* and *The Chronicles of Narnia* over morning tea.

Sam finally agreed to disagree, and moved on to theorising whether Kim Jong-un was more evil than Lord Voldemort or Sauron from *The Lord of the Rings*. That is why everyone is interested in Sam.

It had been a very white African experience so far. We had met a few South Africans, but they were mostly white and mostly tourists. While things have improved, there is still a stark economic divide between black and white in post-apartheid South Africa, with the borders of townships well defined by the sudden shift from rendered brick and high-walled gardens to corrugated iron, dirt and rubbish. Black South Africans still dominate service roles, while whites still mostly own businesses and hold professional positions. What was not evident, however, at least in this part of the country, was animosity or hostility. There was an ease between black and white that I didn't expect, given the raw recent history. It was a remarkable achievement for a remarkable country.

The most important tool of the intervention so far had proven to be our fellow travellers. The backpackers all took to Sam and frequently tried to strike up conversations with him whenever I could pry him away from playing Nintendo DS in our room. Still, it was clear this was hard work for him.

One afternoon, Sam had a typically obscure but none the less productive exchange with four young men—Dutch, Danish and English—about Harry Potter, *The Lord of the Rings* and video games on various consoles. They were remarkably patient. But eventually Sam decided he'd had enough and abruptly took off, with me in pursuit.

I sensed that his conversation skills had started to improve. We discussed what questions were suitable for different people. For example, it was okay to ask someone's age, but not while ordering lunch at a restaurant. On the bus from Mossel Bay to the evocatively named village of Wilderness, something amazing happened to Sam. After meeting a couple from England, Sam asked the woman, Erica, what she did for work. It turned out that she was an actress. 'I was an extra in Harry Potter,' she said. Well, you can imagine Sam's reaction! It transpired Erica played a Slytherin in *Harry Potter and the Order of the Phoenix* and actually knew Tom Felton, the actor who played Draco Malfoy. Sam talked about it for days.

Wilderness is a beautiful place. It's a small village on an endless beach shrouded in mist and surrounded by protected jungle. The evening we arrived, a group of us went to a restaurant with live music. I was worried Sam would be overwhelmed by the music but he did quite well. The people at our table were fascinated as Sam touched my whiskers, ear lobes and hair as sensory calming actions. I didn't mind; I was well used to it.

The next day we trundled along an abandoned rail line through a tunnel to the Cave Man's house. Set up a few years earlier by a man who had a spiritual epiphany, it is a maze of rooms made from driftwood and flotsam set deep inside a cave in the cliffs overlooking a wild beach, lit by candles and decorated with shells and stones. The man allows the homeless to stay, and asks visitors for a 'contribution' for being shown around. Sam was just relieved the man wasn't a real cave man. My boy was definitely more relaxed now. The facial rash was easing.

From Wilderness, two long bus trips took us into and then out of Port Elizabeth, with a short overnight stay in a hostel in the city. We had now moved from the Garden Route to the Wild Coast, a more isolated and windswept stretch of coast, but still beautiful in a different sort of way. The Wild Coast is crossed by a multitude of rivers, which form lagoons and wide mouths as they cleave the wide white beaches pounded by heavy surf.

One of these is the Great Kei River, and the area north of this is known as Transkei, which means 'across the Kei'. Nelson Mandela grew up here. Transkei was nominated as a supposedly independent state for Xhosa-speaking people during the apartheid era. This was one of four 'homelands' established under the separate development policy. These states had their own governments and defence forces but were more a justification of apartheid than anything else, and weren't recognised by any country other than South Africa. They became dumping grounds, beset by poverty and unemployment. Transkei's thirty-one-year history was dominated by a corrupt leader, Kaiser Matanzima, who effectively ran the country as a one-party state. As a result, the area is still lagging behind in infrastructure. It can take a long time to recover from decades of neglect.

In fewer than twenty-four hours we had travelled from what could easily have been part of Europe to a much more 'African' landscape: rounded stone and mortar huts with thatch roofs called *rondavels* appeared, the population and traffic thinned, the flora became coarser, the roads rougher.

The travelling gave me time to reflect on how we were both going. Sam had certainly settled, but I was now much more aware I had to pace how hard I pushed him, not only with organised activities but with chance conversations with strangers on buses or in hostels, or just with the rigours of travelling itself. I needed to make the jelly wobble, but not fall off the plate.

I also wanted to make sure I didn't just focus on Sam making conversation, but also on the way he thought during those conversations. I needed to help him develop his 'theory of mind'.

Theory of mind is more than empathy; it is trying to get inside the head of someone else and second-guess what they are thinking and what they might be about to do. As Atticus Finch puts it in *To Kill a Mockingbird*, it is 'to walk in another man's shoes'. This skill starts developing very early in childhood, even in the first twelve months of life. Professor Simon Baron-Cohen, director of the Autism Research Centre at Cambridge University in England, has theorised that 'protodeclarative pointing'—pointing to bring attention to, or share interest in, an object, which typically develops between seven and nine months of age—is a 'critical precursor' to developing theory of mind.

Trying to figure out what's going on in other people's heads is something most of us do naturally all the time, and impairment in this ability is a central deficit in many people with autism. People with autism have particular difficulty with tasks that require them to understand another person's beliefs. With all my focus now on Sam, I continually peppered him with questions to try to develop this type of thinking. 'What do you think he is thinking?' 'Why do you think she said that, Sam?' 'How do you think that made that person feel?'

My own theory of mind was being tested in regards to our upcoming travel plans. I wasn't entirely sure why but Sam had been demonstrating increasing resistance to going to Namibia, our next major destination after South Africa. He was aware we were going to countries poorer than South Africa and he wasn't happy about it.

He started up again. 'I don't want to go to Namibia.'

'We'll see,' I said.

He leant towards me to emphasise his message. 'I'm too tired to go to Namibia.'

'Let's just see how we go,' I replied, trying to end the conversation.

'I don't like this hard life,' he continued. 'I want an easy life. I want to go back to Sydney.'

'Let's just think about today.' I looked over to the kitchen. 'What do you want for dinner?'

He wasn't budging. 'I don't want to go to seven countries. Seven countries is too hard for me.'

'I think you'll be okay. Let's just see how we go.'

And so it went on. Little did he know we were already booked to fly to Windhoek, Namibia's capital, in two weeks. I wondered if this issue would escalate over that time.

As for me, I was definitely feeling lonely, and we were only two weeks into the trip. While I was meeting people constantly, it was always through the prism of what I was doing with Sam. It was also tiring. I had to make sure I was pacing myself, as well as Sam. It was okay, I decided, to have an occasional day when we didn't do much, especially tourism stuff, which I was determined should remain a low priority in any case. Experiences were fine, but ticking sites off lists was not. We were here to get a job done.

Our destination after the second long bus trip was Buccaneer's Lodge in Chintsa. Sam and I would spend three nights here, taking in the white sand, big rolling surf and panoramic views from the hostel's verandahs.

Our room was named after medical student Steve Biko, the Black Consciousness leader who was arrested, tortured and killed at the hands of the police in 1973. His words were painted on the wall of the room: 'It is better to die for an idea that will live, than to live for an idea that will die.'

On the second day we visited a nearby village where pigs, geese and dogs roamed the dirt roads between *rondavels*. Children peered out of the doorways and women balanced firewood on colourful bandanas wrapped around their heads. As part of the visit, we met a local Xhosa legend, ninety-five-year-old Mama Tofu. She had begun to explain the principles of their culture, standing over a small group of seated Europeans in the community *rondavel*, when Sam started playing up. I had forgotten to give him his ADHD medication that morning, so he was more boisterous than normal, bouncing off the mud walls of the small thatched-roof hut. But Mama Tofu was unfazed, and insisted I not restrain him and just let him do whatever he wanted as long as he was safe.

Sam immediately pointed to a photo she had on display, which showed a topless African woman. 'Inappropriate!'

Mama Tofu laughed uproariously and gave him a hug. He looked at her, trying to extricate himself from the hug. 'You're old,' he said.

She smiled, her deeply lined face with sparkling eyes creasing into a wide grin with angled and missing teeth. 'Yes, I am, Mr Sam.'

'I hope you don't die,' he said.

Fortunately, I think she missed the last comment. Language barriers can be protective sometimes. Mama Tofu was quite taken with Sam. They walked hand in hand around the hut. Animated and engaging, she was remarkable for her age. On a side table she had a photo of her with Jacques Kallis, the famous South African cricketer. Like me, she was a cricket nut. We discussed South Africa's recent disappointing loss in the ICC Cricket World Cup, and how silly mistakes had cost them dearly in the semi-final. With a shake of her head she admonished various team members for their performance. I scrambled to stop Sam knocking over a jewellery display, but Mama Tofu waved me away. 'Let him be. Whatever happens in here is fine by us. You just relax.'

As we were leaving, I took a photo of two young girls with a pattern of white dots painted on their faces standing near Sam. Much to his surprise, one of them burst into song and within a few seconds a chorus line of ten children and adults, including Mama Tofu, clapped, swayed and sung in perfect harmony. The two young girls then leapt forward from the line and swung their lower legs in turn, like gyrating helicopter blades, while skipping on their other leg. We were all gobsmacked. Sam laughed and bounced his way back to the minibus. 'The girls are dancing!'

On the way out of the village, we spied a man walking along the road wearing a road worker's fluoro jacket. As we passed, I noticed his face was painted white. I asked our Xhosa driver why.

'He is a witchdoctor,' he said.

Of course.

The next evening, back in my room with Sam, I started to fret about my capability again. I had lost yet another object, this time my water canister's lid, and was seriously pissed off with myself. I thought about the countries that lay ahead, far more challenging than South Africa, and I wondered again if I was taking too much of a risk with this project, and too much of a risk with Sam. Perhaps I was too old for this crap?

Earlier that day, the South African staff at the hostel had been swapping real-life horror stories—of being robbed at knifepoint or having guns pointed at their heads in broad daylight in Cape Town or Johannesburg—and scaring the bejesus out of the guests, myself included, before adding, 'Yes, but it's not that bad. You just need to be vigilant.' An Australian on the Baz Bus into Port Elizabeth had told me about a close call he'd had with a guy with a gun while walking near Wilderness, exactly where we'd been two days earlier.

Sitting on the lounge in the room, watching Sam listen to music on the bed, I felt a sudden surge of panic. *I must not fail him.* These thoughts had hit me several times a day over last few days. *Just don't fuck up.* I distracted myself by watching a film on my computer.

During our three days at Buccaneer's we met more fellow travellers and, as happens when travelling, quickly formed bonds with them. Sam and I hung out with a couple, Ed and Lana, and Anka, a Dutch physiotherapist, as we went canoeing, walked to the beach and played volleyball. The three of them joined us when we caught the Baz Bus to the next stop, Coffee Bay.

Anka was here to meet up with a South African doctor she'd gone out with in the Netherlands for two years, but hadn't seen since they'd broken up two years earlier. They had planned to go to South Africa together but when their relationship had ended, he had left and she had stayed in Holland. Now she had come to see him again, to find out whether their relationship could be rekindled. It had been hard for her to find the strength to travel here, being a naturally cautious person. I nicknamed her Captain Sensible. Sam liked Captain Sensible; Captain Sensible liked Sam.

Anka was meeting her ex-boyfriend an hour's drive away from Coffee Bay and then staying with him for five days, so if it didn't work out it would be awkward. We divulged our anxieties to each other, mine for Sam and our adventure, hers for her upcoming rendezvous and her future.

Ed and Lana were soon-to-be Australian citizens from Israel and Belgium respectively, and they lived in inner Sydney not far from our home. All three were so understanding of Sam's behaviour and made such an effort to involve him that I was, yet again, deeply touched.

On the bus to Coffee Bay, Ed asked the group where we would go in time and place if we had a time machine. Nominations included Ancient Rome, the Renaissance, the building of the pyramids and Nelson Mandela's release.

Ed turned to Sam. 'Where would you go back in time to, Sam?'

'1992, in California,' he promptly replied.

Ed was taken aback. 'Why?'

'To see Bill Gates releasing Windows 3.1,' Sam replied, with a grin.

CHAPTER 5

Tension in the Transkei

After crossing the Kei River at the Great Kei Cutting—a deep gorge that plunges down to the stony river bed below—the bus climbed on to the two-thousand-metre-high Transkei plateau. A mesa rose above sheer cliffs hundreds of metres tall. Previously, tribal justice had been meted out by throwing poor souls off these cliffs, prompting another conversation with Sam about capital punishment.

Pale emerald hills undulated in almost perfect sinusoidal waves. Sharply edged creek beds occasionally cracked the surface like a cake that was about to fall apart. *Rondavels* sprinkled the hills, spaced out rather than clustered together. Each had a small animal pen with walls of long sticks thatched tightly together, a vegetable garden, and a field of corn or tilled earth. There were glimpses of yellow pumpkins and brown chickens. Pigs, dogs, goats, horses and long-horned cattle wandered between the huts and across the road, causing some sharp swerving and braking from our imperturbable driver.

Anka was getting tense and teary as we approached Coffee Bay. I turned to her. 'Okay. It is 2065. You are eighty-five years old, sitting on a verandah in a nursing home, and I happen to end up in the same nursing home, and I get wheeled out by the nurse onto the verandah next to you. We recognise each other and I say to you, "Hey, Anka, back when you met that guy in South Africa, how did it work out?" At that point, you will have an answer. And really, that is what you are here for: an answer. It may not be the one you want, but at least you will have an answer.'

Anka nodded, smiled and thanked me. She thought for a while. In her Dutch accent and in typically direct Dutch style she replied, 'Yes, James, I will have an answer. But on that verandah you will be ninety-eight.'

The sun was getting low as we neared our destination. Low clouds scurried across the plateau causing shadows to dance over the hills. The *rondavels* seemed to have a set colour scheme, painted one of only four colours: white, aqua green, apricot or pink. They dotted the fields like blobs of paint on a Monet painting. Anka wondered aloud whether there was a cultural significance to the limited colour choice. Perhaps a colour meant a family name or ethnic sub-group?

Anka yelled to the front of the bus. 'Driver, does the choice of house colour mean something?'

'Yes,' he yelled back without looking.

'What?'

He half turned and smiled. 'It means you like that colour.'

The bus burst into laughter as we came off the plateau and bumped our way back down to the Wild Coast at Coffee Bay. The bay had been named for a shipload of coffee that was supposedly spilled in a shipwreck in the early days of European settlement. Upon arriving at Coffee Shack Backpackers hostel, Anka departed to discover her destiny further up the coast. Meanwhile, the hostel manager greeted Sam and me warmly, having heard about our arrival in advance. Apparently, word was getting out about us on the hostel grapevine, and both staff members and guests were reading the blog before they met us, which was kind of weird, but made for an excellent ice-breaker. It also saved me having to explain our situation over and over again.

That evening we suffered yet another compulsory two-hour blackout—called 'load sharing' for South Africa's overloaded electricity grid. This had been the fourth evening in a row where candles were lit, restaurants couldn't cook food and bills and receipts were written by hand.

There was a lot of disgust at the government, and suspicion of corruption. Power rates had risen twenty per cent that year, but nobody thought things would improve any time soon. One South African backpacker was studying economics and told me the power crisis would slash a full one per cent off South Africa's GDP that year, which I well believed. Another commented that this had only become an issue since 1994—the year the African National Congress, under Nelson Mandela, first formed government—and I sensed a hint of racial tension.

Sam was principally annoyed that he couldn't charge his Nintendo DS. After dinner we set out for our cottage, torches in hand. We had to cross a small creek to get to our room and navigating the rocks by torchlight was a little hazardous. As we took off our wet shoes on the verandah, we were struck by the view of the moonlit surf under the bright Milky Way. The sound of drums drifted across the village. It seemed that South Africa took away, but then gave back twofold.

The next day we travelled to a nearby beach with spectacular cliffs and a large rock island, towering vertically up out of the surf, guarding the mouth of a river. Over millennia the relentless pounding of the surf had carved a hole right through the centre of the island, leaving a short tunnel through which wild waves smashed. Other backpackers had walked three hours to get there, but Sam and I had gone in the retrieval truck with the picnic lunch for the group. Sam was disengaged, sitting apart from the others and stimming on small sticks among the rocks lining the beach, flicking them between his fingers and repeatedly dropping and picking them up. It was disappointing, but we couldn't be kicking goals all the time, I reasoned.

On the trip back, Sam suddenly snapped out of his daze and started entertaining the troops. While the truck dodged geese, cattle and pigs on the road, Sam and I took turns making animal noises, doing funny head dances and imitating voices from *The Simpsons*, *The Incredibles*, and of course, Harry Potter. The German and Dutch twenty-somethings looked on with wry amusement and a hint of bewilderment.

In the afternoon we headed back to our hut. Once again we needed to negotiate the creek on the way to our hut. The tide was up but it looked only knee deep so I decided to give it a go rather than go around, a ten-minute walk through the village and over the bridge upstream. But when I was halfway across, already up to my thighs in water, a tidal surge brought the depth up to my waist. Scrambling to keep my phone, money belt and wallet above the water and not fall over in the process, I struggled to the other side.

Sam clearly couldn't follow me across. I shouted to him above the rumble of the nearby surf to stay still while I walked around to get him. A staff member from the hostel saw our predicament and hurried down to Sam's side. She shouted that she'd drive him around to me. That is, I *think* that's what she shouted. I waited at the road above our hut for ten minutes but no staff member, no Sam. I started to worry. Maybe he'd refused to go with her. Did I hear her correctly? I didn't like him being away from me, even in a backpacker hostel.

I jogged over the bridge and back to the hostel, scanning the grounds for him. When I couldn't find him or the staff member, I panicked and ran to the office. People were mobilised and a search began. The two were quickly found down near the creek in the camping area. Sam had refused to accept her lift and tried to find another way across. The staff member had sensibly just stayed with him to keep an eye.

When he saw me, Sam called out 'Dad!' and ran to my side before jumping up and down, flapping his hands by his side. It seemed he'd sensed danger while separated from me, which was a good thing. I also didn't mind he'd refused to go with a stranger in a car, even though the consequences had freaked me out. The staff member drove us both back around to the hut and I changed my wet shorts and underwear. I hadn't quite wet myself, but the creek certainly had.

That night Sam went to sleep early. There was to be a drumming performance at the next hostel over and I allowed myself to go. There was another blackout as the performance began. Four young African men with drums were silhouetted on stage in front of a row of lamps and candles, the rest of the room dimly lit. A weird-looking long-haired white dude with a flute stood behind the drummers. The crowd waited expectantly in the eerie atmosphere.

The drumming began. Powerful rhythms rocked the room. These guys could play. The flute dude actually worked in well, providing a dancing, high-pitched melodic contrast to the thumping low beats of the drums. The drummers beat the tightened skins and worked themselves into a lather, and the crowd, black and white, jumped off their cushions and began to dance. The hands of one of the drummers moved so fast you couldn't see them. Compelling, hypnotic, exhilarating.

The last song was, of course, 'Shosholoza', a traditional Ndebele song brought into South Africa from Zimbabwe by mine workers, and wildly popular in South Africa. It's a call and response song: the singer calls to the crowd and the crowd sings the same line back. Mandela said the song helped him get through eighteen years of breaking rocks in the quarry. To South Africans, it's more than a song.

The white South Africans I had spoken to the night before were also there and quite drunk. They had started drinking shots in the hostel that afternoon while watching rugby. They knew all the words and were as enthusiastic as anyone there in singing the black folk song. Maybe I had misread them. I was still struggling to get my head around the complicated relationship between black and white in modern South Africa, but that night 'Shosholoza' helped bring black and white together.

The next day I decided Sam and I would just chill. We crossed the rising creek to the hostel to check emails and, if possible, Skype home on the wobbly wi-fi. In the office, Sam once again tried to update his Nintendo DS on the web. I didn't realise it at the time, but he had been attempting to do this for nearly a week and it was the main thing on his mind. I was distracted, doing what I wanted to do, as he started to stress out, rocking back and forth on the lounge and whacking his hands on the cushions. I started to pay more attention to him and attempted to calm him down, but to no avail.

I didn't really understand what he was doing with the DS and why the update wasn't working. Soon he really lost it, shouting and jumping up and down in front of the lounge. I tried to soothe him again, but I realised I needed to get him out of there. Staff were hovering nearby with concerned and confused looks. One, a kind African lady who had taken an interest in Sam, came into the room. 'Sam, Sam, you calm down. You be nice to your dad.'

He thumped his fists into the lounge. 'No, no, no! It *will* upload. *NO* to the *no* access to internet. I *FORBID* this!' He grabbed me hard by the arm, then squeezed my head in frustration.

I needed to get that DS off him, so I grabbed it quickly and stood up. 'We need to get out of here. Come with me now.'

He jumped up, raised his fist and shouted at me, '*No!* You give it to *ME* now. The internet only works here. It doesn't work in the *ROOM!*' He tried to stop me leaving by bear-hugging me, the ever-increasing strength of his teenage body taking me by surprise, and then, his forehead buttressed to mine, he squeezed my head again between his hands and grunted and growled. He was now yelling at the top of his voice and I prepared myself for a bite or headbutt, two techniques he hadn't employed to date. The squeezing and grabbing continued but I managed to stay calm. It was so embarrassing but I also felt sorry for Sam. I willed myself to maintain control.

Palms downwards, I patted the air in a calming motion. 'You can't do this, Sam. We are in Africa. You cannot use violence; it will just make things worse. They might take your DS away or you might get arrested by the police if you get violent.'

He shook his fist and jerked his head, shouting, 'I can use violence. I *will* use violence. I will *kill* them. If they take my DS away I will *shoot* them.'

I tensed. Quietly, I said, 'If you shoot someone you will go to prison.'

'I will put *them* in prison,' he shrieked. 'I will kill them *all!*'

This raised the bar. He was making threats that might be misunderstood. I desperately wanted to get him out of that environment and away somewhere private. Eventually I coaxed him out of the hostel and up the road. The creek was so high it wasn't fordable so we had to walk through the village to reach our cottage.

Sam continued to shout and grab at me as we walked along the road. There was now a crowd of thirty or so watching us. He threatened anybody and everybody who could take away his DS. My attempts to talk him through it were getting nowhere. 'I will *swim* to Australia and get back my videos,' he bellowed. 'If they take my internet away I will *make* them get hanged!'

Finally we reached our cottage. But as we rounded the side of the building I was stunned to see a herd of twenty long-horned cattle surrounding the front door. *Bloody hell!* That was the last thing I needed at this moment! To a casual observer it probably looked quite comical as I ineptly and unsuccessfully tried to shoo the large beasts away. Fortunately, a shepherd boy soon appeared and quickly moved them along.

Inside the cottage, Sam and I collapsed onto the beds, a pair of sweaty messes. Over the next twenty minutes, I was able to move Sam from his agitated state to a place of relative calmness, where he could reflect more logically on what happened. I knew I hadn't played my own hand very well either. I shouldn't have mentioned arrests or taking away the DS, but at least I had managed to stay calm.

Sam eventually conceded that violence had not helped, and had worsened the situation. I made him take a solemn oath to not do that again. After a few minutes I turned to him. 'Sam, your DS still works. Even without the update it still works.'

'Yeah,' he sighed.

The tension was breaking. I continued, 'So when we go back at dinner time, we'll try again but if it doesn't work you're going to stay calm, yes?'

'Okay,' he mumbled into the bedclothes.

I gently lifted his chin and looked him in the eye. 'You're sure?'

He nodded firmly. 'Yes.'

And he did. Back in the office later on, I completely focused on his needs and we got the bloody upload sorted out. Four staff members immediately came into the office and congratulated him. Unbeknownst to me, they had all been listening around the corner.

The next day on the news we saw reports of a different sort of violence. There had been unrest on the streets in Durban, where we were due to visit shortly. Great. The source of tension was apparently between local South Africans and black and Indian workers from neighbouring countries who were supposedly guilty of taking jobs. I didn't want us to get caught in any crossfire. Fortunately, we still had a few days before we were scheduled to arrive in Durbs. I had planned a visit to the mountain kingdom of Lesotho first.

Over the next few days in Coffee Bay the African staff repeatedly engaged with Sam. One woman, Susule, took a particular shine to him. She smiled as we watched Sam carry his lunch from the counter to the table. 'He is a beautiful boy.'

I nodded. 'Yes, he is. He looks like his mother.'

She turned to me. 'Yes, but he also has a beautiful heart.'

I grinned. 'Yes, he does. Sam tries very hard.'

After a pause, she hesitantly asked, 'What happened to him?'

'He was born that way. His condition is called autism,' I said.

She had no idea what I was talking about. 'Oh, he was born that way. Where's his mother?' she asked in her thick musical accent.

'She's back in Sydney with my other two boys. She sent me here so I could help Sam learn.'

She nodded and seemed happy with that. 'Oh, that is very good. It is nice to see a father and son together. He's a nice boy.'

As we left Coffee Bay on the bus, a white American woman talked to a black African man across the aisle from Sam. The American woman put forward her point, expression earnest. 'All the colonial powers drew the country borders on the map. Local tribes and cultures had nothing to do with it. That was one of the worst things they did. The borders were drawn by the Europeans.'

'Yes, you are right,' the man replied. 'And after the Europeans stuffed us up with their borders, they are now getting rid of their own.'

We had three bus trips that day to get to Sani Lodge in the Drakensburg Mountains. Between the first and second buses Sam and I sat in an orange and purple vinyl booth in a Shell Ultra City roadside centre and had the first science lesson of the trip. Sam's school back in Sydney had started the new term that day and I figured the best way to maintain the discipline to keep up Sam's schooling was to exactly follow the timetable of his classmates. Today's classes would have been science, religion, English, maths and geography. I had some electronic resources on my computer, which had been supplied by his school. These were better for some subjects than others; I hadn't been able to fit all his textbooks on my laptop. If there were gaps in the teaching materials, I'd just have to improvise.

Sam kicked up a bit of a stink about going to school when he was *not* going to school, which had been one of the consolations of the trip, but grew more accepting when I let him practice writing a narrative using Harry Potter characters. Yes, I improvised. I calculated that about half an hour of one-on-one time with me would easily be equivalent to an hour-long lesson at his school.

On the second bus trip that day we saw a spectacular sunset over the increasingly mountainous landscape. Seven shades of blue steel grey, fading to pale as they approached the horizon, defined the ridgelines. We reached our next transfer at Kokstadt after dark, and we could sense the chill of the higher atmosphere. Our next transport should have been there to meet the bus. It wasn't.

The Baz Bus driver rang to check. There had apparently been a mix-up. He told me the hostel was arranging a driver who should be there in ten minutes. We grabbed some sausage rolls and lukewarm samosas from a nearby dodgy takeaway and watched the bus pull away. I felt suddenly apprehensive. I was alone with Sam, standing outside a rundown roadside cafe complex, at night. I strategically positioned us so our backs were to a wall, with Sam and the bags behind me.

Sure enough, a questionable character soon appeared. He was emaciated, wearing ragged clothes, and stooping with his hands in his pockets. He shuffled towards us slowly, with an occasional glance in our direction out of the side of his eyes. When he got within a metre or two of us he started to mumble, 'Hey, how you doin'?'

I took a step towards him and chopped the crisp air with my hand. 'No!'

He moved away, but continued to circle the complex, glancing in our direction occasionally. I watched him carefully. After twenty minutes and no car I started to worry. While extracting my phone from my pocket to google the number for our hostel I dropped my glasses on the road, breaking the frames. Suppressing swear words and trying to read my phone through broken glasses, I felt the tension rise.

Sam wasn't helping. When he saw me break my glasses he launched into an impersonation of Nelson from *The Simpsons*. 'Ha-ha!'

The car finally turned up. What a relief! It was rattling relic with a top speed of eighty kilometres per hour. The driver spoke little English but I was reasonably confident we were heading to the right place. Well, I *hoped* we were. He was playing a heavy rap song that I soon realised was on a loop. We got to listen to it more than twenty times as we bumped up the dark road through the mist.

After an hour, without warning and in the middle of nowhere, we were moved into a new hire car with a new driver. I could only assume this was so the cars and drivers remained in their local area. At least the music changed. Sam leant on me heavily in the back seat—as he tends to do when he is tired—because of his low muscle tone, which is common in people with autism. This car was faster but, like the first, there were no back seat seatbelts. I started to see why South Africa's road toll was so high. As we neared Sani Lodge, the road became steeper and windier but that didn't stop the driver using his mobile phone constantly while driving.

Finally we arrived at nine p.m., an hour after the restaurant had closed. A kind hostel worker rustled up a loaf of bread from the restaurant to supplement Sam's sausage roll dinner, despite Sam suggesting she was a man because she had short hair (she most definitely did *not* look like a man).

Sam then realised he had left his Nintendo DS in the car. Fortunately, I had the driver's number as I had arranged for him to drive us back to Kokstadt in three days. I rang, he had it, and he'd bring it back tomorrow.

A game of cards in this much quieter and laidback hostel with a German, a Dane, an American and a Chilean soothed my rattled nerves. We were at 1,500 metres above sea level, so the room was fitted out with wall heaters, thick blankets and hot-water bottles.

The days seemed longer and the nights darker but that had nothing to do with seasons or geography, it was all in my head. I was becoming worn down. We were only a couple of weeks in to the trip and already my head was starting to drop. I had nearly managed to lose Sam, the DS was proving to be an albatross and we could have easily got into some serious strife in the mix-up with the transport here.

I wanted to go home and was embarrassed that I felt that way. Sam just seemed unhappy. He didn't seem to enjoy the aspects of the trip I thought he would. The whole thing was a chore to him. Yet we were ticking boxes on what we needed to get done, including the filming for the university, and I could detect subtle improvements in his conversational skills. Must push on, must push on.

CHAPTER 6

The Mountain Kingdom

We awoke to a crisp, clear morning. For the first time we could see where we'd arrived: above the lodge towered the dramatic escarpment of the southern Drakensberg Mountains. Early European settlers called it the *Drakensberge*—Afrikaans for dragon mountains—because they believed it resembled a dragon's back. Sharp ridgelines demarcated treeless rock and grass slopes in subtle mauve shadow and pale green highlights where mist danced in valleys. Muted grey rock pushed up through a lime-green grass carpet that covered the treeless slopes as they headed up, ever steeper to angular ridge lines, cut rough and crooked way above us. Mauve shadows filled the valleys, where mist hung in the still, cool air. The only sound was birdsong.

The lodge owners led us up the mountain, and also into Lesotho, the neighbouring country. We booked a day trip over the 3,200-metre Sani Pass for the second day of our stay. But today I wanted us to relax, and refocus on Sam and on the neuroplasticity exercises. In addition to his school lessons and a one-hour walk on a nature trail, we were able to complete more neuroplasticity activities than on any other day of the trip to date. We boxed in the morning sunshine on a back verandah with a view over the jagged mountains and played chess on the hearth of the fireplace in the lounge room, still smouldering from the night before. Then Sam completed a Harry Potter jigsaw puzzle, as well as half of a game of South African Monopoly—played on a bilingual board with the familiar Pall Mall and Mayfair replaced by Monument Road and Eloffstraat—before his attention, never brilliant due to his ADHD, started to wane.

From my low point the previous evening, this day made me feel we were starting to get into a groove. This was what I needed to concentrate on. While it's pretty hard to visit the Drakensburg Mountains and not do any sightseeing, we didn't have to emulate the twenty-somethings and fill our days with twelve-kilometre hikes, canyoning or abseiling. One of the principal reasons we were in Africa, apart from its dynamic and unpredictable environment, was to find the time and space for neurological growth, undistracted by all the stuff that normally intruded on our days back home in Australia.

That evening, sitting in the lounge room in front of the log fire, I chatted with one of the female Zulu staff members while Sam listened to music in our room. We talked about Sam, our travels and where we were heading next. A bullish, bow-legged and obese white South African dressed in biker leathers loped into the room and joined in the conversation. He was moving gingerly as he took his seat.

'Are you injured?' I enquired.

'No,' he said in a thick Afrikaner accent. 'Just rode eight hours on the bike from Jo'burg through the mountains and I'm feeling like I've been getting a good going over in a prison. Ha ha!'

The staff member stared at her tea with a bland expression and kept to herself from that point onwards.

He started amiably enough, asking about my impressions of South Africa. Then I volunteered that I was pleasantly surprised by the positive vibe, given the recent history, and I thought the country had a lot of promise.

He bristled. 'Oh no, this place is going to shit.' He leant forward, speaking with a pointed finger and clipped tone. 'Look what's happening with the bloody electricity. It's the African way. The whole continent works on corruption and it's going to be like that here, just like it is everywhere else.'

I grimaced inwardly. 'But don't you see the potential?'

'The ANC will just stuff it up,' he said, with a wave of his hand. 'All they have to do is hand out t-shirts every five years and they get voted back in. It's not the fault of these people; they're uneducated and don't know any better.'

I suspected 'they' was code for black or coloured. The staff member continued to look at her tea. I was tempted to take it up to him harder, but what was the point? I sat in silence.

After a long awkward pause, he said, 'So, Sydney? You have lots of refugees there.'

I'd had it with this guy. 'Yes, that's one of the best things about my city. I *love* its multicultural makeup.'

That night a huge thunderstorm erupted over the mountains. The power went out again, but this time it was Mother Nature's fault, not administrative or political incompetence, perceived or real.

The next day we left South Africa for the first time, entering the mountain kingdom of Lesotho on our tour of the Sani mountain pass. I was surprised to learn that Lesotho is the highest country in the world; that is, it has the highest low point of any country in the world. I was excited, but one particular worry was niggling at me. It was going to be very cold . . . and Sam had refused to wear long sleeves at all since he was nine.

The sensation of fabric on his forearms irritates Sam—another quirky and limiting manifestation of his autism. By and large this aversion had been manageable, with the exception of the day he decided to impose his will on his primary school mates. One wintry day in his ninth year, Sam's school had participated in a 'Special Olympics' for primary schoolchildren with special needs. It was held on the oval of a large private secondary school on the upper North Shore of Sydney. As Benison was working that day, it was my turn to supervise Sam.

I was rugged up against the cold but Sam would only consent to don a puffer vest over his t-shirt. I was chatting to the mother of a boy in Sam's class when out of the corner of my eye I saw Sam struggling with a girl he knew. He was trying to wrench her jumper off. Her mother was not impressed. I rushed across to intervene.

'Sam, what are you doing?' I shouted.

'She shouldn't have long sleeves!'

'Leave her alone!' I marched him away from the shrieking girl and her mother but he was clearly agitated, jabbering constantly about all the children with their long sleeves.

'But it's got nothing to do with you! It's their choice!'

'I *hate* long sleeves!'

I tried to get him involved in the activities—T-ball, running relays, mini-football—but it was futile. He just couldn't focus because of those long sleeves. Twice more he lurched and grabbed at other students' clothes, but I was able to step in quickly. I decided to pull the plug on the day early, depressed that my son couldn't even cope with an activity designed for children with special needs. It had been a long drive home. By the first year of high school he had consented to wear his compulsory high school blazer, but outside of school hours, forget it!

Going over a mountain pass higher than a European ski resort with exposed arms was going to prove a challenge. Sam was issued a rug from reception, and I dressed him as warmly as I could otherwise, with two t-shirts, a padded vest, long pants and hiking boots.

Ten passengers piled into two four-wheel drives. I let our driver, Stuart, an ex-park ranger, know why the boy in the passenger seat was wrapped in a rug. He presciently enquired whether Sam would mind if we had an extra passenger in the back of the car: a poisonous snake in a secure container that he intended to release in the mountains. Sam did mind, of course, but I managed to talk him around and off we went.

Stuart and Sam sat in the front seats, two Dutch backpackers and myself were in the middle row, and at the rear was a young female Japanese hitchhiker getting a free ride to the base of the mountains, and that large plastic cylinder containing the mysterious snake. As we headed north towards the range the sealed road gave way to gravel and started to climb. Before us was the mother of all South African mountain passes: the Sani Pass. A family of chacma baboons crossed the road, scratching their armpits and eyeing us curiously. A long-crested eagle sat on a roadside post, and soon our sharp-eyed driver spied a lone eland, the largest of the antelopes, grazing on the steep ridges lining the valley. Red-winged starlings and double-collared sunbirds darted among the marsh pokers and marmalade bushes, sugarbirds fed on proteas, and jackal buzzards and Cape vultures, with their two-metre wingspans, soared and circled high and mighty on the drafts coming off the cliffs. Nature was on show.

Pulling to a stop, Stuart lifted a small sack out of the cylinder in the back seat and deftly opened and inverted it, gently spilling the slithering contents onto the sand near the edge of a thatch of bracken. The short squat adder sat motionless until it was gently prodded with a stick and it slithered off into the undergrowth, safer from the ever-present birds of prey above.

Sam was transfixed. He tried to speak to it in parseltongue, the language of serpents in Harry Potter, but the snake obviously wasn't in the mood to chat. Our fellow travellers were amused.

As we started off in the car again, I decided to pick the brains of our knowledgeable guide. I leant forward from the back seat and asked, 'Why do they call them puff daddies?'

'I am not sure why they would call them puff daddies,' he yelled over his shoulder, 'but they call them puff adders because they puff out their necks when threatened.'

Sitting behind me, one of the Dutch backpackers clarified it for me. 'I think you'll find Puff Daddy is a rap singer.'

I felt my face burn and wondered, *How do I manage to consistently do these things?*

We dropped our Japanese hitchhiker at an outpost where the road started to climb steeply. Stuart couldn't take her any further as it was a commercial tour and she had politely declined to pay. She might possibly have to wait alone for up to four hours before the local minibus turned up, but she seemed undeterred. The buildings were formerly a trading post down to which Basotho herdsmen would drive their sheep and goats from their mountain pastures to be sold, buying wood, grains and other supplies in return. The trading post had become obsolete when the old mule trail had been hacked into a primitive road, and vehicle access meant the trade could happen in Lesotho itself, up and over the pass. The first car, a war-surplus Jeep, came over the pass in 1948, driven by an ex-Spitfire pilot. He needed labourers, equipped with ropes and various block and tackle, to make the summit, a journey that took six hours. The road was made functional in 1950 and the west of Lesotho had transformed its trade route.

We ascended thirteen hundred metres over nine kilometres, bouncing through creeks while we clung to the vehicle that clung to the track that in turn clung to the walls of the cliffs. Hairpin-turn left, hairpin-turn right, we wound our way up. Sam said it was a 'crazy road' and he was right.

The border with Lesotho was at the top of the pass, though the South African border post was sensibly at the bottom. The Lesotho post, a white-plastered one-room building with a side door and one small barred window at the front, had a single bored customs officer inside. On the outside of the building were hand-painted large black letters spelling out WELCOME TO LESOTHO. Behind it lay the treeless plains of the mountain kingdom. Sam sat on a rickety old desk outside the building. Wrapped in his rug he looked like a local. Our entry and exit passes to Lesotho were stamped into our passports at the same time.

Stuart drove the Land Rover across the plains, empty except for the occasional flock of unclipped mohair goats driven by Basotho herdsmen, wearing ragged clothes and carrying metre-length black sticks coloured with decorative twine.

Stuart was fluent in the local language, Sesotho, and known by all the locals. He stopped to chat to a woman in a village to see if we could visit her house later in the day. She agreed and invited us all to watch a herd of goats being clipped in a shed nearby. There, Sam and his rug again attracted attention. He walked up to the herd in the pen outside the shed and started to 'talk' to them in goat sounds, while locals watched him, intrigued.

Then as Sam watched, the shepherds and shearers dragged the beasts up the ramp by their horns as they bleated and resisted. His face creased in concern. He turned to me. 'Is this animal cruelty?'

'Oh, maybe a bit, but not too bad,' I reassured him. 'It's just like getting a haircut. They need to get it done before they move down the mountain where it isn't so cold.'

He smiled and flapped a little. 'They're getting a haircut!'

Sam moved around the shed, watching the goats and the growing piles of wool. He looked again at the shearers and their long sharp shears. With a worried expression, he asked, 'I'm not getting a haircut, am I?'

'No, Sam,' I said. 'Well, not here.'

For lunch we ate a picnic at the highest point of the road to the capital, 3,240 metres above sea level. To the west of us lay the 3,482-metre-high Thabana Ntlenyana, which translates as 'beautiful little mountain'. For an Australian, where the highest peak is a mere 2,228 metres, this seemed strange description, but it actually did appear as a little mountain on this high plain. Thabana Ntlenyana is the highest mountain in Africa south of Kilimanjaro, yet animals graze near the peak and shepherd boys stroll up its summit.

Stuart drove us back to the village woman's stone *rondavel*. These traditional dwellings are built by carefully arranging stones on the circular wall before the gaps are backfilled with a mixture of mud and dung. A similar mixture is used to make the floor.

The thatch for the roof is from the short mountain grasses pulled out by the roots, with the dirty roots on the outside and the grass stems thatched together on the inside.

In the centre of the floor was a fire of slow-burning dung fuel in a hollow, upon which sat a heavy cast-iron pot with a lid. The heat from the fire permeated the floor, effectively giving the hut subfloor heating. The room was smoky, but not unpleasantly so, even to Sam. The warm smoky air rose into the roof before slowly filtering through the thatch into the chill outside.

The Basotho woman wore, surprisingly, a beanie with an Australian flag on it. She opened the pot to reveal some enticing baked bread, which Sam liked the look of, so I bought a segment to go with his lunch. We drank homemade beer, which tasted more like cider. Stuart translated for her and we learnt a few Sesotho phrases. Here we were, in an extreme climate at an altitude too high for trees, in a poor village hut with no running water or electricity, but we were comfortable and well fed.

On the way back to the border we called into one of the few buildings we saw besides shepherd huts: the Sani Mountain Lodge. We enjoyed a surprisingly good Lesotho beer as the mist from an incoming front swirled around the building. Sam drank lemonade while flicking through magazines in front of a log fire. On our return journey, I was glad Stuart had driven this road hundreds of times before as he was navigating the descent in dense fog.

During the two-hour drive back to the hostel, Sam got on a roll about justice systems and modern history. Stuart and the Dutch backpackers were surprised, as was I, to hear his knowledge of the French Revolution and the North Korean government. He must have been googling it. When he gets talking like this, I like to run with it, as it's an opportunity to direct him back to more functional and mainstream understanding and knowledge. We discussed the Cuban missile crisis, the European and Pacific theatres of war, when they started and ended, and the death of Hitler. Between Stuart, the Dutch backpackers and myself, our cumulative general knowledge struggled to keep up with him on occasions. He can really surprise me sometimes.

CHAPTER 7

Thinking outside the square

As we left the Drakensberg Mountains, heading back to rejoin the Baz Bus at Kokstadt, Sam started to work on me again about an early return. 'I don't think we should go to Namibia. Let's go back to Sydney.'

I sighed. 'No, Sam, we have to go to Namibia now.'

'But it's got an ugly name.'

That was a new one. 'What's wrong with Namibia's name?'

He tried a different tack. 'It has malaria.'

'Yes,' I said, 'but we are flying to Windhoek, and there is no malaria there.'

'But if you get malaria you can't get rid of it. I learnt about that in science.'

I bet he hadn't. I bet he'd been reading up on the net. I ducked and weaved again. 'Well, we'll go to Windhoek. It has good internet there, so you'll like it. And we'll take it from there.'

'And then we'll go home in May.'

'We'll see.'

As we rolled into Kokstadt the driver locked the car doors. Perhaps he did that in every place. Maybe. Kokstadt was a large and busy town, but not quite a city. It sat under a bald mountain that resembled a plate of half-melted ice cream. A man carried a bunch of ostrich feather brooms. A gaggle of girls spilled out of a KFC, singing in Zulu.

We had a half-hour wait at the same old roadside facility, outside the restaurant. We ate pizza out of the box. After fifty minutes I rang, to be told the bus would be another twenty minutes. Once again stranded in dwindling light, I kept a close eye on Sam and the bags.

He pestered me to buy ice cream at the convenience store near us so I took a punt and gave him twenty rand. First, he walked in the exit. A bad start. The store security guard was now eyeing him. In the dying light, I was simultaneously trying to watch him inside the store *and* the bags at my feet, while scanning the road for the bus. I could see Sam through the window, springing around the checkout, holding the twenty-rand note and a Magnum in each hand. After a few headshakes from the shop assistants, I realised he was a few rand short. I dashed over and handed him some more money over the exit barrier, while keeping half an eye on the bags. He completed the transaction! *Yes!* Even the shop assistants seemed happy.

This was a step up from his previous shopping experience, buying a cheese and bacon roll at Baker's Delight back home in Leichhardt. This was exactly the sort of experience we were seeking in Africa, pushing Sam's boundaries and expanding his skills into new areas. But that didn't mean it wasn't trying and tiring. The bus arrived, and we pounced onto the bucket seats like children scrambling for the last spots in a game of musical chairs.

On the bus, for the first time ever, Sam challenged me to a staring competition. I didn't know he knew such a thing existed. It was quite strange having a staring competition with someone who has 'significant impairment in quality of gaze', one of the diagnostic criteria for autism. Some studies have shown that autistic individuals look more at the mouth of the person speaking to them, rather than the eyes like most of us. As you can imagine, this often leads to social misunderstanding.

Anyway, I won the staring competition even though I didn't want to. Sam won the second round by pretending to poke me in the eye. Full points for lateral thinking.

Towards the end of the bus trip Sam made a strange request, out of the blue and way too loud: 'Dad, be like Hitler.' I knew what he meant. Months earlier Sam had stumbled across a YouTube clip of the movie *Downfall* where Hitler completely loses it, ranting and screaming at his entourage. Sam had been intrigued and often re-enacted the scene, or alternatively got me or his brothers to do so. He wanted me to shout 'Nein, nein, nein!' I was *not* going to do this in a bus half full of German tourists. I tried to shush him and ignore him at the same time.

He tried again, shouting, *'Dad! Be Hitler!'*

I hissed at him. 'Sam, don't say that!'

Again, way too loudly, 'Why? Because there are Germans on the bus?'

I winced and shrank into my seat.

As we drove through the extensive industrial outskirts of Durban, I realised it was much larger than the sleepy beachside city I had imagined. Sam was happy as a clam. Big cities equal fast internet, which indeed proved to be the case. We spent a fairly relaxed couple of days recharging ourselves and our devices, reorganising packs, and shopping, as well as biking down the magnificent beachfront boulevard full of skateboarders, *tut-tut* drivers, buskers and surf-wetted bodies, black, brown and white. A marching band went by, with dancing teenage Zulu warriors following them. Noise and colour split the high-rise buildings from the sand and surf.

Sam and I visited an aquarium, which introduced us to myriad interesting creatures, including great white sharks, spiked lionfish and odd worm-like creatures that bobbed their blind heads out of sands at the bottom of the Indian Ocean. Trouping through the city, we passed Indian markets where stalls were fronted with open bowls of cone-shaped piles of spices, and draped with silk, and the driving rhythms of Indian pop music piped through the winding alleyways. Durbs has the largest Indian population outside India, with 1.5 million people of Indian descent in and around the city.

At the hostel, the white South African cook, Etienne, was offering an Indian feast for dinner so I decided to sign us up. Etienne had seen Sam pacing around the communal living room earlier and asked what his story was.

'He's on the autism spectrum,' I replied.

Etienne beamed. 'Oh, I *love* autistic people!'

That's not a reaction you normally get. I liked Etienne. 'Really?' I enquired. 'Why?'

'They think outside of the square,' he explained. 'They are the ones who think of things other people don't. The person who invented fire or the wheel, they could well have been autistic.' Etienne was right, of course. Many of the well-known geniuses through history were probably autistic. Great minds often do not think alike and can achieve great things because they think differently.

At the excellent dinner, Sam agreed to eat Indian food for the first time. This was a big step for him, given how aromatic it was. Etienne gently encouraged Sam as he had his first taste of beef curry. Etienne conceded to Sam that using your fingers was okay when eating Indian, as long as you ate with your right hand and you did it in a certain way. He demonstrated, perching curry and rice on the end of his middle fingers and pushing it forward into his mouth with the back of his thumb. I was stunned and proud when Sam was able to do it too.

I also filmed Sam and Etienne in one of Sam's planned conversations for the university study, as well as recording a chat with me. Sam didn't mind being filmed, and he liked the idea he might become a 'famous boy'. Most of the time he didn't notice the camera.

Later that evening, on the rooftop outdoor dining area, I talked to Etienne and Kirk, a young white African carpenter from the Drakensberg, who was in Durban on holidays. Discussion again drifted to politics and the future of South Africa. Kirk had spent a lot of time in other African nations. He also expressed frustration with the politics and admitted he felt more frightened of crime in South Africa than in much poorer nations to the north. But Kirk and Etienne both rejoiced in their nation. Towards the end of our discussion there was a loud bang in the streets below. They looked at me circumspectly.

'A car backfiring?' I suggested.

They answered together. 'A gunshot.'

Our four weeks in South Africa were over. We left South Africa on Freedom Day, a public holiday to commemorate the first free election in 1994. The country had bewitched me. Such complexity, such beauty and such extraordinary people. Crime yes, poor leadership possibly, but full of promise and joy.

As we left, I once again reflected on how the intervention was going. I'd certainly had to recalibrate. My fairly rigid plan of having a routine of activities each day had been blown out of the water by the trials and tribulations of travel, by our plans going awry, by the unexpected. This wasn't necessarily a bad thing.

Maybe I was being a bit autistic; it is a strongly genetic condition, after all. I realised I had to go with the flow more; expect less in terms of achievement but seize opportunities when they arose. The best days seemed to be when we had less travelling and tourism activities and more time to focus on Sam and neuroplasticity. I planned to have more days like this in the countries to come. I had known that South Africa would involve a lot of travelling, but it would be up to me to decide what we committed to from now on. I needed to slow down and focus on the task at hand. I needed to be a less static, more dynamic version of myself. Nonetheless, I was feeling pretty good about things. I knew Sam had already experienced a lot and learnt so much already.

CHAPTER 8

I don't want to be normal

Sam continued to object to Namibia even as we waited at the airport to fly there, but without much enthusiasm. It was as though he was expressing his right to protest rather than an aversion to the country itself.

'We're not going to spend a month in Namibia,' he said.

'We might,' I countered.

'Maybe a few days,' he suggested.

'We'll see.'

As soon as the plane took off, he found a new target: Botswana, the next country on our itinerary. 'We're not going to Botswana.'

'I'm not sure,' I replied, 'We'll decide later.'

He nodded, seemed content with that. 'Yes, later.'

During the plane trip, I spied a good opportunity for a 'nudge' approach. This is when you gently nudge someone into doing something they are almost, but not quite, ready to achieve. It is based on the concept of the Zone of Proximal Development (ZPD) developed by Russian child psychologist Leo Vygotsky in the 1930s. Despite his brilliant breakthrough, poor old Leo died in his forties from tuberculosis and his theory didn't become widely known until it was rediscovered in the 1970s. His concept is now the basis of modern learning theory, and most schoolteachers would be familiar with it.

The ZPD is a learning space. Imagine an individual's skill base as a big bubble. Something they're able to do is inside the bubble, and something they can't is outside. These skills could be as varied as what foods someone can eat, the ability to ride a bicycle or master algebra, or, in Sam's case, whether you can tolerate long sleeves. The ZPD are those skills that are just outside the bubble, in the 'proximal' zone. You can nearly do them, but fall just short. Give someone a task way beyond their skill set and they will probably fail and their confidence may suffer. In contrast, ZPD skills can be mastered fairly easily if the individual is given the right support and encouragement. Their bubble, or skill base, grows. This is how humans learn best, and good teachers aim to hit this zone as often as possible.

Sam's opportunity for a nudge was his lunch. He was served beef ravioli with a tomato-based sauce. Sam had eaten beef ravioli many times—it is one of his favourite foods—but he doesn't like the texture of sauces. I peeled the foil lid off the container.

'I don't like this,' he stated, as soon as the food was revealed.

'You like ravioli,' I protested.

Sam pointed at the meal. 'I don't like this.'

'How about ten forkfuls,' I suggested.

'One.'

'Ten.'

'Five.'

'Seven.'

'Five.'

I stood my ground. 'No, seven.'

'Okay, seven,' he finally agreed. He ate the seven forkfuls, although some were really half forkfuls. The dinner then sat in front of him for a while.

'They're going to take it away soon. If you want any more you need to eat it now,' I said.

He had clearly liked the taste. The hesitance was purely due to the fact it was something new, something he didn't normally eat. It was his neophobia, fear of the new, that was the issue, not the taste or texture of the pasta or sauce. He started to pick at the dish with his fingers, nibbling. Soon he picked up his fork and ate the whole thing.

I smiled at him. 'I'm so proud of you. You don't normally eat sauces, and now you do. That was very mature, Sam. Very grown up.'

He smiled thoughtfully. 'Yeah,' he said.

Why is neophobia so common in autism? One possible explanation is the Intense World Theory. A central issue with people with autism is an inability to effectively filter the sensory information they receive from the world, so they become overwhelmed. The world is too intense for them, so they retreat to only accepting information that's predictable. If something is new to you, it's unpredictable.

Sam had overcome his fear, his neophobia, of sauces. He now eats them. From little things big things grow.

Looking out the plane window as we approached Windhoek, the landscape reminded me of Western Australia or the Northern Territory: flat, dry and empty. I didn't see a single building until the wheels hit the tarmac, and this was the country's international airport! While Namibia is physically much larger than France, it's home to only 2.3 million people.

Sam and I chatted with Fernando, the driver from Chameleon hostel, who picked us up. From Mozambique originally, his English was solid but his knowledge of Australia limited to there being lots of kangaroos. I educated both him and Sam on the basics of the Australian geography, economy and politics.

'Is Australia big?' Fernando enquired.

'Oh yes, very big. About a third the size of the whole of Africa,' I replied.

He raised his eyebrows. 'Oh!'

Sam piped in from the back seat. 'But Africa is much poorer.'

'Yes, Sam, it is,' I said.

'And it doesn't have good internet,' he added.

We had planned to spend a few days in the capital while I organised a rough itinerary with a tour organiser at the hostel. It was arranged that we'd go to Etosha National Park with a tour group leaving in four days' time. We'd be camping, a fact I didn't want to break to Sam just yet. He was already stressed enough: for some reason his Nintendo DS didn't want to connect to the hostel's wi-fi.

We walked into the city on the second day to do some shopping, banking and visit the post office. Windhoek, which is German for windy corner, wasn't that windy, at least it wasn't that day. It's relatively small, similar in size to a regional city in Australia. While there were homeless people and beggars on some corners, the poverty was less obvious than in South Africa—or maybe we were just getting more used to it. I saw little razor wire and few electric fences.

Windhoek gave off a cool vibe. The people were relaxed, even the police and security guards. Women wore elaborate braids in their hair and had a sense of confidence. People smiled a lot. The only hint of aggression was drivers' fondness for their car horns. The traffic, what there was of it, was genteel. It was a likeable and functional city.

The post office, however, reminded me of one from my childhood: vast, bureaucratic and slow. It took forty-five minutes, a half-hour wait in the queue and fifteen minutes at the high stone counter to mail one padded envelope. Each stamp had to have five dots of glue in identical places before the parcel was taped up, stapled, ink-stamped and registered in a multitude of ways. The small package looked so important by the end you would have thought it contained the Dead Sea Scrolls. Sam thought the bank looked like Gringott's, the goblin bank in the Harry Potter books, and while it did have a similar feel, the friendly Namibian woman serving us was a lot nicer than your average goblin.

That evening, three young Germans invited Sam and I to join them for a drink at a nearby five-star hotel, one that apparently had five-star views of Windhoek. The hotel was in a castle on a hill that had been built by early German colonialists; it seemed an incongruous sight in this African desert nation. It did, however, serve as a reminder of Namibia's violent colonial past. In the first decade of the twentieth century, seventy thousand people, more than half of the Herero and Nama tribes, were killed in a brutal 'extermination policy' enforced by the notorious General Lothar von Trotha. It was genocide. Water sources were poisoned, a particularly atrocious act in a desert land, and any tribespeople in German territory were shot on sight. Yet another example of the terrible history of colonialisation on the African continent.

As we got into the taxi, Sam bluntly asked the two German women their age. They were both nineteen. I suspected he was disappointed they weren't closer in age to him. Oh dear. In many ways he is a typical teenage boy. He was soon talking about one of his minor obsessions, Grand Theft Auto, a violent and sexist video game from the US. He has never been allowed anywhere near it, but he knew about it from the web. I repeatedly had to steer him away from 'inappropriate' conversation, but they all tolerated his quirkiness well.

I tried to get Sam to relay to them some of the details of our travels, as they were on their way to South Africa. We discussed Lesotho: Sam described it as 'beautiful, but boring'. I think 'boring' meant 'no internet' but at least he had realised it was beautiful.

Sam then asked a curious question. 'What were the goats saying?'

I realised he meant the goats we'd seen being shorn in Lesotho. 'I don't know. What do you think they were saying?'

In his best angry voice, he replied, '"Take your hands off me; I don't want to go up there."'

We filmed a couple of video interviews with Sam and the German girls for the university project and Sam co-operated well, as did the girls. I thought it would be problematic to get other people to participate in this sort of thing, but everyone seemed very happy to oblige. Maybe that was partly due to Sam's innate charm. His never-ending smile and his quirkiness makes him very engaging, even if he struggles with communication.

The western sky glowed orange as the checkerboard of city lights started to emerge from the growing darkness below us. It resembled a mini Los Angeles. We finished our drinks and called for a cab. It wasn't a long walk back to the hostel, but three people had been robbed in the area the previous week. The taxi driver ripped us off, of course, knowing we had little choice but to go with him.

The next day was a bit of a turning point in the trip for me. I finally had a completely free day, no laundry or shopping, nothing at all. I was able to focus completely on Sam. We finished his schoolwork by lunchtime, and then we had a day of firsts.

It was the first time Sam ever made breakfast for himself—and for me, with my supervision.

For the first time on the trip we did four neuroplasticity exercises in one day—chess, boxing, cards and throwing and catching a ball—and Sam seemed to be engaged and improving on all four skill sets.

I posted the first external hard drive full of filming from the first month back by courier to Australia.

We had our first swim of the trip at the pool at the hostel.

Sam wrote his first ever postcard. It was to his Aunt Helen, and read as follows:

Dear Auntie Helen,
We started out at Cape Town then in Hermanus then in
Mossel Bay then in Wilderness then in Port Elizabeth then
in Chintsa then in Coffee Bay then in Sarni Point [sic]
then in Durban then flight to Namibia and stopped at
Chameleon. From Samuel Best.

What it lacked in description it made up for in detail.

As for the neuroplasticity exercises, the boxing improved faster than the chess, with Sam starting to get a rhythm to our punching combinations. The chess, however, didn't seem to interest him that much; well, not yet. The ball throwing was definitely sky-rocketing, with Sam taking some pride in developing a skill that had previously eluded him. It became apparent to me that this was more than just neuroplasticity and increasing brain traffic: it seemed that self-esteem was also tied up in all this.

And also for the first time I introduced a new motivation for Sam to improve his social and communication skills: scoring the day out of ten. It came about through a discussion I'd had with Sam a few days prior. I had been trying, yet again, to explain why we weren't going home any time soon, and my strategy of just saying 'We'll see' was wearing thin.

He had pleaded with me again. 'But I want to go back to Sydney tomorrow.'

'Sam, we can't,' I'd replied softly. 'We're here to make you better. To make you normal.'

'But I don't want to be normal,' he'd protested.

I'd absorbed the confronting statement, which went to the core of the ethics of this intervention. I went for a long walk to reflect. He may have believed he didn't want to be 'normal'—well, not if it involved this much effort—and perhaps my choice of words was poor, but I knew as his parent that it was in his best interests if we were able to smooth over his areas of weakness as much as possible. At the end of the day, this experiment was not about obtaining a statistically significant positive result in the Griffith University study, it was about Sam being able to have a girlfriend or hold a job.

So I decided to change tack. I needed to get him motivated. I set up a scoring system where the judge, myself, had control of the game. I told Sam if he scored eight out of ten for behaviour seven days in a row we could go home. His eyes immediately lit up; he had something to aim for now. He just failed to realise

I had complete discretion over what his score would be, and therefore complete control over the timing of our return.

It was deceptive, but I believed it was in his best interests. One of the leading voices on autism, Temple Grandin, was interviewed for Andrew Solomon's multi-award-winning book about raising challenging children, *Far From the Tree*. Grandin, who is herself on the spectrum, firmly believes that the higher functioning you make someone with autism, the happier he or she is likely to be, even if this sometimes involves a little 'tough love' on the parent's part: 'Some of these kids, you've got to jerk them out of it. If you're not somewhat intrusive you're not going to get anywhere with them.'

Another leading voice in the autism community, John Elder Robison, who was diagnosed with Asperger's in his forties, explored similar themes in his *New York Times* bestselling memoir, *Look Me in the Eye*:

> Even at sixteen years of age it would have been easy for me to retreat from dealing with humans and move into a world within my own mind . . . It was almost as though I stood in front of Door Number One and Door Number Two, as perplexed as any game show contestant and with much more at stake . . . I chose Door Number One and in doing so moved farther away from the world of machines and circuits—a comfortable world of muted colours, soft light, and mechanical perfection—and closer to the anxiety-filled, bright and disorderly world of people. As I consider that choice thirty years later, I think the kids who choose Door Number Two may not end up able to function in society.

Who better to turn to for advice than those who had walked a similar path to Sam? Their words allowed me to keep the faith in difficult times.

That night we had KFC for dinner. Sam is usually promised McDonald's once a week in Sydney as a reward for good behaviour. He had had it twice in South Africa, but Namibia, amazingly, doesn't have a single McDonald's. I suspected this was also going to be the case in the countries to come. As we sat in the vinyl booth, Sam spontaneously said something positive about Africa for the first time: 'I want to go back to South Africa.'

'Really?' I said, 'Why do you want to go there?'

'They have good internet and McDonald's.'

Of course.

After dinner Sam chilled out in our room listening to music while I chatted to a group of hostel guests including a young woman from Zanzibar called Natalia. When she found out about our trip and its purpose, she went quiet for a while before turning to me holding an old banknote I didn't recognise. 'When I was growing up in Zanzibar there was an old man who always sat outside a store near our house. He used to say hello to me every day when I walked past. When I told him one day I was moving to Namibia with my new husband, he pulled out this banknote.' It was an old Tanzanian five-hundred shilling note, so tattered and worn the images on the note were barely visible. She continued, carefully: 'He gave it to me for luck on my journey. I have kept it on my person ever since. My journey is over, I am staying in Namibia. I would like to give it to you and Sam for luck on yours.'

There was a silence in the group. I smiled, swallowed back my tears, and thanked her.

CHAPTER 9

Lion country

We were due to leave for Etosha National Park the next day, and then I had planned for a few days in the coastal city of Swakopmund before another three-day tour to the south of Namibia. After that our options were limited. Further travel in Namibia was difficult unless we hired a four-wheel drive and it could be dangerous if we broke down in the middle of nowhere. There was no roadside assistance service. Local transport barely existed in this desert country.

And then there was Botswana. I had been told that budget tourism was actively discouraged in Botswana. Government tourism policy was explicitly directed at high-end travellers. Our best option would be to just join an organised tour that took us straight across Botswana all the way to Victoria Falls.

This would put us way ahead of our one country per month schedule, but that was okay. It would mean more time sitting by Lake Malawi. Or maybe we could backtrack from Victoria Falls into Botswana again if we wanted to, or perhaps we could go to Zimbabwe. The travel guide agreed to see if there were two tickets available in around three weeks. I was happy we had a plan, but anxious I wasn't getting Sam involved in these decisions. I'd hoped he'd be more involved in the actual challenges of travel, but these decisions were hard enough for me, and a long way from Sam's Zone of Proximal Development.

Later that day, one of hostel's travel guides, a genial Namibian fellow, caught up with Sam and me as we were leaving the hostel. 'We have spoken to the tour group organising the Botswana trip and they were a bit concerned about Sam and whether he would be okay on a ten-day overland trip,' he said. 'They were worried about whether this would be problematic for the other travellers.'

My face dropped. 'Oh.'

He looked embarrassed. 'They would like to know how he goes on the three-day trip before they decide. So when you get back they'll let us know.' He paused and added, 'Hopefully it will be okay.'

I forced a smile and a nod. 'Sure.' I could understand the company's concerns, but I still felt gutted.

On the truck the next day was a veritable United Nations, with Germans, Canadians, Swiss, a Korean girl and a Japanese man, all headed to a safari at Etosha, world famous for its wildlife. Heading north out of Windhoek, we drove down Beethhovenstrasse, Bahnhofstrasse, Robert Mugabe Avenue and Nelson Mandela Avenue. We soon left the small city and started across the flat plains. Impressive mountains occasionally tipped the otherwise flat horizon that stretched in every direction. I was reminded of old westerns, and outback Australia. Olive green scrub was scattered higgledy-piggledy over the plains and hills, above cream and pale green grasses that sat on the rust-orange earth.

Anthills started to appear; three-metre-high witch's hats of clay. Occasionally they surrounded black tree trunks, and some had bushes sprouting from their peaks, looking like skinny men with crazy hair. Kind of what I looked like.

On the wide open road we passed underneath a storm which covered half the sky, with crepuscular rays of light emanating from its edge. Sam was intrigued. 'God is coming,' he said.

'Perhaps,' I replied.

Once we had entered Etosha, we immediately started spotting animals on the roadside. There was a limping zebra, all alone, easy pickings for the lions. I thought of her awful impending fate.

Sam piped up. 'I can see a giraffe.' I couldn't see it, and nor could anyone else. A confabulation? Two minutes later the rest of us saw it; my boy must have eagle eyes. The giraffe spread his legs, a collapsing quadruped, and lowered his head down to the nearly dry waterhole. Impalas and springboks scattered from the noise of the truck. A lone bull elephant was spied ripping branches off a tree, with one large eye fixed on us.

It was nearly sunset when we reach the campsite, which was more like a village surrounded by a large fence to deter lions. That day we were the ones inside the enclosure, not the animals. Sam slowly realised that there was no option besides a tent. He was not happy.

The Namibian driver and his assistant threw the tents off the roof of the truck and everyone pitched in to help. Sam decided to put his foot down. 'I am not sleeping in a tent.'

'Sam, you have to,' I replied.

'I'll sleep over there.' He pointed to some nearby holiday flats within the enclosure.

I tried to explain the situation to him. 'Sam, we're not allowed to stay there. Other people own those.'

He thrust his fist towards the holiday flats. 'I'll make them let me sleep there.' While my back was turned, he took off. I ran after him, and he ran further. I eventually caught up with him as he ran through a restaurant. He was yelling as I approached him. 'I am not staying in a tent! You can't make me! I want a better father! You are a Voldemort father!'

The concerned restaurant staff came out to see what was going on. Eventually Sam agreed to sit down in the gutter outside the restaurant and chat and calm down. A protracted negotiation ensued. Sam should parley with the North Koreans; he would wear them down soon enough.

Eventually we walked back to the tents near the truck, which were now all assembled. He held my hand as we lumbered along, knowing he had done wrong. The driver said he could sleep in the truck if he wanted to. Sam was happy with this. He grabbed his Nintendo DS and sat in the toilet block, not wanting to have anything to do with the tent.

The rest of the group walked over to a nearby waterhole and watched the spectacular sunset but I dared not leave Sam in the toilet block so I had to sit that one out. The limitations of travelling with a child with special needs, I suppose.

After dinner I was able to talk Sam into walking with the others back to the waterhole. There was a viewing area above the lion-proof fence, and we looked down on the waterhole, which was surrounded by rocks and lit by floodlights. Like a choreographed pantomime, a black rhino sauntered down to the edge for a drink. A few minutes later a large herd of zebras played their part and came down beside him. Off in the distance a lion roared, which spooked the herd. They hesitated, appearing to decide if continuing to drink was worth the risk. But Sam's patience had worn thin. I had to decide between forcing him to stay, so that I could see what played out in this game of predator and prey, and the risk of over-stressing Sam. We headed back to the tents.

On the way, negotiations continued. 'Tents are for poor people,' Sam said.

'There's no other option.'

'I'll sleep in the truck.' He looked at me. 'The man said I could.'

I didn't want him sleeping in the truck, as I didn't want him alone at night and I certainly didn't want to sleep there when I had a mattress in a tent. 'How about just trying ten minutes in the tent, just to see how it goes.'

'Okay,' he acquiesced. 'But only ten minutes and then I'll go in the truck.'

Ten minutes became thirty, and then Sam remembered. But the truck was now locked. *Good.* 'So now the tent is the only option. It's not too bad,' I said.

'Unfair!' he whined. 'I want the truck.'

'Just lie down and see how you go,' I said gently.

The others returned from the waterhole. The lions had appeared after all. At least Sam went to sleep in the tent. As the group chatted, jackals flitted around the site looking for scraps from the tables and during the night I tried to discern between the snores coming from the tents and the lion roars and elephant calls off in the distance. It was difficult sometimes. Hyenas joined the chorus before dawn.

We arose at 5.30 a.m. to get a start on the animal spotting at the best time of day. The group scrambled to break camp to hit the waterholes early.

As we drove through Etosha on the rough dirt roads, animals seemed to be everywhere. The zebras and springboks were so common the sightings soon became uneventful. Wildebeest, giraffes, ostriches, black-faced impalas and red hartebeests were spotted. At a waterhole, a yellow and red tawny eagle sat on a dead tree. A large wildly plumed secretary bird pecked the sand and rocks for grubs. It reminded Sam of the phoenix in Harry Potter. Flamingos filled a large waterway, and a hyena bloated with his night's kill lay digesting.

At every intersection of the winding dirt roads, a sign instructed you not to get out of your car. This was lion country. And sure enough, soon two lions loped towards us across the plains. The serious cameramen on the bus went nuts with their telephoto lenses. A Japanese guy had a lens on his camera that looked like it belonged on a surface-to-air missile.

A German teenager who was sitting next to Sam teased him. 'Do you think they have smelt you, Sam?'

'No!' he said quickly.

Smiling cheekily, she continued. 'They like the young ones. You will be first to be eaten.'

'No!' he grinned, getting the joke.

The lions veered off. No one was eaten; well, not that day.

Etosha, which means 'wide great place' in Oshiwambo, celebrated its centenary in 2007, which makes it one of the oldest national parks in the world. Flat rocky plains scattered with scrubby mopane trees and saltbush surround a salt pan 130 kilometres wide. The pan was an inland sea a million years ago. We drove down onto it and walked around. It felt eerie, knowing there was nothing but salt-covered dry mud so far in every direction.

As the truck climbed off the pan, we saw some oryx in the tall grassveld, a beautiful hardy antelope that can go for days without water. It is Namibia's national icon, surviving in the oldest desert in the world.

During lunch at a campsite, we walked to another waterhole. Five elephants slowly rolled in. Sam thought it was hysterically funny when one of them did a large poo in the water. So did I.

They were magnificent, and we were all transfixed, Sam included, as we watched them from a viewing platform only metres away. Their gentle perambulation, and the way they splashed themselves down, flinging water and mud with their trunks, showed a grace and serenity that belied their size.

Upon returning to the campsite to eat lunch, we heard there were now twenty-five elephants at the waterhole. Milner, our driver and guide, encouraged us to return, but Sam was by then playing his Nintendo DS in the truck.

'Sam, do you want to stay in the truck?' I asked.

'Yes,' he replied, not looking up.

'Don't wander off anywhere,' I said firmly.

He continued to be transfixed by the game. 'Okay.'

I left Sam in the truck and joined the others at the waterhole. By then the elephants numbered fifteen. Young males wrestled with their trunks, infants snuggled next to their mothers, and an old matriarch watched us warily from the side of the pack.

When I returned to the truck, Sam was gone. Milner said Sam had run off towards the restaurant area without answering questions about where he was going. In a quickening trot I checked the toilets and the shop. No Sam. My search widened as my fears about what might have happened grew. Surely he wouldn't have run out the entrance to the village, past the lion-proof fence? Surely there was nothing out there he would be interested in? *Surely he wouldn't try to get himself back to Sydney?*

Fuck.

Images of Sam being attacked by lions swirled through my head as I sprinted around the complex yelling his name. Milner and some of the others from the truck quickly joined the search. After fifteen excruciating minutes he was found in a toilet block in the other direction. He was merely constipated. He'd circled back behind Milner to find a quiet toilet without the latter realising. Living in your own autistic world means you are sometimes harder to notice.

'Sam, you nearly gave me a heart attack!' I was almost crying with relief as I struggled to catch my breath.

Sam looked concerned. 'Don't die, Dad.'

'I'll try not to.' I thought of the difficult phone call I'd have had to make to Benison if Sam had been killed by lions—not something the parent of an Australian child normally has to worry about.

That night Milner told me the company had asked him to assess whether it would be suitable for Sam to travel with them from Windhoek to Victoria Falls. 'I told them Sam will be fine,' he said, with a smile and a thoughtful expression.

'I don't know about sleeping in tents. It stresses both of us out,' I said.

He looked up from the fire. 'You can book a room at all the places we stop, you know.'

I felt relief sweep over me. 'Oh, excellent! We'll definitely do that.'

Milner smiled. 'He'll be fine, James.'

Before going to bed—again in a tent but this time without any resistance from Sam—I took him to the nearby bush bar so he could buy himself a lemonade, a reward for not fussing about our accommodation. I gave him twenty Namibian dollars, which should be enough, and stood back to see how he would go. He had been improving over his many attempts at retail transactions. Two Namibians were in the bar: a woman behind the counter and a man sitting on a chair nearby.

Sam went up to the bar and spoke to the woman. 'Lemonade. Sprite.'

The woman gave him the drink and, in her thick Namibian accent, asked for fourteen dollars. Sam misheard her, and thought she said forty.

He pointed at her across the counter. '*Liar!* That's too much!'

She spied the twenty-dollar note in his hand. 'Fourteen. One, four.'

'Oh,' Sam said. He handed over the money and got the change. He then looked at the man and said, 'You're bald,' before promptly walking out. I followed, apologising profusely. Well, I *thought* he'd been improving.

A busy few days followed: the long drive back to Windhoek, neuroplasticity exercises and school lessons. We were getting into a real rhythm here, with Sam and I negotiating at the beginning of the day which lessons and exercises were on the agenda. As always, I would push him a little into his discomfort zone. His chess game was starting to progress, and there was now more of a competitive edge to the games. The boxing was easier for him, so I invented more difficult combinations. The cards continued to be a struggle. We took another long shuttle bus ride, this time with local Namibians, not tourists, over to the German coastal town of Swakopmund.

Skipping over the flat central Namibian plains, we watched the sun set on the wide flat horizon after yet another cloudless sky. I reflected on how the trip was going. There were some improvements in Sam, certainly, but it was still early days. The trip had still been way too busy—I was struggling to reel in the pace, and unfortunately the next few weeks were also heavily booked up. There was little I could do about it. I would have preferred to be staying in Swakopmund for a week rather than the three nights we had planned.

Sam continued to grumble about being away from his electronics, away from the certainty of binary. Yet he didn't seem nearly as stressed as he'd been a week or two earlier and his facial rash had resolved. Since we'd introduced the scoring system, he seemed to be more focused on improving his own behaviour. He did, however, still need to improve his willingness to face his fears. To pick hot toast out of the toaster, to eat scrambled eggs, to wear long sleeves.

I was also feeling the strain. The burden of responsibility was challenging my body and spirit. My heels were bruised from so much walking with heavy luggage and I'd developed 'tennis elbow' tendonitis in my left arm from swinging our twenty-kilogram packs around. Backpacking had been much easier in my twenties. My forty-ninth birthday was the following Sunday, and I was feeling like an African taxi with 400,000 kilometres on the odo: still running, but wondering which part is going to breakdown next.

As well as the flesh, my spirit was also feeling weak. I was missing my wife terribly. I was increasingly excited about chances to talk to her on Skype and when I couldn't get through I would feel very down. I worried about my other two boys and what they were up to, and issues happening in their lives.

While we were consciously working on Sam's adaptive skills—a psychology term to describe the practical, everyday skills a human needs to function in their environment—mine were also being tested and expanded. The countless challenges each day—technology, writing, teaching, filming, blogging, supervising Sam and just travelling—left me exhausted each evening. I never knew what was around the corner, but I was getting better at going with the flow. There was the constant niggle in the back of my head that I had to get this right. This was the only opportunity I would have to help Sam in this way. I had to make it count.

CHAPTER 10

Sand safari

Our first day in Swakop, as Swakopmund is affectionately known, was spent chilling out. We walked into town, surrounded by rolling dunes on three sides and rolling waves from the South Atlantic on the fourth. Swakop was once the main harbour for German south-west Africa, so it's full of colonial German architecture, with dormers in steeply pitched shingle roofs, symmetrical facades and small casement windows. It seemed fitting our lunch was a wurst sandwich.

On the long walk back, a tiring Sam asked how far it was to the hostel. 'Is it right?' I broke out the video camera to record our conversation as we walked down the road, holding it out on an extended arm, selfie-style.

'Say it properly,' I replied.

'Is it the next one right?'

'No,' I said again. 'Slow down and say the whole thing. "Dad, do we turn right at the next intersection?"'

He tried again. 'Dad, do we go right at next section?'

I encouraged him to give it another go.

'Dad, do we go right at the next insection?'

'In-ter-sec-tion.'

He focused all his attention. 'In-ter-sec-tion.'

I smiled and patted him on the back. 'Good.'

After a pause, he looked up at me. 'I'm trying hard, Dad.'

My heart welled up inside my chest. 'I know you are. You really are.' I was so proud of him.

I was trying hard to slow down, I really was, but when I discovered there was a day excursion to the Namib Desert from Swakop the temptation was just too great. It would be a good geography excursion. Well, that was my excuse and I was sticking to it. We joined two older English couples and a German fellow in a small four-wheel drive truck that pulled up outside our hostel. Our driver and guide, Burger, was an ex-waxhead from Namibia. In his misspent youth he had walked his red kudu leather shoes on every beach in South Africa and Namibia. Well, so he claimed, and who was I to doubt him?

Heading south, we passed through desert to Walvis Bay, an ex-British protectorate that had been subsumed into Namibia when apartheid collapsed. Now a playground for Namibia's well-heeled, architect-designed houses and condos lined its boulevards. The large lagoon was home to vast flocks of flamingos, making all sorts of malarky. Two large males flared their tail feathers at each other in an elaborate dance to impress the females in the flock. A long line of pelicans, looking like beads on an invisible string, soared over the truck.

Burger clearly enjoyed his job. Without warning he yanked hard at the wheel and suddenly we were off-road, sliding on the narrow beach between the dunes and the surf. The coastline south was five hundred kilometres of sand, with nary a dwelling or even a tree. We were on the longest beach in the world, which was also home to the largest diamond field in the world—the backbone of the Namibian economy. The highly secret and secure mines were located somewhere in the great desert spreading below us.

The dunes towered above to our left before plunging steeply down to the waterline. Their mustard-cream hues were striped with lines of crimson where garnets remained, long broken into dust by the toiling winds, while the lighter crystals of other stones had blown away. The grey sand of the beach was new. As it aged, the iron-rich magnetite crystals would oxidise and become a richer, more vibrant colour. Blown over the ever-expanding and changing dunes, the sands darkened over the eons to yellow, orange and finally red.

The dunes of the Namib were living beasts. Our footprints would be swept away by the South Atlantic winds within minutes. They were being moulded before our eyes. It was relentless. If our truck was left for a day, its wheels would have to be dug out. It was a beautiful but unforgiving vortex, absorbing all and governing all.

'We are in the desert!' Sam chimed from the back seat. 'It is the oldest desert in the world.'

Burger asked how old it was.

'Fifty-five to eighty million years,' Sam promptly replied. Burger raised his eyebrows, impressed. Our geography field excursion, coupled with our earlier Google searches, was proving a success.

Late in the morning, we climbed one of the larger beachside dunes. It took about half an hour to make the ascent. As I stood on the edge of the dune, exposed skin rasped by the flying sand, I experienced vertigo while looking into the shadowy valley below. The view from the top was dunes stretching north and south and inland as far as the eye could see. The dunes stretched over one hundred kilometres inland, in fact. Fifty thousand square kilometres of sand, sand, sand. I was reminded of the science-fiction movie *Dune*. I hoped there were no giant sandworms.

Sam pretended to be dying of thirst at the top, and rolled around on the sand. Unfortunately, the Vaseline we'd applied to his face to stop his rash returning collected a goatee of sand. Not a good look.

After lunch, our truck surfed the dunes, as Burger cut the engine and let it slide a hundred or so metres down the sixty-degree slopes. It was the best, and certainly the most natural, rollercoaster ride I've ever been on.

On our way back to Swakop, vegetation slowly started to reappear. Hardy animals came with it. A lone springbok, a pair of jackals protecting their hidden young in their lair, a dune lark watching over its nest. We were well satisfied after an exhilarating day. Sam was happy he'd been brave and made the difficult climb up the dune. Tomorrow we were heading to the largest and reddest dunes in the world, smack in the middle of the desert at Sossusvlei. This would be a new challenge.

Our driver for the next three days was Gabriel. Thin, bespectacled and congenial, his placid manner permeated the small truck. As a married Herero man, by custom he was obliged to always wear a hat and carry a walking stick. Gabriel's tribal name was Veruanaije, which was also his father and grandfather's name. If Gabriel were to have a son, it would continue to be passed on. His name translates to a question. When the Germans fought the Herero back in 1904, older women in the villages were told the Germans fought with guns and horses. '*Veruanaije?*' was their reply, meaning 'What do the Herero men fight with?'

Our small group contained only two other travellers: TJ, an effusive Dutch fellow in his fifties, and Corinna, an eighteen-year-old

Londoner on a break from volunteer teaching in the north of Namibia. From Swakop we headed inland to skirt the Namib sands on their eastern border. At first, the road was salt, kept intact by the regular moisture of the coastal fogs. Once away from the coast, it became gravel corrugations.

The flat landscape, suffused with salt, was the faintest yellow. Mirage lines hovered on the horizon, and heat and glare reflected off the pale and flat rock-strewn terrain and still paler road. Salt lines streaked the dirty brown and black hills on the horizon, resembling nothing so much as giant mounds of tiramisu. We crossed the Tropic of Capricorn and then an ancient dry riverbed marked only by a line of deep-rooted trees.

The road wound down and through a deep gorge that wasn't visible until you were almost on top of it. We descended to the dry, shaded, sandy riverbed below. During World War II, when Namibian-based Germans were recalled to the fatherland to fight, two young geologists went AWOL and hid in this gorge for two years, living off game and digging into the riverbed for water, before they were finally caught and imprisoned. It was a good place to hide from the heat, and from the world.

Sam completed his schoolwork in the truck and then read more of *Harry Potter and the Philosopher's Stone.* I was so glad he was finally reading fiction. Now he had started it seemed like there was no stopping him. During the trip I asked Gabriel if there were lions about.

'No, but there are leopards,' Gabriel answered. 'There are three big cats you need to be careful of, Sam: lions, cheetahs and leopards. When you come across any of these you need to know what to do. If you see a lion, you should look him in the eye, slowly walk backwards, and you should be okay. If you see a cheetah, make a lot of noise and rush towards it, and they will usually run away.' Sam was looking worried. Gabriel continued. 'But with a leopard, you are in big trouble. They are very aggressive and very strong and if they decide to attack you, you will be killed. You run up a tree, they climb after you. You cross a creek or river, they follow you.'

Sam wasn't happy. 'No! Not die! I will get away.'

I piped up. 'Don't worry, Sam, we won't come across a leopard.'

After the gorge, we travelled through undulating plains leading up to red rock towers. Occasionally we spotted zebras, ostriches and oryxes grazing near the road. Large mountains appeared first as faint blue ridgelines in the distance before looming large and ominous either side of the road, which cannoned straight between them like a cathedral aisle. Cliffs, mesas—the lines of this landscape were either vertical or horizontal, with little deviation.

We reached our desert campsite at sunset after being delayed by a flat tyre sustained on the gravel. Sam was happy the 'tents' had power, en suite bathrooms and, incredibly, wi-fi (well, more or less). This was soft camping. Benison would have liked it: there was even somewhere to plug in her hair dryer. The only thing missing was a fence. Hmm.

Over dinner, Sam had more opportunities to experiment with new foods: pup, a cornmeal mash, and curry sauce and cucumber. I also encouraged him to practice his conversation skills with these relative strangers, and used the video camera to record some footage for the university study. We discovered that Corinna had taught Namibian children with the following Anglicised names: Precious, Big Boy, Silence (well, he'd be easy to teach),

Marvellous, Surprise, Treasure, Rejoice, Promise, Given and Gift (twins, with a younger sister Bienvenue), Trust, Angel (a boy) and, my favourite, Brangelina. (Angelina Jolie and Brad Pitt had a long association with Namibia. Their daughter Shiloh was born in Swakopmund in 2006.)

The morning reveille went off at 4.30 a.m., and we were ready at the nearby park gates before dawn. Cliffs and rocks slowly emerged in the low light while we waited. Sam had never been up before dawn before; at least, not in his conscious memory anyway. At dawn, the gates opened to admit a long line of tourist vehicles and four-wheel drives into the park.

As our truck passed through the park, red dunes started to appear around the sandy road, increasing in stature as though working towards the dramatic final act. A hot air balloon hovered nearby as the sun rose above the horizon. The road down the valley arced right and the main dune range was revealed: three-hundred-metre-high ancient monsters rendered in deep apricot, light and shadow, serpentine arcs. There was no Atlantic wind moulding the sands here. This was a graveyard of ancient rusted sand: spiritual, still and sombre.

Leaving the vehicle, we ventured over the sands to Deadvlei, a small pan long cut off from water by the encircling dunes. Here camel thorn trees had germinated nine hundred years ago and died six hundred years ago. They still stood, forlorn but proud, their dead limbs and branches reaching for the sky like men dying of thirst. It was an arboreal Pompeii, created not by super-heated ash but super dry and still conditions. Human footprints were visible in the cracked clay from the last time the pan was wet, six centuries ago.

Sam and I took the opportunity to have a quick game of chess. It was a good flat surface for the board. I let him win again, but he was definitely getting savvier. Sam asked questions about the footprints and why the trees died. He didn't like the fact that there had been no water for hundreds of years, and worried we might 'die' from thirst, but fortunately was easily reassured. He asked what score he'd got the previous day.

I decided to give him some encouragement. 'Eight.'

'Yay!' He was truly excited. The ethics spun in my head.

The temperature soared as we tramped up a dune ridgeline. Despite being encouraged and then harassed by me, Sam couldn't make it all the way to the top, but that was okay, it was pretty tough going in the soft sand. Two-thirds of the way up we aborted the attempt and bounced down the steep face at a slow jog, sinking ankle deep with each step. We plonked onto the pan at the base and emptied our shoes of a kilogram of warm red sand apiece.

It had been a great day.

Back at camp, Sam splashed in the pool while I supervised. Gabriel, TJ and Corinna had gone off to visit a nearby gorge, but Sam had had enough. Some toddlers from a group of Germans nearby wandered over towards the pool. Sam wasn't happy. He feels uncomfortable around toddlers, especially without his shirt on. Pointing awkwardly, with a crooked wrist, he said, 'Go away, you.'

The German adults startled. 'Sam, don't,' I cautioned from my chair nearby.

He continued to be bothered by the presence of the toddlers. I hovered carefully until they were whisked away by their parents, who seemed to have caught on that there were issues underlying Sam's behaviour. They weren't fussed, but I was. It was this type of behaviour, unsupervised in years to come, that could get Sam into some seriously troubling situations.

At dinner, Gabriel bailed up to me, excited. 'You know, Sam asked me my middle name and where I came from!' His enthusiasm and insight into Sam was touching.

And with another dinner on safari was another success with Sam trying new food: this time *poike*, a chicken and vegetable stew with rice. On the food front, Sam was kicking goals with both feet.

The next day I turned forty-nine. Sam gave me a tantrum for my birthday. I had told him when he woke up that he hadn't received eight out of ten the previous day after all, but only seven, because of his behaviour at the pool. Sam wasn't happy. 'But they started it,' he said, referring to the toddlers. His anger and frustration rose. Once again I was a bad father whom he variously wanted replaced, gone or dead.

'No, they didn't start it,' I said, firmly but calmly. 'They just wanted to go near the water.'

'But I don't like them doing that,' Sam protested.

'They're allowed, Sam. You're not allowed to order around other people, especially little children.'

Negotiations continued. Tempers rose, and voices. I eventually went to breakfast without him, to give him time to calm down. As I arrived at the breakfast table, Gabriel brought out a chocolate cake with HAPPY BIRTHDAY JAMES piped across the top in white icing, and a small present wrapped in foil and tied up with a ribbon. It turned out to be a box of camping matches. He must have realised it was my birthday when I filled out the forms for the tour, cobbled the cake and present together in Swakop before we left and kept them hidden somewhere in the truck. I was taken aback at the effort and kindness involved. This moment, the birthday cake in the Namib Desert, would stay with me forever.

I retrieved Sam from the room. He was calm now, but more withdrawn and autistic than usual. Knees up, gaze averted, licking his lips, not engaging. The tantrum had distressed him, and he was retreating. I let him have whatever breakfast he wanted, let him eat with his fingers. I just backed off.

At least I was starting to read my son better—getting to know when to push and when not to. I now knew that his previous meltdowns had been followed by long recovery periods in which he needed some downtime. Throughout the morning he remained withdrawn, even during a visit to a cheetah reserve. Sam liked seeing the cheetahs, especially on foot from only ten metres away, but he was still in his shell and bothered by the glare and flies.

By lunch his mood was improving. Copious amounts of Vaseline had kept his resurgent facial rash—as much a consequence of the harsh corrosive environment as his lip-licking—mostly in check. He asked whether he could still get a score of eight today, despite the tantrum. I avoided answering.

The truck swung north, up through the Naukluft Mountains, German for 'small gorge'. Red rock faces hung over us, ominous and foreboding. The mountains had sheltered tribal guerrilla leaders who were subsequently crushed by von Trotha and his Schutztruppe, rebel chiefs and warriors who were now commemorated on banknotes.

Our vehicle tumbled up onto the central Namibian plains. Arid certainly, but verdant in comparison to the parched earth and air of the ancient desert at our backs. There was a bonding in the vehicle, and we were all pleased with the few days we had had together. The others had seen Sam presenting the challenges he does and had seen that he was hard work in an extreme environment, but Sam had also been the entertainer, reframing the world in his own unique way, which had led to wry grins and chuckles. It seemed everyone who met Sam would not forget him.

CHAPTER 11

Namboobia

The tour over, we returned to Windhoek for the third time. I felt like I was starting to know the place. The staff at Chameleon greeted us, particularly Sam, with big smiles. He hurriedly bumped his way through the pool and bar areas determined to check-in as quickly as possible in order to use the wi-fi.

Our trip to the delta and Victoria Falls had been confirmed for eleven days time. For the first occasion in the trip I felt the pressure lift. I was able to focus fully on the task at hand: school and neuroplasticity exercises; neuroplasticity exercises and school. Algebra and geometry; a PowerPoint on the Namib Desert; cells, cell walls, and the role of nuclei; attempts at writing narratives. On Sam's third narrative writing attempt he came up with the following:

The Adventures of Captain Pumpkin.
He is a Famous Captain who watches out for pirates. He has a big American boat called Steamwall boat.
It was built in January 1st 1900 at 12.00 am in New York in a town called hoyatas.

Captain Pumpkin was born in January 1st 1930 at 12.00 am in England in a city called London in UK in Europe. He moved to America in January 1st 1940 at 12.00 am in New York in a town called hoyatas which make him turn 10 years of age. He used this boat to travel since January 1st 1960 at 12.00 am when he just turned 30 years of age. In September 1984 he was 54 years old he enjoyed the big American boat called Steamwall boat. He started watching out for pirates in 1990. He was retired in 2011.

Story 7.5/10
Grammar 8/10

The marks were mine, the rest was his. Not too bad, I thought, though a bit keen on the dates and times. I suppose Captain Pumpkin could have been catching pirates in the 1990s off the Horn of Africa.

We continued with our boxing, cards, chess, catching a ball, and started drawing and checkers. I had wanted to include music, as Sam already had basic keyboard skills from a year of piano lessons, but there wasn't a keyboard we could easily access.

The boxing and chess remained interesting. Sam was getting the idea of chess, certainly, but I'd expected him to be more of a natural given his impressive memory. He wasn't as cautious or strategic as I thought he'd be. He did make the interesting observation that the queen was evil. He'd always had a problem with female monarchs since he encountered the White Witch queen in *The Chronicles of Narnia*.

Maybe the motivation just wasn't quite there yet. I had let him win every game so far. Perhaps I needed to turn the screws a bit, but I also didn't want to push too hard and make it a negative experience. I needed the jelly to wobble, not fall off the plate.

Sam found boxing the most challenging exercise, as it involved force and with it the risk that he might jar a wrist or finger joints if he didn't get his technique correct. Over the days I introduced new challenges, such as uppercuts.

Sam didn't like them. 'Uppercuts are for losers.'

'Oh, I don't know,' I replied, 'good boxers should have all types of hits.'

Sam clenched his fist inside the glove. 'I want to do a power spin instead,' he said, and spun around 360 degrees. I think he was referring to a Mario Kart manoeuvre.

'I don't know how to do one of those, but I wish I did,' I said, truthfully.

We pushed on: uppercut, jab, right cross, left kick, right kick. No more power spins, but he was getting better.

A couple of days into our enforced hiatus, I decided to tackle another adaptive skill: planning, buying for and preparing an evening meal. This was a good example of an activity I intuitively knew we should have been focusing on with Sam back home in Sydney, but it just never seemed to happen. Benison and I just ended up doing it ourselves because it was easier.

Sam and I wrote a shopping list together and walked down to the local supermarket. Sam collected the items and paid at the checkout, while I watched. It took about three times longer than it would have if I had been shopping, but he got there. That evening at the hostel I cooked the sausages while Sam prepared the noodles in the saucepan and tore up some lettuce leaves. His fear of being burnt meant I had to drain the noodles, but that was okay. There was a hint of pride in Sam's smile as the plates hit the table.

Our prolonged stay in Windhoek meant that we also came to know a range of different people from different parts of the world. As well as backpackers and aid workers, we met academics, professionals taking a break, and some interesting free spirits. There was a softly spoken Scot with long dreadlocks and a beard doing his master's in environmental studies in northern Namibia. A couple from Wisconsin—a biologist and a geologist—were deciding in which direction they wanted to head, torn between developed-world academia and the wilds of Namibia's natural environment. Two young pilots, Swiss and English, were trying to build up their flying hours over southern Africa's long stretches. A charming older Spanish man, who was travelling the country with his new Namibian bride, enjoyed a glass of red wine and cigarette at sunset each day after working on a LandCruiser parked in the driveway. A Caribbean-born Frenchwoman with a crew cut had been travelling hard solo through Africa for two years. She had a Range Rover so well equipped for her nomadic lifestyle it included a solar panel, a soldering iron, a sewing machine and an angle grinder. She could replace a drive shaft or make panel-beating repairs on her car in middle of the desert.

Sometimes Sam would interact with them, sometimes he wouldn't. They were often curious about Sam, and our day-to-day activities: our lessons on the computer, boxing in the driveway, playing chess and cards in the lounge.

But I would find out that Sam did occasionally approach some of the girls in the hostel when I wasn't around. A pretty young

German woman with straight dark hair told me, 'He came up to me, stroked my hair, and said "Ginny Weasley," and then walked off. What's that about?' And a youthful-looking Canadian woman had a similar experience. 'Sam came up to me in the lounge room and asked, "How old are you?" I said, "Twenty-six" and he just said, "Oh," and walked off.' I can only assume Sam thought she was too old to attract his interest.

One afternoon we were doing Sam's maths lesson in our room at the hostel. The first exercise was a mini-test, which I got Sam to attempt by himself while I tidied up the room.

'Sam, how many questions are there in the test?' I asked.

'It goes up to "u",' he replied.

'How many is that?' I asked, expecting him to have to work it out.

Without hesitation, he answered, 'Twenty-one'.

I worked it out on my fingers. I don't know why I bothered; I knew he was going to be correct. By the end of the exercise he had also answered questions 'v', 'w', 'x', 'y' and 'z'.

'I thought it only went up to "u",' I said.

'I made up five more questions so it went up to "z",' Sam said.

I smiled to myself. Of course he did.

Writing postcards was proving to be a good way to develop Sam's handwriting and narrative skills. Sam knew he had to write neatly enough for it to be legible, and that the other person's needs, for example, wanting to know how the trip was going and whether he was enjoying himself, should be considered. From Windhoek he wrote cards to his maternal grandparents and to his aunty and uncle. The former was a pretty good effort. The latter, well, I don't know what to say.

Dear Gran and Grandad
We've been to Etosha National park. We saw lots of
elephants, zebras and lots of other animals. It was a bit
boring because we had to stay in a tent.
  We also went to the sand dunes in the namib desert. It
was a bit okay. I climbed a sand dune.
Cheers Sam XX

Dear Roslyn and John and family
Is your surname a biskit?
  Do you have a rabbit?
  We drove down this road.
  Roslyn your name sounds like a royal family. There is a
picture of a lion roaring.
Cheers Sam

To be fair, there was a picture on the front of the postcard of the road that he was referring to, and there was a lion roaring in a small emblem imprinted at the bottom of the card. But for the life of me, I had no idea what their surname, Driscoll, had to do with a biscuit!

One day in Windhoek, we walked down to the hostel driveway to throw and catch the rubber ball. Halfway through the exercise I had an idea. 'Hey, Sam, see if you can just hit it back to me with your hand and not catch it.' I demonstrated. He did it straightaway, and before I knew it we were having handball rallies with five or ten shots in a row. He was really good! I was amazed. This was a fundamental lunchtime activity at any boy's secondary school but I had never expected he would be able to do it, let alone pick it up so quickly. It was such a *normal* thing for a fourteen-year-old boy to do. It's amazing what will grow in the rich, tilled soil of opportunity.

At 3 a.m. that night, I awoke with nausea, cramps and a rumbling stomach. I rushed to the bathroom, the first of about twenty visits. The vomiting and diarrhoea eased off mid morning, but I was left a mess. I knew I needed some oral rehydration solution and anti-nausea medication. Leaving Sam at the hostel, I struggled slowly down the hill to the shopping centre. My muscles ached and I was shivering but I was wary of looking too vulnerable in an African city. Even so, I needed to stop and rest in the gutter a few times. I was sweating profusely by the time I reached the shops, and stumbled past the beggars and street vendors hovering near the entrance, hustling for baksheesh or to sell cheap sunglasses and jewellery.

The pharmacy was open, and I got what I needed. Back to the hostel, this time uphill. I was relieved to make it through the locked gate and back to the room. There was certainly not going to be any boxing or handball for Sam today. I ended up sleeping for most of the day.

The next morning I had mostly recovered, but the day would prove much worse than a stomach bug. From the get-go Sam was in a bad mood. He didn't want to get his breakfast. He didn't want to walk to the shops. He didn't want to do anything, really. I hoped he hadn't caught my virus. Maybe he just hadn't slept well?

When we arrived at the shops, I tried to get him to buy some takeaway food for lunch. It was Sam's worst African retail performance. He stood in front of the shop counter in a daze, twitching and grunting. The two female attendants behind the counter waited for what must have been over half a minute. They glanced at each other occasionally as they tried to figure out what this guy was about. Eventually, with some prompting from me, Sam mumbled an incomprehensible order, and I had to jump in.

I told them the order and took the money from Sam to pay them myself. Angered, Sam attempted to snatch the change from me. 'Give me back the money!' he demanded.

I held the change aloft. 'Sam, I had to pay, you were taking too long.' It quickly escalated.

He grasped again at the money. '*No! I will do it.*'

'It's too late. I've paid.' I was cross now too. Through gritted teeth I told him it had been only a three-out-of-ten performance.

'*Not three! No!*' he screamed at me. He grabbed my head and squeezed and growled. I eventually calmed him down, but not before attracting the attention of security.

We scuttled into the supermarket to get some supplies for the spaghetti bolognaise I planned to cook for us that night. He did better at the checkout, and scored a seven (a fairly generous concession from the judging panel).

Later in the day, Sam and I were meant to be meeting up with the chairperson of Autism Namibia. Benison had found Petra's details on the web and established contact and Petra had kindly offered to show us around her association's resource centre and take us to visit her home afterwards.

Petra had two sons and her eldest, Michael, had autism. Michael was twenty-six years old and non-verbal. I wondered how Sam would interact with him. He knew lots of autistic children through his primary school and our family's social circles, but he had never met an autistic adult before.

As Sam and I sat in the penetrating Namibian sunlight outside the hostel, waiting for Petra to pick us up, he began his usual objections to the trip but in an unusually aggressive tone. 'I want to end the trip now,' he snapped. 'I *demand* to go back to Sydney.'

I was resolute. 'No, Sam. You know the deal. You know what you have to do.'

'You're being too strict,' he complained. 'You're being mean and cruel. I don't want to go to the M countries.' By that he meant Malawi and Mozambique—he had trouble remembering their names but he knew they were very poor. I tried to ignore him but he grabbed my arm and looked me in the eye. 'Go home now, Dad.'

'No, we're not going home until the job is done,' I said through a clenched jaw.

He pointed at me in his unique style, with a straight arm and wrist bent down. 'I will go home. I will go without you.'

'You can't, Sam. I have your passport and you need to buy a plane ticket and you have no money.'

'I will *steal* some money.'

'Don't be silly.'

Petra and Michael drove up. I wondered how this was going to go, given Sam's mood. I sat in the passenger seat and Sam sat next to Michael in the back seat. Michael had a solid build and grunted and rocked as he looked at us with curiosity. He didn't appear threatening in any way to me but Sam looked worried. 'Are you a bully?' he asked, with his head tilted.

Petra reassured Sam. 'Michael can't talk, Sam, but he won't hurt you. He's not a bully.'

The resource centre was housed in a lovely hundred-year-old small stone building in Klein Windhoek. It had originally been the primary school. Klein Windhoek was a well-to-do part of the city that reminded me of the Hollywood Hills: hilly and picturesque in an arid sort of way, with date palms and stylish old houses.

The centre was still a work in progress, but also a place of great energy and activity. Books, magazines, boxed games and toys overflowed from shelves. Sam looking for anything Harry Potter or Pokémon themed, Michael played with some plastic blocks, and Petra and I chatted about autism, therapies, funding and disability in Africa.

Earlier in the week, I had seen a quadriplegic man in a motorised wheelchair being escorted around the city by his carer. It had caused me to reflect on how a serious disability would be handled in a country with next to no social security, where children would be stunted from chronic malnutrition and preventable infectious diseases ravaged the populace. Even in the developed world, the disabled have historically been disenfranchised, their exhausted carers frequently lacking the strength to rally for resources and rights. In many people's eyes they were regarded as a burden, a drain; people you didn't want to think about, in case it happened to you or your kin.

Petra was impressive; her extensive knowledge and commitment to autism and disability soon became clear. She outlined the same old depressing themes I was familiar with in Australia: a lack of awareness, understanding and funding. But, of course, it was all the more brutally evident here in a developing economy. She and her colleagues did the best they could with what they had, which was never enough. Her type, many of whom I know in Australian autism and disability circles, are our unsung heroes.

Petra's house was also pleasingly dominated by books. I met her architect husband, her three dogs and an Afrikaans-speaking grey African parrot. Sam refused to talk and kept escaping to explore bookshelves in other rooms, but he was somewhat interested in the parrot. Petra and I chatted some more on the verandah while

Michael sat between us and played music on his iPad. Every day he would delete all the music he'd listened to, and every evening Petra would re-sync it. Tedious, but that was the score.

Michael had good taste in music. He was listening to a South African string quartet play traditional African music. He seemed to like that I took an interest. He pointed to the trees and said what Petra interpreted as *bahn*, German for train. Did the lines of the branches look like railway tracks? He didn't mind that the message wasn't quite getting through. He was a very accepting individual, happy in his own space.

As we left, Michael spun some plastic pool filter covers like tops. Apparently he liked the sound they made as they wobbled to a stop. So did I, actually. Sam watched him with curiosity, while keeping a careful eye on the dogs that were eager for attention and ready to jump up on him. The visit had been illuminating, and we promised to keep in touch.

While rather graceless, Sam at least hadn't lost the plot. That was to come. I should have known better than to try to get him to help cook dinner. I should have read him better. Halfway through the dinner preparation, with the pasta boiling and the sauce cooking, in the middle of a large bustling kitchen, he ran off. I scrambled to get the pots off the heat and follow him.

As I searched for Sam from room to room, a South African backpacker ran up to me. 'James, your boy is at the gate. He's trying to get out.'

I ran out. There he was, trying to figure out how to unlock the gate. 'Sam, what are you doing?'

'I'm going home,' he said.

I was flummoxed. 'You can't, Sam. You can't go home alone.'

'*I will swim home!*' he shouted, thumping his fist into his hip and standing on tiptoes.

'Sam, it's too far. Nobody can swim that far,' I gently reasoned with him.

Now Sam screamed at the top of his voice, pointing at me as he marched up and down next to the gate. '*You! You are a bad father! You are being mean and awful! Awful father! You! You are a dick! You are a dick-head!*'

Well, that was a new one. The whole hostel would have heard, but at the gate at least we were partly out of sight. He grabbed and squeezed my head as hard as he could, and headbutted me, fortunately not too hard.

It took a long time to talk him down. I followed him as he paced back and forth, now through the hostel. 'Sam, do you realise it is really dangerous for you to go out in a city in Africa by yourself at night? You might get robbed.'

'Or kidnapped,' he added.

'Or kidnapped, yes.'

'I will escape. I will shoot them.'

This was getting ridiculous. 'You don't have a gun.'

'*I will get one,*' he yelled. '*I will shoot them and kill them.*'

Eventually he calmed down enough to agree to sit on his bed and play his Nintendo DS. That night we were staying in a dorm for the first time, as there had been no private rooms available. Great timing! Sam tended to make a huge mess. My plan was to just leave everything in the packs as best I could. At least he was quiet now.

I returned to the kitchen to salvage the meal. Sam flatly refused to eat anything. The other backpackers were aware of my distress and gave me space. I ate my meal alone and then distracted myself with a game of pool.

Eventually Sam approached me at the pool table and agreed to eat some spaghetti. He had written a note on our drawing pad. As he ate, I read:

Take me back to Sydney and not go back to Africa. This must Happen Tomorrow. If you don't you will be sentenced to life in gaol.

Give me 10/10 for this

I couldn't help but smile. Then it dawned on me that our drawing pad had been at the bottom of one of the packs. I entered the dorm in trepidation: our stuff was scattered from one end to the other, all over other people's bunks. I tidied up, feeling very down and fending off annoyed glances from other backpackers.

I was full of doubt. *What the hell was I thinking?* He didn't even have the insight to realise how dangerous going out that gate would be. *And swimming to Australia? Imaginary guns to defeat criminals?* He was so naive.

That night, sinister thoughts crept up on me from dark spaces. They clubbed me from behind, as brutal an assault as Sam squeezing my head from the front. I wanted to go home too. I was overtired, overstretched, overwhelmed. The trip was meant to be recharging, yet I felt depleted. Tomorrow was another day, but I wouldn't want too many more like today.

The next day I Skyped Benison. I was relieved I could get through on the hostel's wi-fi. I needed to talk to her. She told me to give myself some space. Afterwards, Sam seemed to accept his score for the day—four out of ten, his worst yet—and we talked about the reasons.

The movie *How to Train a Dragon* was playing on the TV in the lounge. Sam had always had trouble paying attention for the duration of a movie, especially one he hadn't seen before, so I set this as a challenge that would be easy on me. We negotiated: watching the whole movie would be equivalent to two activities. It worked; he watched it. It was a small but important victory for Sam and it revived my sagging spirits.

For the next few days Sam's behaviour was outstanding. Maybe his all-time low score shook him up. He was co-operative and pleasant, and also made some significant progress. He started organising his morning medications himself, had a prolonged game of checkers with a fellow backpacker, and made his breakfasts and washed up without even being told to. He did some excellent boxing and handball, and spontaneously conversed with a woman behind the bar while buying a Sprite. Mind you, she was young and pretty. I didn't hear the conversation; goodness knows what he said.

I gave him his second score of eight out of ten, but the next day only 7.5, marking him down for spending too much time on his Nintendo DS. This scoring system was keeping him focused and motivated, as it had been designed to do. I had begun to realise, however, that I had made a rod for my own back because I had to keep the scores and his expectations constantly in check.

The day we would leave Namboobia, as Sam was now calling it, was fast approaching. 'Namboobia sucks. Namboobia is poorer than South Africa. Butts-wana will be even worse.' *Wait till we get to the M countries*, I thought to myself. But what I said aloud was, 'Don't say Butts-wana at the border, Sam.'

That evening I met a young coloured guy from Johannesburg. With short sharp braids and a winning smile, he chatted to me about South Africa: where it was going, and where he had been and where he was going.

'So where are your family from?' I asked him.

'I don't know. I never knew my real dad, and I don't think my mum knows where she's from. I'm a lost sheep.' He took a swig of beer. 'It's great that democracy came in 1994, but there are a lot of cut strings. I am one of those strings.'

I wanted to know more, to understand. 'Do you think South Africa has a good future?' I asked.

'I don't know. Maybe there will be a war.' *What?* That hadn't been on my radar. He smiled ruefully and said, 'Maybe it will be necessary. Things are not yet sorted. Not in my world.'

One of the advantages of stopping for a while in Windhoek was the Tornado cafe. I had heard on the grapevine that this place had very reliable wi-fi and good coffee, both rare and highly prized by Sam and me, respectively. We went there most days to Skype Benison and other family members. Benison was taking her aunt to the Sydney Writer's Festival, seeing a play at the Sydney Opera House with a friend and going to the State of Origin with her sister next week. Culturally diverse, that's my girl. It was great she was getting out and about. In many ways she had the harder job: being stuck at home, working, and looking after our older boys, Matt and Nick. She missed her darling Sam terribly—and hopefully me a bit too. She always looked forward to seeing the top of Sam's head on Skype: that was about all she could see, as he always looked down and had never been much of a conversationalist with her.

Our last day in Windhoek was a busy one. In the morning I gave Sam a challenge: to write a post for our blog. I outlined the brief: it needed to be at least three hundred words and I left the topic purposely vague, just something 'about our trip'. Sam sat at the computer and I went to get a coffee at the bar. On my return, he had come up with the following 312 words:

We have Started off at a Australian Airport and then Fly with a Singapore Plane to Singapore and then to Johannesburg and another 2 hours to the airport and drive to Cape Town and stayed in a hotel for 6 nights and we went to the top of the rock and drive to a safari and saw lions, elephants, rhinos, hippos and zebras then we went to visit a prison where Nelson Mandela was in he was there for 18 years he was released eventually then we went to Hermanus for 2 nights and stayed in a quite big house and then we saw Erica who played a Slytherin Girl and had McDonald's and we went to Mosel Bay for 2 nights and we went to the half top of the rock with a lighthouse then we went to Wilderness for 2 nights and we saw a cave lady and then we had to go to Port Elizabeth for 1 night and then we went to Chintsa for 3 nights and rowed a boat and walked down the beach and then we went to Coffee Bay for 4 nights and we walked on a river and then we went to Sani Pass for 3 nights and we went to a trip to Lozutu on to the top of the mountain and drove back and then we went to a city called Durban for 3 nights and we went to the aquarium and went on a bike ride and then we flight to Namibia and went to Windhoek for 5 nights and went to Etosha for 2 nights and went back to Windhoek for 1 night and went to Sossel bay for 3 nights and went to a desert place for 2 nights and celebrated dad's 49th birthday and went back to Windhoek for the rest of Namibia and went to some restaurants.

Apart from anything else, I was amazed at his memory. It was interesting what had stuck and what hadn't—rowing a boat, walking on a river and riding a bike—he was retaining experiences as well as places. Surely this must be expanding his view of the world, and how he fitted into and participated in it.

In the early afternoon, a group of us from the hostel went to a meat market on the outskirts of the city. It wasn't as busy as the barbecue restaurant we'd visited in Cape Town, but the flies, glare and smoke still made for a challenging environment for Sam. Men and women swung axes, splitting wood for the fires. Butchers carved sides of beef and lamb into meat cuts, and smoke from the sizzling meat, oil and fat billowed into the surrounding alleyways. All I could hear were the sounds of axes on wood, of axes on bone, of haggling and banter.

We cruised through the market, tasting small cuts. It seemed you handed over twenty Namibian dollars and got a fistful of meat sliced into small pieces, wrapped in newspaper, with a small pile of mysterious orange spice on the side of the meat. I ended up buying liver, although I had thought it was beef. The spice was agreeably hot and peppery but certainly not something Sam would like. He bought bread rounds that had been cooked on the barbecues.

We found some unoccupied plastic chairs at a table towards the centre of the market and plonked ourselves down. Sam was freaked out by the chaos and withdrew into silence, legs up on the chair. He nibbled at a few token pieces of meat and drank lemonade.

Sam on the beach at Camps Bay, Cape Town, on our first full day in Africa. He calmed himself by running his fingers through the sand.

Our first encounter with African animals on a visit to a game reserve north of Cape Town. (*Photographer: Max Bourke*)

At Robben Island prison, where Nelson Mandela was incarcerated for eighteen years.

Sam shares a joke with Madam Tofu, near Chintsa, on the Garden Route, South Africa.

Sam outside the immigration office at the Lesotho border. Wrapped in his rug he looked like a local.

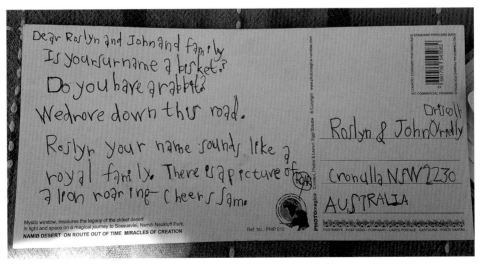

Sam's postcard to his aunty and uncle from Windhoek, Namibia. Writing postcards proved to be a good way to develop Sam's handwriting and narrative skills.

Sam strolls down the 'endless' beach where the dunes of the Namib Desert meet the South Atlantic Ocean.

Climbing a dune ridgeline near Deadvlei, in the Namib Desert.

Exploring the waterways of the Okavango Delta, Botswana.

Sam shares a joke with Alex, our guide to Livingstone Island on the Zambezi River, overlooking Victoria Falls.

A primary school in a village near the Zambezi River, Zambia. The kids are being taught outside in the sun, under a Zambian flag on a pole.

Sam teaches some Zambian teachers computer skills.

Public transport near Livingstonia in northern Malawi. Sam is at my feet, and the compulsory chicken is on the right.

Sam wanders along a street market near Lake Malawi, intriguing the locals.

Waiting on a beach on Likomo Island, Lake Malawi, for our launch to the *Ilala*.

Juliette, Sam and I wait in the tray of a utility in a remote town in Malawi, hoping to hitch a ride to the Mozambique border.

With some guilt, I realised I would have loved to have been here by myself, playing pool and maybe having a beer at the bar off to the side. But that was for another life.

Sam turned to me with a longing expression. 'I want to go back.'

'Hold on, Sam. We won't be long.'

But Sam wasn't dissuaded. He leant forward and grabbed my arm. 'Let's go back *now*. It's too smoky.' He was becoming increasingly agitated, smacking his hands on his thighs and the table, and humming loudly to himself. I could see things going pear-shaped quickly if I didn't bail.

So I hailed a cab, calling out a hurried goodbye to the others. When you hail a cab in Africa it doesn't matter if someone is already in it. Sometimes the driver even boots out other passengers if he thinks he's going to get more money out of you. The meek acceptance of these discarded passengers, who were frequently plonked on the side of the road in the middle of nowhere, was surprising and at times embarrassing. Money talks.

On this cab trip, we rode with a mother and her two-year-old daughter. The little girl regarded me as she nuzzled into her mother's chest. I smiled at her and asked her mother if I could take a photo of her daughter.

'Heh heh, no problem. But she is very sick. I am taking her to hospital.'

Sam looked concerned. 'She's not going to die?'

'Sam, shush!'

Sam leant forward towards the mother, and said earnestly, 'I hope she doesn't die.'

'Sam, be quiet!' I snapped.

The mother looked confused, and then realisation dawned. 'She will be fine, don't you worry,' she reassured him.

Sam sat back, looking more comfortable. After a minute or two, he leant forward again to talk to the mother. 'Sorry for being inappropriate,' he said.

She smiled. 'No problem, Sam.' In the rearview mirror I could see the driver was also smiling.

CHAPTER 12

Easy eights

The next morning, we left Windhoek for Botswana. A cold snap had hit the city: it was going to be only 26 degrees Celsius, as distinct from every other day we had spent here, where it had been 27 degrees Celsius. We hadn't seen a single cloud since Etosha.

A comfortably small group of eight wayfarers shared the truck that would be our home for the next nine days: an older German couple; two young women, English and Swiss; a greying and pensive American aid worker; an elderly Chinese woman who spoke next to no English; and, in the back seat, an Australian doctor with his quirky kid, who was reading Harry Potter aloud.

The B6 national highway took us across the semi-arid plains of central Namibia. It was quiet, flat, smooth and gun-barrel straight. The crimson Cambrian chalk dotted with desert shrubs gave way to cream grasses and dense coarse scrub, a landscape of dirty lime, mauve and grey. A warthog patrolled a fence line; a family of baboons crossed a dry riverbed; falcons hovered like Harrier jets over a potential meal far below in the grass and sand.

We reached Gobabis, our last stopover before the border and the final chance to get personal supplies before the camping began. I was worrying about Sam's refusal to wear long sleeves, and how his exposed arms increased the risk of contracting malaria.

I gave it another shot. 'Sam, how about I buy you a long-sleeved shirt that's so light so you won't even feel it?'

He shook his head. 'No!'

'It would help protect you against malaria,' I pleaded. 'Come on!'

But he wasn't having a bar of it. 'No! No long sleeves.'

The border staff moved like they were in treacle; a triumph of torpor. The lag only added to a long day for Tuhafeni, our guide and driver, and his assistant, Alfeus. But eventually we entered our fourth African country. The dense coarse scrub now contracted to reveal the vanishing point of the horizon, wobbling in haze and glare. We were approaching another desert, a land of endless thornbush and clicking tongues, the Kalahari.

Farm animals started to appear on the road so Tuhafeni slowed down. Sam began to fret at the prospect we'd have to sleep in a tent. We were planning to upgrade our accommodation at each destination but this would depend on availability.

The sun set behind the truck. The tops of the olive trees were briefly lit orange before the grip of the evening shadows took hold. We were all lost in our own thoughts, Sam included. All we could see now were headlights on bitumen. Ten hours after we left Windhoek, the truck peeled onto a four-wheel drive road. After bouncing along for another half hour, we finally rolled into our destination, Dqae Qare San Lodge, Ghanzi.

Tuhafeni negotiated with the eager-to-please South African manager. As they talked, I became anxious to get some insect repellent on us—particularly Sam, with his exposed arms and legs. In the cold evening air, he lay next to the packs on sand lit gold by the lights of the truck.

The good rooms were all booked out, however Sam and I could take a room that was empty, but had a broken toilet, for free! After settling in, the group watched a talk and dance show from the local San people who owned the farm.

Around a large fire, we heard two traditional stories—first in the twinkling clicks of the San language, then in English, and finally in song and dance. They told of a race between an ostrich and a tortoise, and a jackal, disguised as a teacher, attempting to woo lion cubs away from their parents. The plots were reminiscent of Roald Dahl stories I read to the boys when they were little.

The dancers wore strings of stone beads on their ankles, which rattled like tambourines with each stomp on the soft sand. The women swayed smoothly in neck beads, head scarfs and flowing robes, and the men wore loin cloths, coloured headbands and twirling wands of eland tail hairs. There were gentle melodies, soft harmonies. But I'm not sure if Sam got much out of it; the long drive had worn him out. He stroked his fingers through the soft sand around his feet, preferring to sit directly on the sand rather than on the large logs with the rest of us, and paid no attention to the performance.

The group trundled back from the dancing to where our indefatigable guides had prepared our evening meal. As we headed back to our room after dinner, I noticed the cold and was secretly glad Sam refused to sleep in tents. The generator switched off at eleven. Lights out, power off, wait for dawn.

The breaking light revealed a landscape full of colour, beauty and birdsong. The flora of the Kalahari featured candle thorn bush, acacia and bush willow filled with a myriad of birdsounds. A crimson-breasted gonolek flashed his striking colour; two red-billed spurfowls squabbled in the scrub nearby; three Cape starlings engaged in a dogfight in the sky above.

After breakfast, one of the dancers from the previous evening, Tshabu, took us for a bush tour. He led the group over the ochre sands, pointing out plants and their various uses, as well as animal tracks and droppings, explaining how his people would trap and kill birds and animals. The dunes and scrub were his pantry, his pharmacy, his home.

Tshabu was slightly built, and the same height as Sam. His scalp was a maze of centimetre-length braids, and he had a gentle manner and a lilting accent. He wore a loincloth made of steenbok hide, leather sandals, and a faded striped polo shirt. A quiver made from African wildcat hide carried bows, spears and firesticks made from bush willow.

With each discussion of a plant, a rock, a track, he would first describe it in his own language. He was connected to his culture and his land. The traditional San lifestyle was truly nomadic; home was where the animals went.

One of the plants Tshabu showed us was the source of the poison with which they would tip their arrowheads. The Englishwoman asked how quickly the poison would work.

'Quite quickly.' Tshabu didn't wear a watch.

Sam initially paid attention, registering his surrounds and what was being said by Tshabu and the others, but became antsy towards the end, asking when we were going to finish, and how long it was going to take.

We navigated our way back to the farm and truck through the disorientating endless scrub by following the noise of the generator.

As soon as we got back on the truck to leave, Sam resumed reading Harry Potter. But after a few hours he perked up and got me to do a 'head dance', where he'd get me to dance with only my head. There were different types: the sideways head dance, the round head dance, the tongue-poking-out head dance. Gabriel in Sossusvlei had introduced a cool new variation, the African head dance: a sharp tilt of the head followed by a slow return to vertical.

It was just as well that Sam only required my head to dance, because all sense of rhythm stops at my neck. I'm a tall white guy, after all. Throughout Africa—at restaurants, in bars, on buses and trucks—I'd been repeatedly ordered to 'do the head dance'. If I was reluctant Sam would often force the issue by pushing my head around with his hands. Folks invariably seemed enchanted by our routine.

The road stretched on, seeming endless. It reminded me of scrubby roads from the Australian outback. Perhaps Queensland's Bruce Highway, about halfway to Cairns? Then a herd of ostriches was surprised by our noisy truck and scattered off the road, all raised knees and bobbing heads. No, we were definitely in Africa.

When we stopped for lunch our sixty-nine-year-old Chinese companion, who was travelling by herself, started doing tai chi on the sandy shoulder of the road. Everyone but our guides and Sam joined in. It must have made for a very odd sight: seven Westerners being taught tai chi by an elderly Chinese woman by the side of the road in Botswana in the middle of nowhere.

The road narrowed and deteriorated. Tuhafeni manoeuvred the truck around potholes, donkeys, cattle and goats. Soon we were on the worst road Sam and I had been on in Africa; incessant corrugations gave the 'African massage'.

At another stop, Sam sat in the dappled shade of a willow and drew in the white sand with his finger. I knew he was drawing coins and banknotes, which were currently rising with a bullet on his hit parade of obsessions. The villagers tried to figure out what he was drawing. They asked him his name and age and he drew the answers in the sand. Kids jumped, waved and yelled at us through the wire fence of their sandy school playground as we left.

We bounced and heaved, up and over dunes, through creeks and rivulets. In the late afternoon glow, after the better part of two days of hard travel, we reached our destination. Guma Lagoon Camp was a stylish retreat set on a large lagoon on the edge of the Okavango Delta, where the handle meets the pan. Here the water from Angola came down the wide Okavango River and spilled into the vast delta before drying out, fading out, as it stretched south to the Kalahari.

The campsite was set invitingly on lush grass under willows and waterberries. Sam thought it looked like a golf course—but that didn't mean he wanted to camp there. Fortunately, a room was available. We also heard that there was a very sociable pet owl who liked to gently brush his wings on you as he swooped by. Sam loved the idea, and christened the owl he was yet to meet Hedwig, from Harry Potter, of course.

Guma Lagoon Camp had been set up fifteen years earlier by a couple from Johannesburg, Beverley and Guy. Sam was especially fond of one of their dogs, Diesel, because he had a special job to do: chasing away hippos. Sam was paranoid about hippos as he'd read that they kill more people in Africa than any other animal, if you exclude mosquitoes, microbes and man. Hippos were a real threat here and we were instructed to take care at night. I didn't really understand what 'taking care' meant and asked Guy. 'Just keep an eye out, and if you see one, head in the other direction. You should be fine. Just don't shine your torch in their eyes, they really hate that.' I certainly didn't want to piss off a hippo.

Sitting on the retreat's broad verandah, which had panoramic views of the large lagoon, the group relaxed and drank in the atmosphere. The reeds across the lagoon looked like giant clipped hedges, lit orange by the dying light. The silhouette of the nostrils and brow of a croc glided by fifty metres away. Sam returned from the toilet where to his surprise and joy Hedwig had visited him.

The wetlands filled with sound: millions of insects and thousands of birds competing for attention. Rhythms would sometimes merge into each other before parting again. Like a poorly synchronised orchestra, the notes would jar at times before harmonising again. The symphony continued, with no conductor, relentless.

Beverley and Guy ran a smooth operation. They had many local employees, and also had sponsored a local primary school by supplying simple machines and supplies, such as a photocopier, staplers and paper. I asked if the school had any special-needs kids and how they coped. It turned out that in this environment even relatively minor learning difficulties were exacerbated. 'You see, before there was equipment and supplies, the teacher used to have to read exam questions aloud,' Beverley explained. 'Simply having a printed exam paper sitting on the desk can make the world of difference for a student with learning issues.'

With their sponsorship, the pass rate at the school had risen from thirty-two per cent to seventy-five per cent in one year. Now families from villages nearby wanted to send their children to the school, but there weren't enough teachers.

Later at the bar, I overheard a Botswanan driver from the retreat joking with Tuhafeni. They ribbed each other about how inept the armed forces of their respective countries were, given neither country had been in a conflict for a long time. 'If war came, your soldiers would not need to be worried about the Namibian soldiers, because they can't shoot straight.'

The Botswanan driver laughed. 'Well, I can guarantee you that the Botswanan soldiers would shoot first, because they would be so frightened!'

But as the topic switched to poaching the banter became more pointed. 'What are you doing over there in Namibia? Why don't you get tougher? Do you want to give them a tap on the back or something?'

Tuhafeni shook his head in disgust. 'You know, it is getting much worse now. So far this year, there have been sixty rhinos shot in Etosha alone. And it is only May.'

'Oh my God, that is terrible,' the Botswanan replied. 'You know, there were three poachers shot dead near here just yesterday.'

'Dead?'

'Yes. Shoot on sight, that is what you guys need to do.'

That night, through the chorus of the wetlands, I heard a stomping sound underneath our hut, which was on stilts over the water's edge. The unmistakable hyper-echoic honk of a hippo came up through the boards. Yikes! I hoped hippos couldn't climb stairs. Where the hell was Diesel?

Having survived the night, we emerged the next morning wearing enough fly spray to have serious neurological consequences. The plan was to boat out to the wetlands and then ride in dugout canoes through the reeds to an island in the delta. Well, that was the official plan. But it wasn't Sam's plan. 'No, I don't want to get on the boat.'

'Sam, you have to get on. It's already organised and everyone is going.'

He dug in. 'No. There are hippos. I don't want to die!'

I couldn't reassure him. He took off and refused to return to the boat ramp. I pleaded with him for five minutes as the rest of the group boarded. He wouldn't budge. I thought laterally. 'How about I give you a reward if you go?'

'What?'

'I'll give you an eight.'

'Okay.' Sam got into the boat straightaway.

Dodgy life jackets, an open-topped motorboat, slightly nervous passengers. The boat zoomed across the lagoon, and then down a watery passageway between seemingly impenetrable walls of papyrus. A spur-winged goose zoomed with us down the winding passage like a fighter jet escort. The passage narrowed as it snaked along. Like a giant organic maze, the wetlands were criss-crossed with these passageways. Occasionally islands jutted above the waterline, home to majestic towering hardwoods—jackalberry and waterberry trees, and marulas.

The passages narrowed even more. Our captain slowed the boat to a crawl. I was reminded of Hepburn and Bogart in *The African Queen*, chest-high in the muck, struggling through the reeds, their bodies covered in leeches. Well, at least we had an outboard motor. I wouldn't have wanted to be walking in these waters, and it wouldn't just have been leeches I'd have been worried about.

On a wetland island we met our guides. They would use long poles to push us—two passengers to a canoe—through the reeds to another island; ninety minutes' hard work each way. The chief pole man was Royal, long and lanky with muscular arms. Sam and I were to be his charges; he had been told the teenager who didn't look you in the eye needed to be watched.

The canoes were pushed off the mud and we glided away. Royal stood at the back, long pole in hand. He had been on these waters all his life, and it showed. It was peaceful on the water, gliding. 'So calm that it disturbs,' as Coleridge put it. There were day water lilies everywhere, and spotted pumpkins sitting on the long stems which descended through the crystal clear waters.

The four canoes were in single file, the first bow cutting through the reeds, grasses, lilies and papyrus like a scythe. A hippo honked, sounding close, and us tourists exchanged anxious looks. As we rounded the head of an island, an enormous bull elephant appeared one hundred metres away. He checked us out with a glare and splashed away.

We landed on our island destination with a crunch under the canoe. The white sand of the island was sprinkled with lime-green grasses, dotted higgledy-piggledy with candle thorn and aromatic kuntze shrubs, and punctuated by grand trees. There was a sausage tree with metre-long hanging fruit. A large and ancient baobab tree crowned the small peak of the island, its bark stripped up to ten metres by elephants. Ilala palms with sour tennis-ball-sized fruit soared above.

The air was pungent from the large elephant droppings combined with the acrid kuntze. We toured the small island, walking single file to reduce the risk of snakebite, before settling in the shade to drink from our water bottles and eat our packed lunch. Nobody spoke. It just seemed right to be silent.

Eventually, roused from our torpor by Royal, we reluctantly headed back. I was so glad I'd been able to get Sam on the boat.

I wouldn't have wanted him to miss this experience. It had been eight points well spent.

That night there was a loud ruckus on the water: a crotchety elephant and some hippos. I couldn't sleep anyway. I was tossing and turning, thinking about the trip and Sam's progress. My thoughts tumbled. The acute anxiety I'd felt earlier in the trip had passed, but now I was starting to worry that I wasn't anxious enough, that I was getting lax. *Shut up, James,* I told myself. *Just get on with it.*

Eventually dawn broke over the clipped hedges. The lagoon was still, the reflection of the multicoloured clouds like a painter's palette.

When he awoke, Sam was excited to officially receive his eight. 'How can I easily get an eight on other days?' The bugger had out-thought me.

CHAPTER 13

Marshmallows and googols

I t was Africa Day, celebrated across the continent, as we left Guma
Lagoon Camp, which seemed an appropriate time to reflect upon
my impressions of Africa so far. While we were yet to reach the
poor M countries, we had now seen a fair bit of the place.

Africa was an event. It was complex, surprising, unpredictable.
It threw up issues and problems to be dealt with or overcome, and
then either threw up solutions and alternatives, or just a shrug
and a smile. 'No problems, boss!' I felt Benison and I had selected
the location and route of the trip well. The unpredictability was
perfect for our intended purpose. We'd started in the relatively
familiar cosmopolitanism of Cape Town and now things were
becoming progressively more challenging. I felt that if we'd been
facing the current circumstances when we first set out, neither
Sam nor I would have coped. Both of us had developed new
skills and coping abilities. Sam was now pining to return not so
much to Sydney but to Cape Town, Durban or even Windhoek.
I reflected back on how dependent I'd been on Max and The
Fixer's help in the first week.

Mind you, experienced traveller as I might now consider myself, I'd still managed to leave my torch behind at Guma Lagoon Camp. I knew exactly where I'd left it, under the pillow. Oh well, another item to add to the list of lost things.

Our physical ailments remained. Sam's facial rash had flared, worsened by the Kalahari's parched atmosphere and the stress of hard travelling. My tennis elbow still troubled me. I would forget occasionally and heave a backpack with my left arm, only to quickly pay the penalty.

Another long day on the road, another border crossing. These guards showed more lassitude than attitude. We headed up to and along the Caprivi Strip, an elongated thin extension of Namibia that the German colonists annexed to give Germany access to the Zambezi and a route to their eastern colony Tanganyika, now Tanzania. We stopped overnight at a campsite; another river full of hippos and crocs, another indemnity form to be signed. Fortunately, I was again able to upgrade our accommodation, and Tuhafeni told me this would be possible for the remaining stops on the tour. It would be expensive, but it was a relief. I announced that we were hitherto to be known as the rich wankers of the group.

Sam polished off his poached chicken and potato dinner while I had another cup of rooibos tea, for which I'd developed quite a liking in the absence of good coffee. Sam was still trying new foods, but unfortunately called Alfeus bald to his face, and lost some points as a consequence. As I walked from the dinner fire back to our hut—in darkness, because I no longer had a torch—I whacked my right shin on a low post lining the path. I gingerly inspected the injury: a nasty laceration and a bruise to add to my list of injuries. A *Simpson's* style 'Ha ha!' was Sam's not-so-sympathetic response.

The next morning we visited a traditional village: a gaggle of thatched *rondavels* inside a two-metre-high fence made of thin sticks. There were displays of traditional animal traps. Women sieved, and pounded with mortar and pestle. An old man pumped bellows to fire a small smith used to shape iron spear tips. The women then danced to a drum beat before a witchdoctor emerged from a hut chanting—according to our interpreter—about how we would all have a safe journey home. I wondered how authentic it really was. It was clear there was a commercial drive behind it—I doubt most traditional African villages have their own gift shops.

However, once the young fellow who'd showed us around finished the short tour, he relaxed. Yes, it was contrived, put on for the tourists, he admitted, but he pointed to a village a hundred metres away where they all actually *lived*, and it looked very similar, although messier and with more dogs. They still used these tools and wore these clothes, though the traditional dress was now mixed with recycled clothing, handed down from rich Westerners. They did regularly sing these songs and dance these dances. They took pride in their culture.

Sam was taking next to no notice, and seemed more interested in his fingers, declaring the performance boring and saying he didn't like the music because it wasn't rock. He was certainly correct there. The witchdoctor freaked him out too—and me a bit, truth be told. The American aid worker in our group wryly observed that he was secretly hoping the witchdoctor would 'cure' Sam's autism, which would have been a major scientific break-through but would have made the rest of the trip less interesting in the process.

We reached Katima Mulilo, the regional capital of Caprivi, and stocked up on supplies. On a large billboard near the shopping centre car park the mayor of the city declared that he used a condom, so every man should. The devastation of the HIV epidemic was revealed in the frankness of the message.

In the supermarket Sam wanted a Sprite. I didn't want him to have one in the morning; our rule was that we had no fizzy drinks at least until lunchtime. I suggested a flavoured milk.

Sam persisted. 'No, I want a Sprite.'

'I said no. If you insist on having it, it will mean an automatic six.'

He lifted his chin high and pointed to the floor. 'No. I want an eight *and* a Sprite.'

I tried to be firm but fair. 'No, them's the rules, Sam. It's your decision.'

I left it up to him and refused to discuss it further. He ended up buying the Sprite, but was in two minds about whether it was worth getting an automatic six, and hesitated to actually drink it.

It was Sam's own marshmallow experiment. In the landmark series of experiments conducted at Stanford University in the 1960s and 1970s, a child was offered the choice between an immediate reward, usually one marshmallow, or two rewards if they waited a short period, like fifteen minutes. The tester would leave the room and often video the child's behaviour as they grappled with the dilemma of delayed gratification.

Mastering delayed gratification demonstrates self-control, and can predict better outcomes in education, professions and life generally. It was a skill I was interested in developing with Sam, but I was also conscious of not wanting to push him too hard. Sam sat at the back of the bus looking longingly at the unopened can of Sprite in his hand. I loosened the criteria a bit. 'You only have to wait until midday, and then you can drink it and not get the automatic six.'

'What time is it?'

'11.30 a.m.'

He squirmed through the half hour, but he made it. Proud of himself, he drank the Sprite and the rest of the truck, myself included, smiled with relief.

As Tuhafeni steered the truck out of town, I noticed a large government development being built, once again, by a Chinese construction company. Throughout our two months of travel, we had frequently seen Chinese-funded developments. Even in Lesotho, the roads were being upgraded by Chinese companies. Apparently this is a continent-wide phenomenon, and it's not only China, but also Brazil, Russia and India investing in African development. These countries are referred to by the acronym BRIC: they're all rapidly developing economies increasingly looking beyond their own shores for financial opportunities. Some economists see them threatening the global dominance of G7 economies in the next few decades.

Witnessing it on the ground, I wondered whether this was potentially just a new wave of economic colonialisation for Africa. I suppose foreign investment is a healthy thing, but considering what happened with colonialisation the first time around, I couldn't help but think it would be preferable to see Africans driving change in a developing Africa.

At lunch, Sam got talking to a fellow traveller, Peter, who had an extensive academic background that included arts, biology, cognitive psychology and IT. I started the ball rolling by asking him what the mathematical term was for a one followed by a hundred zeros.

Peter and Sam replied in unison: 'A googol.'

Peter knew it just because he knew it. Sam knew it because it was the origin of the name of Google.

Sam turned to Peter. 'What year did Google start?'

Peter thought about it. 'Mid nineties?'

'1996.'

Peter nodded and raised his eyebrows, impressed. 'Yes, that would be correct.'

Sam and Peter then discussed, in a friendly but competitive fashion, the release dates of various Windows programs, the origins of the computer, the history of Nintendo and a whole bunch of stuff that no one else on the bus had any idea about. Sam was enjoying the challenge of talking to someone who knew a lot about what he liked. When Sam gets on a roll, he gets on a roll.

The truck churned up the kilometres, interrupted only by police checks; foot-and-mouth disease stops where we walked our muddy shoes through gooey black water, presumably to stop the virus hitching a ride; cows meandering onto the bitumen; and our third border crossing in four days.

The border crossing into Botswana was the most spectacular I'd ever seen: beyond the cyclone-wire fences elephants gathered beneath huge baobab trees, a fish eagle perched on a nearby tree and buffalo grazed on the vast river valley stretching into the distance.

We asked Tuhafeni if we could walk up to the fence to get a closer look at one of the elephants. 'That would not be a good idea,' he replied.

'He's behind a fence,' I said.

'That fence is nothing to him. He is a wild elephant. He would sweep it away in a second and kill you.' It was a convincing argument. We stayed put.

It turned out to be so picturesque because Chobe National Park was immediately across the border. There was wildlife everywhere. Chobe National Park contains one of Africa's largest concentrations of game, but unfortunately it also seemed to have one of the largest concentrations of tourists, usually rich ones. The village in the park was complete with a supermarket, ATM and currency exchange, and a large resort. It had decent wi-fi, so Sam was happy. I winced to think how much it was going to cost us to upgrade to a room here for two nights. I consoled myself that we'd soon be able to live on diddly squat in Malawi.

That night, Sam saw the resort's impressive buffet and took off for it, like a moth to a flame, with me in hot pursuit.

'No, Sam, we're not allowed to eat here!'

Sam stopped and turned. 'Why?'

'That's for rich people.'

After surveying the diners, most of whom were now watching us as Sam's loud voice and bouncing walk gathered attention, he corrected me, again way too loudly: 'It is for rich OLD people.' *How to Insult Fifty People at Once*, by Samuel Thomas Best. I tried to bundle him out of the dining area as he continued. 'It *is* for old people. They *are* old. They have grey and white hair. Even more grey than you, Dad.'

Make that fifty-one people. Sam pointed at some poor guy. 'Look, white hair!'

We awoke before dawn to be loaded into one of many open four-wheel drive trucks. The drivers constantly chatted with each other on the two-way radios, to direct everyone to wherever the interesting animals were. It was very cold in the open truck. There were animals everywhere—giraffes, warthogs, hippos, hyenas, monkeys, birds—but the driver was trying to track a lion. Occasionally he'd slow the truck, open his door and lean out as the truck rolled along to examine the sandy track. I thought he was bunging it on at first, but it was authentic; he was a real bushman.

We drove past a thousand-head herd of buffalo and a congress of baboons. The two species have a synergistic relationship: the baboons are sentinels high in the trees and shake fruit down for the impalas, which, with better hearing and vision, can alert the baboons to approaching predators. This cooperation collapses during famine and drought, when baboons steal and eat newborn impalas. The natural world is brutal.

There were radio reports of a sighting of a leopard at the far end of the park. We were the fourth of eight trucks to arrive, which all collected at the bottom of the tree, from where glimpses of the leopard's coat and face could be seen with binoculars through the dense foliage. Apparently, after she'd killed an impala, a pride of lions had chased her up the tree and taken the kill for themselves. Jackals and vultures hovered, hoping for a share.

I felt like a vulture, too. The leopard was engaged in a life-and-death struggle, all the while being gawked at by a herd of strange primates in noisy machines. Eventually the trucks departed, one by one, leaving her alone to her fate.

Sam was struggling with the cold and his facial rash was bothering him. He huddled in the vehicle wrapped in a blanket, legs drawn up onto the seat and staring into space. He only occasionally looked out to the animals at my prompting. Sam can't use binoculars well so he never saw the leopard. He did, however, like the baby baboons clinging onto their mother's abdomens, and the monkey trying to steal biscuits from our group when we stopped for a cuppa.

After the tour we had a break to recharge, both our electrical appliances and ourselves. I let Sam play his DS; he'd had a very early start to the day and seemed tired. In the afternoon, we were meant to go on a river cruise. I wasn't sure whether he was up to it or not. But when I asked around about what the trip was like it was strongly recommended, so I pushed through and took him.

Sam became angry and argumentative as we waited on the dock. I was worried he was going to get physical, but he managed to reel it in, just. The boat, carrying more than fifty people, had the same touristy feeling as the morning drive. For much of the three-hour tour Sam was struggling; he lay on the floor of the boat, stimming by flicking his fingers in front of his face or staring into space. He shouted to me about banknotes or other obscure obsessions while the guide was making announcements about the wildlife, or when we were meant to be quiet so as not to spook the animals. I was beginning to regret my decision to come.

I gave him my notebook and pen and he proceeded to draw his favourite obsessions: Harry Potter, Super Mario, gaming consoles, the alphabet, numbers and notes and coins from different countries. It took him over an hour; it was like a form of meditation. Psychologists would call it self-regulation.

But when the boat approached a large pod of hippos Sam looked up. While honking a warning, the alpha male breached and bared his massive gaping mouth and teeth. It's hard to appreciate how big a hippopotamus can get until you see a large male up close and personal. He was bold as brass and probably stupid enough to attack the big boat, but we were certainly safe.

Sam loved it, as well as the long line of elephants perambulating up the banks of the river as our launch glided alongside. Soon a buffalo, stranded on one of the islands on the river, decided to try to swim to another island. The islands were safe havens from predators, but when the grass ran out, the buffaloes had to get past the crocs to move on. As the buffalo took off, a croc a couple of hundred metres away saw an opportunity and set off in pursuit. It was touch and go whether the buffalo would make it, and Sam was fascinated by the life-and-death race, cheering for the buffalo. He made it!

As the sun set over the river and the flat expanses of the valley beyond, the sky lit up in myriad colours, reflected in the waters below. The river cruise ended up not being too bad, despite the poor start. I made a mental note that this was not the first time this had happened with a tired Sam on the trip; a floundering start but finishing with a wet sail.

CHAPTER 14

Zim

We were heading to Zimbabwe to visit Victoria Falls the next day. I was in two minds about it, given the political state of the country: while the situation had improved, and the Zimbabwe side of Victoria Falls provided better views, it was still unnerving to take a young lad with autism to such a troubled place.

Tuhafeni had last visited Zimbabwe—or Zim, as it's commonly known—eleven years earlier, and was still bruised by the experience. While escorting a group like ours, he'd been fleeced of all the tour company money by bogus demands from the border guards. They'd held him in a police cell for ten hours, trying to squeeze more out of him. Eventually, finally convinced that he had indeed run out of money, they'd released him into the night.

Understandably then, Tuhafeni seemed on edge the next morning. We all did. He had visited the border the previous afternoon to make sure all the paperwork for our visas and the truck was organised. We filed into the immigration office. A portrait of Robert Mugabe dominated the room. The immigration officials weren't smiling, in contrast to every previous border post. I was chastised for not having the immigration form in my passport and the correct money, in US dollars, for the visas. It cost us thirty dollars each, except for the Englishwoman who had to pay fifty-five; the price of colonialism I suppose.

Flustered, I awkwardly retrieved the immigration form and notes as Sam observed that I was being a dork. He was right, of course. 'Chop, chop, hurry up,' they said, which became retrospectively hilarious during the ensuing delay. An official scowled at Sam, who was stimming in the corner of the room. It soon became clear there was a problem. What a surprise. It seemed the man who had spoken to Tuhafeni the previous day had been mistaken: the fee for our tour group was twice what had been quoted.

We moved outside where we languished in the glaring sun for over an hour. Sam played with the sand while Tuhafeni tried to keep his cool. The group postulated on the reasons for the delay. Corruption? Maladministration? Just toying with us? Eventually the border officials waved their hands and said we could go. A visibly relieved Tuhafeni hit the pedals and we zoomed past the boom gates. It was corruption, of course; they had just been trying to rip the company off.

At the dusty, dirty town of Victoria Falls, we stopped to ask for directions to our accommodation. As soon as we pulled up, a man approached the windows trying to sell small wooden carved statues. Another waved Zimbabwean banknotes in an attempt to change money. The notes I saw were for five billion and twenty billion Zimbabwean dollars. Sam was impressed. At the resort, our room was expensive, basic and poorly lit, the staff edgy, the security intense. The whole feel of the country was different to anything we had previously experienced. I was on high alert.

I managed to Skype Benison. 'We're in Zimbabwe,' I told her.

'What?' she said, in alarm.

'At Victoria Falls, on the Zimbabwe side.'

She frowned at me through cyberspace. 'I didn't know you were going there. Be careful.'

⋄

Victoria Falls, by far the largest waterfall on the planet, had long been a planned highlight of our trip. We'd been in Africa over two months now, but the moment of our first sighting of it had seemed to rush up on us, just as the broad and mighty Zambezi rushes up on the nearly two-kilometre long gaping chasm in the Earth's surface, over which a million litres of water plummets every second.

The water, falling over the one-hundred-metre drop, creates a roar that you have to shout over, a force that literally thumps you in the chest, and a beauty that, as Livingstone described it in 1855, was 'so lovely [it] must have been gazed upon by angels in their flight'.

I was in awe. Sam was too. We all were. You couldn't help it.

But as we cruised along the cliff opposite the falls, the viewing points became progressively wetter and Sam became progressively more bored. He'd liked the falls, but he wanted out, telling me he'd had enough, he'd seen enough of the falls, and that he wanted to go back to the hostel. I made a deal: he'd get a bonus half point for the day if he completed the whole five-kilometre walk and went to all the lookouts.

'Make it a whole point,' he said.

'Half is plenty.' We negotiated as I followed him up the soaking path. 'All you have to do is walk. That's not hard.'

'Half a point is weird and odd. Let's round it up to a whole point.'

He wore me down and I relented. A whole bonus point it was. As we exited the vast and sodden cloud that surrounds the falls and re-entered the sunlight, now all drenched, we visited the last viewing point on the cliff-top walk, which looked over to Victoria Falls Bridge, spanning the second gorge. The job done, Sam took off back up the path we had just come down. I half jogged after him. *Well, there's nowhere for him to go,* I thought to myself.

But then I came to a fork in the path: the left turn was a shortcut to the exit, the right another path to viewing points along the cliff. I went left, and soon passed an African couple resting on a bench. 'Did a teenage boy just come past here?' I asked.

He hadn't. *Bugger.* Adrenaline pumping, I jogged to the exit. He hadn't been sighted here either. I asked the woman at the exit to not let him out. Over the next quarter of an hour I worriedly explored the maze of paths around the lookouts before finally hearing he'd returned to the exit. It hadn't been as bad as the previous instances of losing Sam, but it had still not been pleasant.

Our group dined at the restaurant at our accommodation, not wanting to venture out the gates at night. It was scary enough during the day. A group of male singers appeared in the dining room, singing traditional songs in tribal dress. They were very good, but we waited for the inevitable request for money for the unsolicited performance. Did the facility get a kickback? Probably.

They sang a fascinating African version of 'Swing Low, Sweet Chariot', which brought the song full circle: it had started in Africa, had been taken to America on slave ships, and was now returned home. The last song was 'Shosholoza'; the song I had heard so often in South Africa had originated in these parts.

The group had decided to splurge on a fifteen-minute helicopter ride. It would be expensive but unmissable. So the next morning we were bundled into the helicopter company's minivan and driven to the heliport.

We were drilled on the safety protocols and procedures and Sam started to worry. 'I am not going to die. I am not going to be chopped.'

'No, Sam,' I assured him, 'just keep calm and keep your head low as you get on and off. I'll look after you.'

As we approached the incredibly loud rotors, Sam sank lower and lower. He was practically crawling the last yard or two but I got him aboard okay. With headphones and mike in place, away we went.

Neither Sam nor I had ever been on a helicopter before. Within two minutes we were doing figure-eight loops over the smoke that thunders. As the helicopter banked, dipped and climbed, we were alternately pressed into the windows, and then away, thrust forward and then forced back into our seat. It was a rollercoaster hundreds of metres in the air.

From that height we could appreciate how the wide flat river was compressed first into a deep narrow gorge before the washing machine-like waters, frothing and swirling, would tumble through the subsequent series of gorges gouged out of the arid landscape. Wild rapids raced down alleyways, zigzagging into the distance.

Sam was remarkably calm and cool, and smiled the whole time, as he so often does. But as soon as we landed I had to stop him running to the safety of the terminal. *Fair enough.* The whole experience was a complete buzz.

That afternoon we went shopping in town. The first hawker approached us even before we'd passed the security guards and boom gates that marked the boundary of our resort.

'Hello, sir! How are you?' he yelled over the boom gate.

I didn't respond.

'You want white-water rafting? Bungy? Zimbabwean billion-dollar bills? Change money? Taxi?'

No response. I was used to being hassled, but not like this. His street colleagues queued up, one by one. They were also more aggressive and persistent than I'd been used to. When I ignored them, the tone became insistent. They walked beside me for minutes at a time. To them I was a big bag of money, bigger than anything they could imagine.

Sam had the perfect manner for street hawkers. He didn't have to pretend to ignore them, it came naturally. He didn't even notice them. I tried to follow his lead.

By GDP purchasing price parity, Zimbabwe is the second poorest country in Africa and indeed the world, second only to the Democratic Republic of Congo. The resource-rich country had been devastated by corruption, mismanagement and violence since Uncle Bob came to power in 1980. He's been rated as the second-worst dictator in the world after North Korea's Kim Jong-un. Zim is also consistently ranked as one of the world's most corrupt countries.

There are two major ethnic groups in Zimbabwe: the majority Shosa and minority Ndebele. In the mid-1980s, twenty thousand Ndebele were massacred by Mugabe's thugs to prevent any political uprising. In 2000, Mugabe's ZANU-PF supporters, led by unemployed war veterans armed with axes and machetes, invaded and seized white-owned farms with the president's open support. In the same year Uncle Bob was awarded the winning prize in a lottery run by the state bank. No corruption there.

Politically motivated beatings, rape and murders were common, and their frequency rose prior to planned elections. In the 2005 election, the opposition, mainly supported by the urban poor who suffered most under the regime, dared to win some seats in parliament. In response, the government burned markets and homes across the country. Seven hundred thousand people lost their homes or livelihoods, and two million people were driven further into poverty.

In 2009, hyperinflation of over five billion per cent finally led to the suspension of the currency, but not before ridiculous one hundred trillion dollar banknotes were issued. The economy was bleeding out. Food became scarce. Life expectancy, exacerbated by rampant HIV, plummeted to the mid thirties.

The country was now paralysed by corruption, waiting for the abominable old criminal to die. But who knows what will come next.

As we walked back to our accommodation a warthog marched importantly down the footpath towards us. We crossed the road to avoid him; he had big tusks so he got right of way. After we crossed the road, a large male baboon glared at me from atop a parked car. The hawkers were not the only hazard on the streets of Victoria Falls.

That night Sam and I shared a warthog schnitzel for dinner, which was another impressive win on the food front. I felt a bit guilty eating our friend Pumbaa from *The Lion King*, but it did taste good.

In the morning, the English woman from our group discovered monkeys had broken into her tent and ate her antimalarials. At least one Zimbabwean monkey was going to have bad diarrhoea that day. When we returned, we found small vervet monkeys had surrounded our chalet. Sam approached one, and it screeched and advanced towards him aggressively, before I shouted at the small creature, frightening it off. Sam thought it was hilarious. Once we were safe in the chalet, the monkey glared at us through the window while he sat on the sill.

Later in the day when Sam and I visited the supermarket, we saw a blind old lady begging outside. She had sunken eye sockets, sunken cheeks, and a sunken spirit. Inside, as I looked at which juice bottle to buy, a young girl approached me and offered me 'favours' if I bought her one too. When we returned outside, a young boy, presumably the blind lady's grandson, led her away by a stick. Sometimes all you have left is family.

I felt a seething anger well inside. This should never have happened to such a resource-rich country. I hated that ubiquitous portrait photo.

On the group's last afternoon in Zim, we treated ourselves to high tea at the opulent and grand Victoria Falls Hotel, the oldest hotel in the area and the preferred way station of intrepid early white travellers who worked their way from Cairo to Cape Town or vice versa, by land or air. It was all very British, very indulgent and very cool.

With the camera rolling, Sam debriefed me, conducted a formal interview with Stephanie, a Swiss woman on our tour, and ordered drinks and food. His talk with Stephanie was a high point. I was heartened to see his reciprocal conversational skills were definitely advancing.

His questions were:

- *What's your name?*
- *Where have you been, where have you been travelling from?*
- *Where is Switzerland in?*
- *What town, what city do you live in?*
- *Have you ever been in Australia?*

- *Where abouts in?*
- *Did you went to any shops in Australia?*
- *Have you been to Coles?* (He explained that it was a supermarket.)
- *Have you been to New Zealand?*
- *Where else besides Africa have you been?*
- *Have you been to Japan?*
- *Have you enjoyed the trip?*

Sam also made an appropriate welcome and farewell, but there were two long pauses, one over a minute long, that Stephanie tolerated and waited through. Stephanie, like so many people we'd met on the trip, was so supportive of what Sam and I were attempting.

As the sun lowered, rainbows formed in the iridescent mist rising up from the falls. The hotel had views up the second gorge to the elegant Victoria Falls Bridge, linking Zimbabwe to Zambia. The bridge, opened in 1905, was constructed by the same company that would go on to build the Sydney Harbour Bridge, and at the time of its construction it was the highest bridge in the world. The placement of the bridge, directly over the point where the water exits the first gorge into the second in a flurry of white water, referred to as the 'boiling pot', was specifically designed to give train travellers a view of the falls as they headed to the next destination for Sam and I, Zambia.

CHAPTER 15

The dementor at the falls

Our tour had ended after an amazing eight days. Early the next morning, the group parted ways. Sam and I headed off in a bus transfer to Livingstone, half an hour's drive away in Zambia. Our friendly driver allowed us to walk across the bridge over the Zambezi River, below the falls, to get a good look. We stared down at the tumultuous waters far below.

Sam turned to me. 'Would I die?'

'Absolutely.'

He didn't like that. 'I might land in the water and be all right, just injured.'

'Perhaps.'

As soon as we crossed the Zim–Zam border you could feel the poverty and oppression of Zimbabwe lift. While certainly not a wealthy country, Zambia felt completely different. We booked into a very cool backpacker hostel, the curiously named Jollyboys, and settled in. I wanted to emulate our week in Windhoek and focus back on schoolwork, on neuroplasticity, and on Sam.

Benison had sent me an interesting article she'd found on autism, discussing the issue of disability. A growing neurodiversity movement, mainly driven by high-functioning individuals with autism and Asperger's, proposes that autism is simply a 'different way of thinking'. The author of this article disagreed with this proposition, arguing that we need to acknowledge that it's also a disability. A disability, by definition, stops you doing things that most other people can do. This, he continued, can be tough, seem unfair and lead to discrimination, but to not tell an autistic person they're disabled is to not prepare them for what life might throw at them.

I thought it was a valid point. However, as I sat in Livingstone, Zambia, I explored the idea further in my mind. Disability itself is a fluid concept. An individual's level of disability is entirely contingent on the social context.

What's socially expected of a person living in a village in Africa is entirely different to what would be expected of a person living in an urban environment in a developed country. An African villager with moderate autism might receive the same level of schooling as every other child, might well get married and then go on to work at a similar manual job to the one they would have had were they not autistic. A similarly affected individual living in Australia would likely go to a special-needs school, flounder in the modern teenage dating scene, and potentially have no chance of finding gainful employment, where appropriate communication and social skills are generally deemed essential.

In his 2008 book *Unstrange Minds*, American anthropologist Roy Richard Grinker, who has a daughter with autism, explored how different cultures around the world respond to individuals with autism. 'There are still cultures today that do not have a name for autism,' he wrote, 'or that do not even see as pathological the symptoms that we call autistic.'

What we as individuals or as a broader society *expect* can determine whether a child or adult is disabled, or just different.

Livingstone was about four times the size of the town of Victoria Falls. Tourism for the falls had developed almost entirely on the Zambian side of the border, despite offering the less spectacular views. Such was Uncle Bob's legacy. But bad news for Zimbabwe was good news for Zambia: the city was booming.

Jollyboys had table tennis, so I decided to grab the opportunity to teach Sam a new skill. Table tennis certainly involves a lot of motor traffic across the midline; that is, it requires the use of both sides of the body. Sam had never played before, and could barely hit the ball on our first effort. *Not to worry.* We filmed some more interviews with myself, fellow travellers and staff members of the hostel. We'd managed to keep up our planned schedule of four interviews per week, and all this practice was improving Sam's speech skills and focus on others. Well, I thought it was. I reminded myself I'd have to wait for the results of the study to be certain.

That afternoon, the hostel posted a notice about an excursion to a local orphanage to play football with the children. I signed Sam and myself up.

The orphanage was set on the edge of Livingstone in a poor section of town. On the drive there, our ebullient taxi driver, Evans, told us that two years earlier the orphanage had taken in a newborn baby found abandoned in a bathtub in bushland. This sounded almost biblical.

The orphanage, run by nuns, survived on money from churches, private donations and what the staff and children could earn by selling eggs, tomatoes, eggplants and potatoes from the orphanage garden at the local market. Fifty children, aged two to sixteen, lived simply but comfortably in dorms similar to a backpacker hostel, sharing a communal dining room, a single large school room, a small library full of second-hand books and, of course, a small but lovely church.

The kids were keen as mustard to play football against all comers, which today included a young Swedish guy, Oskar, and his girlfriend, Frida, as well as Sam and me. Sam didn't last long, complaining about the dusty hot playing field. After a compulsory minimum five kicks from Sam, he sat in the shade of the school building nearby and stimmed in the dust, gathering small rocks together and running his fingers through the pile. He was having one of his late afternoon cranky-pants sessions. An eleven-year-old girl sat near him, eyeing him with curiosity while she played a version of marbles, with a circle drawn in the ochre sand and small rocks as makeshift marbles.

The manager of the home, an impressive and determined lady in her forties, was proud of their work and protective of her charges. There were to be no photographs or videos, and questions about the children were answered carefully and slowly; no disrespect was to be tolerated. She had the aura of a woman who had had to deal with a lot of crap. She got Sam straightaway; no issue there.

Oskar asked how the children ended up at the home.

'Sometimes their parents have died or abandoned them, or they bring them to us because they cannot afford to feed them anymore. Sometimes we agree to house, feed and school them for a while until the parents can get themselves back on their feet.

'Sometimes relatives will take care of the children for a while after the parents have died, if they have left them some money, or valuables like a fridge or furniture. Then when the money runs out they abandon them, and if we don't take them in, they end up as street kids in the city. This never used to happen years ago. Family ties are not as strong as they used to be.'

I asked if any of the children were orphaned by the HIV epidemic.

She replied after a considered pause, and I wondered if the question was too direct, too personal, whether I had crossed a social boundary. 'Yes, five of them.'

On the way back to the hostel, Evans took us to the local market where the produce from the orphanage was sold. Frida's eyes lit up. This, she said, was what she had always imagined an African market to look like: chaotic and crowded, a cacophony of music blaring over the buzz of conversation and laughter down the dirt aisles of the market. Bikes and dogs and breastfeeding mothers. Food stalls sold vegetables, herbs, spices, dried nuts, grains, and . . . caterpillars.

Evans got some of the last to take home. 'They are my children's favourite,' he said. 'If I say I'm going to bring home some caterpillars, they get very excited.'

Sam had a look of disgust on his face. 'Sam, do you want to eat caterpillars for dinner?' I asked him.

'NO! Not for me!'

Oskar and I rose to the challenge and each downed one of the brown comma-shaped morsels in a single bite. I expected piquancy, but discovered a mild musty taste that did not remind me of chicken. Sam was grossed out, and looked at me with an amalgam of disgust, amusement and curiosity. Did Dad really eat a caterpillar? Evans seemed a touch crestfallen in our lack of enthusiasm for the snack, and told us they tasted better when you ate them alive.

Over the next few days, Sam resumed his campaign to go home, demanding the requirement of scoring eight or more for seven days in a row be relaxed. I held firm, but he frequently escalated the argument, becoming threatening and aggressive, bordering on violent.

On the third morning in Livingstone I gave Sam an eight for the day before, even though he may not have quite deserved it; he'd had a bit of a tantrum shopping in the markets. I just sensed he needed it for his morale, which was starting to drop.

I wondered what was distressing him. It wasn't missing his mother, his brothers, his home or his school. I didn't even think it was missing his electronics and games. My suspicion was that Sam was missing control in his life. This was something I couldn't remedy. It was exactly the purpose of the trip, and it was proving very difficult for him to cope with.

We visited the Livingstone Museum, which was literally across the road from Jollyboys. It was a good opportunity to give Sam a history lesson. The solemn and venerable institution covered natural history, the anthropological, cultural and political history of Zambia and, of course, the life of Dr David Livingstone. While the atmosphere in the museum reminded me of the mustiness of caterpillars, it was still a worthwhile visit.

I had always wondered why Livingstone was so celebrated, and particularly why Africans revered him. Now I got it, as did Sam. Driven by missionary zeal, he had brought modern medicine to central Africa, as well as exposed the ongoing slave trade decimating the region, at a time when it went largely unacknowledged in Europe. He was unstoppable: mauled by a lion, repeatedly ravaged by dysentery and malaria, on and on he went, expedition after expedition.

Apart from advancing the world's understanding of the geography and nature of Africa, he helped rid a large chunk of Africa of the nightmare of slavery. His exploits became headline news in England, and questions over his health and sanity added a dimension of mystery that fired the public's imagination. When rumours circulated that he had died on the upper Zambezi, the *New York Herald* arranged the publicity stunt of sending journalist H.M. Stanley to track him down and see if he was still alive. With two hundred porters in tow, Stanley found Livingstone in what is now northern Zambia, and greeted him with the famous line, 'Dr Livingstone, I presume?'

The two journeyed on together and became close friends and exploring companions, before Stanley returned home. Livingstone refused to stop his work in Africa, and his disease-ravaged body eventually succumbed. He died kneeling in prayer. They buried his heart in Africa while his salt-preserved body was stretchered by two close African companions hundreds of miles to the coast, before being shipped to England. The Royal Geographic Society doctors confirmed it was Livingstone's body because of the deformed humerus bone in his arm—a legacy of the lion attack—before he was interned in Westminster Abbey.

We ambled through the city that bore his name, banking and shopping. Women in bright tribal dresses effortlessly balanced trays of fruit on their heads. Soldiers casually carried Kalashnikovs as they smoked and waited in line at the ATM. A car drove past, megaphones hoisted on the roof, blasting out political messages. Schoolchildren in royal-blue uniforms, the boys in ties and blazers, the girls in vests and long skirts, laughed and jostled at a bus stop.

Once again, Sam and I got into a rhythm and efficiently worked through neuroplasticity exercises and schoolwork each day: table tennis, boxing, chess, checkers, drawing, throwing, catching, handball. Algebra, writing narratives, writing postcards, the history of Africa, the geography of Africa. Jab, jab, uppercut, uppercut, kick, kick.

Word about us spread among the staff and guests at the Jollyboys. When you box with your adolescent son in the backyard of a backpacker hostel, people want to know why. Yet again I was moved by how supportive people were. They were interested, fascinated, motivated to help. It reinforced to me that there's an innate helping drive present in all people. Well, in most people.

Sam was turning his week around. He was calm and co-operative; a couple of day scores of eight had improved his confidence. His boxing was now miles ahead of what it had been when we had started on Table Mountain, and in a few days he had grasped some table tennis to the point of being able to sustain short rallies. Apart from the occasional blow-ups he was always fun to be with. Everyone around him enjoyed his quirky sense of humour, his constant smile and his fascinating take on the world.

But Africa continued to frustrate. The wi-fi sucked. Only some ATMs would recognise my bank card, and they changed from day to day. People only dealt in cash. Everything moved languidly, and we needed to match that pace, whether it was walking down the street, going through the supermarket checkout or buying stamps at the post office. There's an expression the locals use to explain these inevitable delays, inefficiencies and frustrations. This Is Africa. What other explanation is necessary? If you can't beat 'em, join 'em. With time it became easier and easier to adopt as my own mantra.

One evening, I chatted with a group of the backpacker hostel staff and their friends over a few beers in the bar. Dutch, English, Finnish, white South Africans, white Zambians, black Zambians—they all lived in Livingstone and they all liked it. Christie, a Zambian woman, worried about the Chinese buying up too much of the infrastructure. The Chinese workers on development projects lived in a self-contained village on the edge of the city and kept to themselves.

Graham, a South African, commented how Zambia and Zimbabwe had completed a role reversal in the last fifteen years, with Zimbabwe's economy now even worse than Zambia's used to be, and Zambia on the rise.

Tim, a stonecutter who'd fled Mugabe's regime when the farms were taken, worried that if South Africa went the way of Zimbabwe, the whole of southern Africa would collapse.

Some days Sam and I would cruise down to the local supermarket to buy bottled water, snacks or toiletries. Ancient taxis with peeling paint and broken door handles would toot as they passed us, their drivers hoping for a flicker of interest. Sam was becoming more accomplished at negotiating the unpredictable traffic on the broad dusty boulevards. He was nearly able to do it by himself. Close, but not there yet.

One day as we walked to the backpacker hostel, Evans drove past in one of the taxis and hollered, 'Hey, Mr Sam, I have saved you a bag full of caterpillars.'

Sam beamed at Evans and pointed at him. 'No!'

Near Jollyboys, I paused to buy some bananas from a street barrow. Reasonably healthy looking bananas sat on top of cardboard sheets, while a reasonably unhealthy looking man in a threadbare suit and thongs sat behind the cart. Very pleased to get the sale, he didn't have the right change and ran off down the road to another local guy to change some money.

Watching their exchange, I realised he was mute. When he ran back I noticed a dense cataract in his left eye. 'Keep the change,' I said.

The next morning as part of his schoolwork, in an exercise that sat halfway between English and religion, I set Sam the challenge of describing himself in hundred words or more. He came up with the following:

Description of Samuel Thomas Best

Personality: Funny, Kind, Noisy, Cheeky, Relaxing and Happy.

Appearance: Brown Hair, Tall, 14 years old and Pale Skin.

Likes: Playing Video Games and watch VHS Tapes and have Software.

Dislikes: Charlie the Cat*, Being Hurt, Errors, Losing in Video Games, Coming Last Place in Mario Kart and Data being deleted.

Examples of Good TV Shows: Simpsons, South Park, Family Guy, Pokémon, Futurama, Drawn Together, Cleveland Show, Beavis and Butthead and American Dad.

Examples of Good Movies: Harry Potter, Lord of the Rings, Pirates of Caribeen, Shrek, Hunger Games and Batman.

Example of Good Games: Mario, Sonic, Legend of Zelda, Kirby, Pokémon, Metal Gear Solid, F Zero and Grand Theft Auto.

Sport: Tennis, Golf, Bowling, Boxing and Swimming.

School: Maths, Geography, Science, TAS and Religion.

*Charlie is our cat. He and Sam have an ongoing dispute.

That afternoon, the funny, kind, noisy, cheeky, relaxing and happy boy and I ventured to Livingstone Island for high tea. I had stuffed up the timing of the trip to the island, and we were running late. Kim, a Canadian co-owner of Jollyboys, kindly gave us a lift to the departure point: a ramp at the rear of the five-star Livingstone Hotel, on the banks of the Zambezi at the edge of the city.

'So how is the tourism business going?' I enquired in the car.

'Oh, okay, I suppose. Tourism is so fickle. We've been hit hard by the Ebola crisis. Also the Japanese market has evaporated, especially since ISIS beheaded that poor fellow. They're just too afraid to leave their country now.'

Kim had a sixteen-year-old stepson and a two-year-old daughter. She knew about Sam and was curious about our trip and its purpose. 'Are you sure he's going to be okay on the island?' she asked. 'Don't let him too close to the edge.' I was concerned about safety on the island too, and was determined to keep Sam close to me, although I thought Sam would likely be more afraid of the current and cliffs than I was.

At the hotel, tame zebras grazed on manicured lawns, a bizarre backdrop to the five-star hotel and the river. Alex, our guide, met us at the ramp.

Sam cut to the chase. 'Are there hippos? Are there crocodiles? Am I going to die?'

'Well, I don't think so, but we'll see how we go,' Alex teased.

Livingstone Island was no bigger than a small football field, an outcrop that defied the massive torrent that surrounded it on all sides. It perched astride the edge of the falls, halfway along the precipice, marking the eastern edge of the main falls. Livingstone had first seen the falls from this island in 1855, the first non-African to do so, and named them after his queen.

The speedboat zoomed across a swirl of eddies and rapids towards the ominous edge, demarcated by a wall of mist and an increasingly sonorous roar as we approached. You wouldn't have wanted the engine to fail. As we approached the island, I informed Alex about Sam. A father of two, Alex was professional and responsible. 'Right, we'll get onto it. We'll not take any risks with Sam. Don't you worry.'

The boat crept into the reeds on the upriver shore of the island and we disembarked and trooped up the muddy path through the dense trees and shrubs. Mist started to drench our clothes, and we were handed heavy green canvas ponchos in preparation for our walk to the edge. Alex personally escorted Sam and me. We manoeuvred Sam to within a few metres of the edge; I started to get nervous, but Alex was cautious, carefully instructing Sam where to place every footstep while tightly gripping his hand.

As we sat on the rocks, the air resonated with the sound of the relentless tumble of millions of litres of water roaring past. I smiled. It was like sitting astride a great beast. The river felt alive.

I teased Sam about his green poncho. 'Hey, Sam, you look like Yoda.'

'No, I look like a *dementor*!'

I grabbed his upper arm and teasingly nudged him in the direction of the edge. 'If you were a dementor you could fly over the edge.'

'*No!* I don't want to go over the edge.' He laughed, in on the joke. Alex patted him on the shoulder through the thick, drenched poncho. 'Don't worry—you're not going over the edge, Mr Sam. I'll make sure.'

We escorted Sam back to a large tent where the group were to have lunch and Alex offered to take me back to the edge alone, to walk across the rocks to a pool literally on the edge of the falls. Sam could stay at the tent where other staff could keep an eye on him.

As we crossed the rocks, I spied a small wooden plank bridge, just underwater. Alex explained that we needed to cross this to get to the edge. If you slipped, there was nothing to stop you going over. No barrier, no rope, nothing. Alex leant in and asked me carefully over the roar of the falls, 'Are you afraid of heights?'

I gulped. 'No.'

'Are you okay to go across? I'll help you, but don't go if you think you might panic.'

I hesitated for a few seconds. 'No, I won't panic.'

We inched across the slippery board hand in hand, like two giant green molluscs, moving sideways only centimetres at a time. It was hard not to lean away from the threat of the falls, but Alex's firm grip kept me in check. On the other side we sat on rocks at the edge. I crawled forward and, lying flat on the wet rock, poked my head over the edge of the falls and looked into the white wet abyss below. I could only watch the torrent crashing down for a few seconds at a time before having to turn away to keep the vertigo in check.

Back at the lunch venue Sam was patiently waiting. The Dementor and I were seated in a separate tent apart from the others. While I had greatly appreciated the extra service offered to Sam and me by Alex, we could still eat with people! But their intentions were good; they were just trying to help us out as best they knew how.

On our last day in Livingstone, I saw a poster on a tree advertising the services of a Dr King Tunga:

We are helping the society healing different diseases like madness, epilepsy, manhood management and hard on medicines, business luck, enhance your love, recovering stolen properties, healing STIs, swollen legs, chambu, charms able to make you rich through the spirit of your ancestors, asthma and many more.

Despite Dr Tunga's impressively wide range of skills—and the fact I was personally concerned about a couple of the maladies on the list—I decided against a visit.

CHAPTER 16

Jungle Junction

Our next stop was a place recommended on the backpacker's grapevine: Jungle Junction. The hostel, situated on an island upstream on the Zambezi River from Livingstone, sent a guy called Fergus to pick us up in a beaten-up LandCruiser. It had a cracked windscreen, broken side mirrors and doorhandles, there were panels missing and the rear door latch was held together with a coat hanger. Oh, and there were 451,000 clicks on the odometer.

Manchester United and Futbol Club Barcelona stickers festooned the windscreen, reflecting the African obsession with European football and, in particular, the English Premier League. On the way out of town, Fergus picked up two female teachers from a college. The three Zambians in the front seat chatted, joked and laughed in their local language, Tonga, while modern African music played on one of the teacher's mobile phones. It felt good to be moving again.

From the back seat, Sam pointed out a sixty-five kilometres per hour speed limit road sign, a new one to add to his mental collection. We left the bitumen after an hour or so and, with what remained of the side mirrors turned in, we bumped down a narrow bush track on non-existent suspension while the thorns of juvenile teak bushes and African balsawood trees scraped against the windows. The track led down to the Zambezi River valley. The teachers exited with their supplies at a small primary school in a village on the banks of the river. Apparently Sam and I were visiting the school the next day.

At the river's edge, we piled into some balsa dugout canoes, operated by oarsmen who stood in the back with a single long oar, used for pushing or rowing. Sam was in one canoe, I was in the other. I tried to explain Sam's challenges to Godfrey, the oarsman on Sam's canoe. 'He may not understand you completely,' I said. 'Sam is a bit different.'

Godfrey calmly nodded. 'Okay, sure. Just stay still, Sam.'

'Are there hippos?' Sam asked.

Godfrey leant on his long oar and pushed off from the muddy bank. 'Yes, but we'll stay away from them.'

As we glided down the smooth waters, the honks of hippos echoed through the reeds. Elephants grazed on the bank. We reached Bovu Island where a white Zambian man, Brett, had set up the magnificently relaxed Jungle Junction. Sam and I were the only guests when we arrived, which was both good and bad: good that we had the facilities to ourselves, bad that it limited the chance for Sam to talk to strangers.

Bovu Island is also referred to as Simaleu Island after a Mr Simaleu. The story goes that many years ago he found a dead hippo on the island and tried to remove her uterus as material for some black magic. Unfortunately for Mr Simaleu, she was not in fact dead but asleep, and no doubt awoke in a surprised state. She contracted her private parts, trapping his arm inside her, and marched to the water, dragging Mr Simaleu behind her to his impending doom. With an axe in his free hand, and options running out fast, he did what he needed to do: he chopped off his trapped arm, and lived to tell the tale.

In the afternoon, Godfrey took Sam and me on a sunset canoe ride, a chance to have a fish from the canoe. Sam only reluctantly agreed. He doesn't like fishing. The first time he caught a fish, from a boat when he was about ten, he was so frightened by the flapping white streak on the end of his line he promptly tried to jump out of the boat himself.

On the water, I lamely tried a few casts of the lure but I was really just going through the motions; I didn't want to risk Sam jumping out of the canoe in these waters. The sunset over the Zambezi was heroic: we could glimpse the western orange sky here and there through the wild vine-filled jungle on the banks. A cacophony of insect noise and birdsong emanated across the swirls and eddies of the mighty river. Godfrey kept us clear of the rapids, where Muriel Spark's 'rocks that look like crocodiles and crocodiles that look like rocks' ominously sat. He pushed hard on his pole as we inched upstream in the reeds and shallows, struggling against the incessant current.

As we turned and headed back for Jungle Junction, gliding easily now that the current was our friend, Godfrey mentioned to me that Brett had told him Sam was autistic. 'My sister is autistic,' he added, as he glided the canoe in the current.

'Really, how old is she?'

'Twenty-five.' He paused. 'So does Sam go to school?'

'Yes, he's in year eight.'

'And does he shout at people?'

I wondered where this was going. 'Not very often.'

'My sister doesn't want anyone near her. She lives by herself.' Godfrey was clearly interested in Sam and the fact that he went to school, and could excel at maths and computer science. 'People in the village think my sister has autism because she has been bewitched. Perhaps her father or someone else put a curse on her. She is actually my half-sister.'

I decided this wasn't the time or place for a lecture on autism causality.

At dinner, we were joined by Brett in the dining hut: a thatched roof built around a giant African ebony tree. We chatted about autism, science and Harry Potter as I pushed Sam to eat a meal that was challenging for him: chicken cacciatore, rice and vegetables.

As we ate we were suddenly joined by a genet, perched on the railing beside me. Her body was the size of a small domestic cat but with her thin tail she was a metre long. Despite appearances genets are not cats, but are actually related to the civet. Her blonde coat was checked with dark brown markings, her tail striped. She eyed the three of us, and then the chicken. Before I knew it, a chicken bone on my plate was gone, and up with her in the tree. She was fast, very fast. Sam ate his chicken a tad quicker.

Our thatched hut was set away from the bar, restaurant and office. We had lighting in the room until the generator went off but no other power apart from at the office. The hut sat on stilts over the water. There were toilet facilities up a path but Brett suggested weeing off the verandah at night was probably safest. There was no Diesel here to protect us from hippos.

Elephants trumpeted. Hippos honked, stomped and splashed. Cattle mooed off in the village. A small something landed on the roof. A large something trampled in the reeds near the verandah. All that separated us from the river was a mosquito net and five wooden stairs.

Before dawn the hippos started up a ruckus. I crept out onto the verandah. In the dim moonlight I could see their hulking silhouettes a stone's throw away, but I sure didn't throw any. I reminded myself again that they can't climb stairs and retreated inside.

Dawn lifted the mist from the Zambezi, the vapour rising off the fast current looking like a pot about to boil. Squadrons of reed cormorants glided by in tight formation, a large hadeda ibis, resplendent with his emerald-green sheen and ruby beak, hark-harked for a mate as he lazed on a hanging branch, a pied kingfisher shot from the reeds. The northern waters tumbled east to the rising sun in their relentless journey to the falls.

After breakfast we headed over to the village, a short canoe ride across the channel on the northern side of the island. Godfrey showed us through the village, a scattering of huts over a dozen or so acres, housing one hundred and thirty-six people at last count.

The village, with no electricity and water carted by bucket from the river, was authentically traditional. I had promised Brett and Godfrey that Sam and I would take my laptop over with us and give a lesson on the basics of word processing to the teachers in the primary school.

At the school, the kids were being taught outside in the sun, under a Zambian flag on a pole. The lessons were in Tonga and they spoke little English; that skill only became possible if their families could afford to send them to high school in Livingstone.

What the children lacked in English they made up for in enthusiasm. Fascinated by seeing themselves on the monitor of the movie camera I was carrying, they tumbled over each other and Sam and me to get into frame, yelling, screaming and laughing as they did so.

As the children broke for lunch the three teachers—Maureen, Marita and Alice—sat in a classroom with Sam and me. I showed them the basics of using a keyboard and a mouse, and cutting and pasting. Sam gave them a display of what could be done with word processing when you're fast. They very much appreciated the lesson, but I wondered how many years it might be before a school like this would get a computer.

After the lesson we waved goodbye to the throng of jumping children and made our way back to the village. Cruising up the track behind us was Godfrey's sister, Manga, the one with autism, and her friend. This was going to be interesting.

Manga was certainly wary of us and aloof, but shook Sam's hand and said hello before walking on ahead of us to her hut, next to Godfrey's.

'So what does she do?' I asked Godfrey, as we strolled along the dusty track.

'She fishes and sells oil. She is very good at fishing.' Manga, just ahead of us, heard him and half-smiled. As she moved further away, Godfrey explained that she was very skilled at catching fish using a simple wooden pole, a piece of string and a worm on the end. She would sell the fish to people in the village, but only particular people on particular days. No one knew why, but she never relaxed her self-imposed rules.

She would also buy a large quantity of oil from a wholesaler before dividing it up and selling it to the villagers in small bottles. Once again, only to certain people on certain days. And she never made a mistake with the money. She lived alone, with only minor support from her family, and spoke well, although only when she felt like it.

'Do you think she's content with her life?' I asked.

Godfrey stopped walking and turned to me. 'Yes. I do.'

It was fascinating to see how an autistic woman, probably one who would be classed as high-functioning in a developed world environment, coped in a village in Zambia, and also how the village coped with and reacted to her. After a while Godfrey started talking again. 'You know, every now and then—say, every few months—she just takes off. Just walks. She can walk all the way to Livingstone. Sometimes she turns up at the police station there, asking for a lift back.'

I thought to myself that it was a bloody long way to walk. 'Why do you think she does it?'

'It tends to happen when she's stressed. Maybe it's a release.'

Sam, Godfrey and I reached the community centre, a small open-walled hut where a village woman cooked over a makeshift fire. A friend held the woman's one-year-old baby, and the two women chatted while she cooked. Skinny dogs slept on the dusty roads, chickens followed by their chicks scratched under the thickets and thorn bushes nearby. Rectangular mud huts, some with doors and windows, some not, but all with thatched roofs, stood here and there. African music floated over the village from speakers somewhere distant.

Sam was wary of the food. Our cook prepared okra, eggplant and tomato, and ground peanut with rape, all to go with the cornmeal pup. It looked and smelt good to me, but even though Sam might have managed some of this in a more familiar environ-ment I knew it wasn't going to happen today so I didn't push.

Godfrey chatted to the women in Tonga. I heard Sam's name mentioned and computers and teachers. He explained he'd been telling the ladies how Sam, even though he was like Manga, had still taught the teachers some computer skills. There was an unmistakable note of defiance and pride in his voice.

As we headed back to the canoes after lunch one of the men in the village shouted across a cow field to Godfrey, pointing at the river. On the far bank was a hippo with a gaping wound in its leg, likely from a croc or another hippo. Our canoe was about fifty metres from the wounded beast. Godfrey manoeuvred carefully, keeping a close eye on the animal, but we were safe.

The next day—after the hippos fortunately had a quieter night—we headed back to Livingstone and Jollyboys. Our last day in the city was spent trying to catch up with schoolwork and neuroplasticity exercises. Sam's table tennis had improved markedly throughout the week and he was chuffed with himself. He had stopped seeing it as a chore and actually asked to extend our game a little at the end, which in turn made me feel chuffed.

CHAPTER 17

Two *wazungu*

It was time to leave the city of Livingstone and head north. As Livingstone had said, 'I am prepared to go anywhere, provided it be forward.' And forward we went. We caught the Mazhandu Family Bus Service No. 3 to Zambia's capital, Lusaka. The road and the railway, both in pretty good nick, flirted with each other as they headed east. Mopane scrub became baobab and Zambezi teak, which became sugar cane, which became cattle farms interspersed with the Miombo woodlands, with the red saplings maturing into yellow and green canopies.

The rollicking blue bus picked up passengers from towns on and near the highway, and soon filled up. There were towns that seemed to exist only for the business from the buses. Dogs slept in the sun. Women balanced sacks of grain or trays of tomatoes, carrots, okra, capsicums, eggplants and oranges. Men hawked green bananas through the bus windows. A yellow plastic booth sold mobile phone data vouchers. Streets were lined with wooden and tin booths, second-hand clothes laid out on the pavement.

A Seventh Day Adventist church was surrounded by abandoned brick buildings, where a gander pecked at the rubbish. A sky blue herbal clinic, a mustard-coloured auto shop with PRAISE THE LORD written on the wall, an empty superette. A minivan passed that was so full one passenger balanced outside the window with his legs inside and his fingers gripping the window's frame. THANK GOD was scrawled across the van's rear. Leaving one town, our impatient driver nearly collected a woman who was a bit slow getting off the bitumen. Thank God, indeed.

We stopped for a ten-minute lunch break under a towering grain silo by the railway. It was the usual roadside diner with greasy and dirty toilets, for the use of which you had to pay the cleaner. I encouraged Sam to read some Harry Potter.

'I don't think so. I would like to decline your offer,' he said.

Where the heck did that come from? We negotiated a different challenge; he was to write a summary of me, written in the form of a letter to Harry Potter.

Dear Daniel Radcliffe the actor of Harry Potter,
Let me tell you about my father.

My father is 49 years old, his name is James Andrew Best. We call him Jabber. He takes me to the Africa trip up to 7 months. Dad has seen the 50 billion dollar note in Zimbabwe.

It is now just over 2 months since dad had start of the trip.

He is a Doctor. He has white short beard around his face. He is a little bit tough and sometimes angry and has wine and beer and coffee.

He did the head dance. He has been to Africa without me in 1970s or 1980s.

He is kind usually. Overall, he was born in May 10th 1966.

Cheers Samuel Best

When I sent it to Benison, I assured her I was occasionally drinking beverages other than wine, beer and coffee.

As we approached the capital, traffic thickened, on roads being widened and upgraded by the Chinese. Crossing the railway, teeming with pedestrians on the tracks, we entered the city. A billboard from a church announced a CITY WIDE MIRACLE CRUSADE. THEME: JESUS.

Lusaka, with its jammed roads, jostling sidewalks and medium-scale high rise, is the sort of place where you don't carry a bag that could be potentially stolen unless you have to and you don't go out at night alone unless you're desperate. It was a relief to get behind the hostel's electric fence. Fortunately, we were only overnighting here before heading across the border into Malawi. I noticed as we travelled further towards the centre of Africa that white people, referred to by the Swahili term *mzungu*, were fewer and fewer. Sam and I were the only *wazungu*—the plural—in the hostel. The word literally translates as 'aimless wanderer' and was first used to describe European explorers from the eighteenth century who had a disconcerting propensity for getting lost. I considered it a very apt term for the two of us.

As I organised dinner while Sam lazed in the room, I was approached by a couple of guys playing pool and asked if I wanted to join them. I'd been feeling fairly out of place so I appreciated and accepted the kind offer. Kelvin and Mdala, a refrigeration technician and scientist-turned-car-salesman respectively, were locals who used the hostel as a safe watering hole. They were intrigued to learn about the trip and Sam and me.

'So where is Sam now?' Mdala asked.

'Here he comes,' I said. Sam bounded down into the open

lounge area and loudly said, 'We are the only white people here!' Kelvin and Mdala and several others in the bar cracked up.

'Yes, Sam, that's true,' Kelvin said.

Sam turned and pointed to Mdala. 'Are you poor?'

Yikes!

'No, I am not, Sam. Are you?'

'No, I'm not. I'm glad you're not poor.' Sam bought himself a Sprite and rushed back to the room shouting, 'They are not poor!'

Mdala and I swapped email addresses and I headed back to the room, shaking my head. I decided on my own version of 'This Is Africa': This Is Autism.

The next day was a catch-up day of school, shopping and running repairs. On Skype, Benison laughed about Sam's description of me, so I decided to get her back. Sam was given the challenge of describing her to Hermione and Ron.

This is the description of my mum called Benison Anne O'Reilly. She has bushy multibrown hair like Hermione. She likes Reading, watching shows like Tuders [sic] and Miss Fishers.

She dislikes eels, messy rooms and camp in the rain. She gets cross at Matthew Best sometimes. She also dislikes dog poo, anacondas and Tricky* stealing Charlie's food. She goes to work at North Sydney. She makes books about autism.

Benison's joke name is called medicine. She also likes tidiness, Lulu the cat and emails. She is kind and makes house tidy but not as tidy as Singapore and organises home-work that I have to do. Her brother and sister are called Cameron and Roslyn and her parents are called Gran and

Grandad. Gran and Grandad are old but healthy and their
bodies are well.
    Overall she is lovely and makes her house clean.
    Cheers Sam.
        *Our dog. She and Sam get along just fine.

Well, at least I was not a neat freak. I did, however, agree she was lovely.

I left the bar early and read my Kindle in the room while Sam played on his DS: it was another quiet evening in a concrete cell-like room behind electric fences and security guards. The next day was going to be a big one.

3.15 a.m. The phone alarm sounded.

3.50 a.m. We scrambled our packs together and left the room. At the gate, the sleeping security guard awoke with a jolt and demanded our room receipt, which I couldn't find. We were five minutes late for the taxi. *Would it still be waiting?* I still couldn't find the receipt. Would the room key do? It was in the door. Packs down. 'Stay here, Sam.' I ran back to get the key.

The security guard, finally satisfied he had fulfilled his duties, opened the large metal gate. No taxi. We walked with our packs down the murky deserted Lusaka street. At the nearest intersection, we found a taxi, its driver asleep. He woke on our approach.

4.10 a.m. Out of the cab at the bus depot, we threw our packs into the baggage compartment underneath the bus, hoisted our daypacks onto the above-head luggage shelf, and plonked onto the blue velvet seats with relief. Sam broke out the DS.

The host checked my ticket. 'Can you come with me please, sir?'

Wrong ticket, wrong bus. The bus to our destination, Lilongwe, the capital of Malawi, wouldn't leave until 2 p.m.

'This bus only goes to the border town of Chipata,' we were informed. 'You will have to change there, get a taxi to the border, cross, and then get another taxi and bus to Lilongwe. Here is a one hundred kwacha refund.' *Great.*

I seethed in my velvet seat. Hawkers roamed the aisle spruiking headsets, memory cards, phone chargers, power packs and crisps.

5 a.m. *Why hadn't we left yet?* More hawkers: sweets, crisps, gloves and underwear.

5.20 a.m. More hawkers: mobile phone vouchers, lottery tickets and socks. People were still getting on. We were meant to have left nearly an hour earlier! Somebody thumped the side of the bus, I don't know why. And then finally the wheels on the bus went round and round.

And round and round. The road seemed to be being repaired all the way from Lusaka to Chipata. Every time we veered off what remained of the bitumen onto yet another dirt-road detour, the bus would fill with the rust-coloured dust and the passengers would all cough. I would dust off the screen of my Kindle and Sam would dust off the screen of his DS.

The bus was full to capacity, and not only with passengers; it seemed some locals travelled with half a houseful of possessions. The aisle of the bus was an obstacle course of wheeled suitcases, vacuum-compressed bags of clothes and taped cardboard boxes, all now covered with dust. Occasionally we'd stop to let a passenger on or off, who would have to negotiate the obstacle course. Rather than find a way down the aisle, one guy just jumped out the window.

Mid morning the bus pulled to a halt at a small village with a few old shops. I asked the fellow next to me if this was a toilet stop. He nodded. I negotiated the obstacle course and ran off to the rear of the shops where there was a toilet block with no actual toilet inside, just, well, an area that didn't smell so good. As I did my business, I heard the bus start up. *Shit!*

I sprinted back. The bus was just pulling out as I approached; the driver braked and let me on. I wondered what would have happened if I had missed it. I hoped Sam would have yelled out something. I reached my seat with relief.

The landscape of south-east Zambia was semi-arid scrub. We ascended and crossed a ridgeline. With the appearance of greener vegetation, clumps of sugar cane and banana trees and fruit on the trays on the heads of women in the villages, I realised we had left the central African plateau. We were approaching the physical feature of the planet most visible from space, the Great Rift Valley.

Named by British explorer John Gregory in 1892, the system of valleys extends from the Middle East, down the Red Sea, through the great lakes of eastern Africa, and branches to Madagascar and the Indian Ocean. In east Africa, including Malawi, a tectonic plate under the Horn of Africa is splitting away from the rest of the continent, creating a giant split in the earth's crust, leading to vast deep valleys and lakes.

Anthropologist Richard Leakey has also described the Rift Valley as 'an ideal setting for evolutionary change', and indeed this is where the oldest origins of man have been found. The abundant flora and fauna and varied ecosystems provided fertile grounds for new species to develop. This was where we all came from.

As the afternoon sun beat down, we finally approached the border town of Chipata. Sam was sitting a few seats away from me. He yelled across the aisle, 'Are there going to be any white people, Dad?' Difficult though it was in a sea of dark faces, I tried to pretend he wasn't my son.

A taxi driver approached me as we got off the bus. 'Hey, I remember you guys! I took you to a hostel a few days ago.' I tried desperately to place him. By the time I had figured out he had just made that up to get our attention, he had our bags in the back of his taxi. I realised where Sam got his naivety from. Oh well, whatever; we needed a taxi anyway.

Our old friend took us to the Zambia–Malawi border. After an uneventful border crossing we found our third taxi of the day, me in the front seat, Sam in the back. It was immediately apparent that the prices had dropped. As always, the taxi wouldn't leave half full so we waited next to the dusty customs building for the next potential customers. Two women of what author Alexander McCall-Smith would describe as 'traditional build' approached. The driver helped them to load their copious baggage into the boot of the taxi. They wedged into the back seat on either side of Sam. In their bright floral dresses with matching head-wraps, resting wooden trunks on their laps, they looked like they were setting out on a Grand Tour.

I could see Sam's increasing irritation with the close quarters in the back seat as they chatted and giggled and shuffled on either side of him. I closed my eyes and waited for the inevitable.

'You're too fat,' Sam said.

Yep, there it was.

They glanced at Sam but fortunately decided to ignore him, perhaps dismissing him as just another rude *mzungu*, then continued to chat in Chichewa all the way to our destination, the town of Mchinji.

Sam and I were both over the day. Neither of us had slept a wink on the bus. But there was one more trip to go. In Mchinji, we had our first experience of an African minibus. You figure out which is yours by reading the hand-drawn signs on the front dashboard or hearing the driver yell out the destination. Given the thick accents, this can be tricky. Basically, they wait until they fill up and then they go.

Seventeen passengers were tightly packed into our minibus for the two hours to the capital. The sun, and our spirits, sank lower. Sam and I both willed the capital to appear. Finally, we came to Lilongwe.

The footpaths were mostly dirt tracks. Dishevelled shanty suburbs lined the dirty garbage-filled river. Lilongwe was no Windhoek. The minivan pulled into a chaotic 'bus station' where drivers negotiated who had right of way over the lumpy bumpy dirt by shouting and waving out the window.

We snatched our packs and stumbled out of the bus in the twilight. A *tut-tut* driver bustled up to us and half-dragged us to his vehicle. A fight broke out between him and some taxi drivers. I had no idea what it was about. *A turf war? Did he break protocol by grabbing us too early?* I was too tired to care. There was lots of pushing and pulling and some of the taxi drivers kicked and thumped his *tut-tut* as we sat on the back seat.

We landed at Mabuya Camp backpacker hostel after six trips over fifteen hours. There was a restaurant at the hostel where we could get a beef stew and rice. I had promised Sam pizza but I sure as hell didn't want to head out in a taxi to a restaurant, and I didn't want to figure out how to order pizza in, especially since I didn't have a SIM card for Malawi and my computer battery was flat. I just wanted to eat and go to bed.

But in the reception area, in front of ten people, Sam lost it completely. 'You changed your mind! You said *pizza*!'

'I know but it is just too hard, Sam. We'll have pizza tomorrow night.'

'*No! Fuck off! Give me pizza!*' He clamped his hands around my throat and growled at me. I hustled him up to the room, where we had a ten-minute shouting match, during which Sam threw the room key and water bottle at me and landed some reasonably effective punches to my shoulder. Teaching Sam boxing had come back to bite me.

'I *hate* you! I want a *new* father!'

I eventually left him to cool down but only after I had stupidly threatened all sorts of punishments that knew I wouldn't implement, such as throwing out the precious DS. I was breaking all the rules of effective parenting. But I just wanted to eat and go to bed.

Eventually he calmed and the restaurant managed to rustle up some buttered bread instead of the rice, which Sam accepted as a reasonable compromise. While I read my book he collapsed asleep on the bed. He had barely slept in thirty-six hours.

The next day on Skype, Benison reminded me that:

a) even typically developing teenage boys can have issues with anger management, and
b) she would have wanted to strangle someone if she had gone thirty-six hours without sleep.

True, true. It's not always about autism.

CHAPTER 18

Mr Friendly

I felt human again after a twelve-hour sleep. I hoped Sam did too. We went into town on a minibus to sort out SIMs and money. Once you got used to the minibus system, and getting up close and personal with your fellow passengers, it was kind of efficient and cool.

I broke out the *Lonely Planet* and started booking accommodation for the next week or so. I tried to get Sam involved in the planning, even if only peripherally. We did have pizza for dinner, but that didn't stop Sam having another blow-up in the evening. His scores for the last two days had been five and 5.5. I hoped things would turn around soon.

And they did. Sam finally got into the swing of things again. There was no table tennis at Mabuya, but there was a pool table so I taught him the rules. Once again Sam applied himself well, despite his gross-motor limitations. He also understood the concept of the game already as he'd played an electronic version on a Nintendo Wii.

At reception, the co-owner of Mabuya overheard my conversation about trying to organise bus tickets north to Mzuzu the next day. She came over to help out. 'Your best option is the AXA

Executive bus which leaves at midday from City Mall, which is quite a way away. You should get over there today and book because it does fill up.'

'Okay, I'll book a cab,' I said.

She waved her hand downwards. 'Oh, look my car is here, I'll get our tour manager to drive you guys over.'

It was just that sort of place.

Later in the lounge, we got chatting with a few of the staff and some of their friends. James, a pony-tailed English editor, sailor and raconteur, had a great talent for kicking along a conversation. Posh accent, wide grin stretching under an aquiline nose, and an open posture that seemed to necessitate him having a wine in one hand and a cigarette in the other, he was instantly likeable. I wished Sam would pick up a few tips from him on social engagement, but he was too distracted by James' ponytail.

'Are you a woman?' Sam asked.

It was patently obvious James was *not* a woman. Sam just wanted to make the point that a man shouldn't have a ponytail.

The conversation drifted to annoying and unpleasant people in general. A young woman in the group mentioned 'tobacco wives'.

'They're kind of like Malawi's equivalent of WAGs,' she explained. 'Pretty young women, usually blonde, partnered up with rich tobacco farmers, who think they're better than everyone else because they have a big boat on the lake.'

Matt complained about the goats on the roads at this time of year. 'They're everywhere. I have a theory it's because it's maize season, and all the kids who normally look after the goats are off helping in the fields, so the goats just wander about.' He joked he was trying to keep his 'goat kill count' down to single figures when he went for a drive at night. Well, I think he was joking.

The two big stories in Malawi were who was going to take over as coach of the Malawi Flames, the national football team, and Cashgate, a corruption scandal involving civil servants and high-ranking officials in the ruling party and tens of millions of dollars. The story became public in 2013 after a civil servant was shot and nearly killed outside his house supposedly in relation to widespread looting of government funds. There were also allegations some of the funds were being used to finance ministers election campaigns. All in one of the world's poorest countries.

The next day we hit the road again on the AXA Executive bus. The bus was late, and then made even later by the presidential motorcade. The entire city seemed to be shut down to allow the long line of shiny black limousines through. There were more passengers than seats on the bus, and while I scrambled to ensure Sam got a seat, I missed out myself, along with three Africans. My best option for the six-hour trip was to sit up near the driver on a step next to his seat, facing backwards. I was trying to read my Kindle but every time he braked I would career backwards towards the dash. Executive bus, my aunt! About halfway through the trip I was seriously getting the shits when a few people disembarked and I got a seat.

We were heading to the north of Malawi, rising up through young and volcanic mountain ranges. Umber parched grass fields were flecked with patches of curry-coloured and withering winter corn, their stalks standing in the fields redolent of ragged prisoners on parade. Mango and citrus, cane and banana. Off in the distance, plumes of cyanosed smoke hazed the hills and horizon.

The busy road was filled with packed minibuses, bikes and open trucks, slow, beaten and bashed, carting sagging grain sacks, building materials, or humanity, sometimes all three. We passed a wooden truck brimming with nuns and schoolchildren. Two yoked donkeys looked bored while a man filled their cart with straw. An old man operated a foot-pedal sewing machine on a verandah outside a rendered white building. Goats, bikes, children, a man in a suit.

The heavy sun lowered into the haze and became a giant vermillion beacon as we careered up through the mountains. Round, jagged or conical, like blankets drawn up by pinched fingers, the slopes now covered in forest or pine plantations. Wispy mauve clouds danced across the treetops.

Our driver seemed unhappy about driving along the darkening mountain road, but rather than slow he flung the bus forward, crunching gears and thrashing the clutch. Overladen timber trucks and oil tankers were passed on blind curves. White-knuckled, I seemed to be the only one noticing.

Another day spent on buses came to a close as we pulled up to Mzuzu. In front of a crackling fire in the hostel's lounge room sat an older South African man who had abandoned his quest to kayak around Lake Malawi after catching malaria five days earlier. He looked, to put it bluntly, like shit. Later that night, a mosquito snuck inside the net over my bed. At fifteen hundred metres altitude, Mzuzu winter nights are cold, but I was motivated enough to get out from underneath the blankets and swat the blighter.

Mzuzu seemed to me to be an intimidating town; in the short time we were there I could not see its purported charms. I did, however, stumble across a FedEx office and was able to organise the transfer of more video footage back to Australia, which was a bonus.

John, the hostel owner, was a British expat in his sixties who had lived in Australia and all over the world and had truly excellent taste in music. He had the indurated look and manner of expats who had spent a lot of time in Africa. While Sam and I were ordering lunch in the hostel dining room, out the window I saw three youths, one holding a machete, at the open front gate. John was sitting on the verandah and they were asking him something. John seemed unperturbed, continuing on with his crossword. As I walked out, he sent the three around the side of the house, saying the boss wasn't there at the moment. But he was the boss.

I sat down near him on the lounge. 'Everything okay?'

'Oh yes, they are just after some bamboo from the yard for some project they're doing.' I tried to see if his indifferent manner was bluster, but he remained inscrutable, applying all his attention to the puzzle. *Why then lie?*

In the morning, as we waited for the cab to the minibus station, one of John's friends from out of town joined him for coffee on the verandah.

'What's new?' John asked him.

The man shook his head. 'A woman in our village killed by an elephant.'

'Oh, I'm sorry,' John said. 'It happens.'

The minibus station was the usual topsy-turvy chaos on bumpy rutted dirt, and as our taxi driver told us which bus to get on, a young African starting gesticulated wildly at him. The youth had little or no speech and erratic behaviour, and I tried to perform a ten-second diagnosis. *Schizophrenia? Autism? Developmental delay? Something else?* When he realised we weren't going to Lilongwe he left us alone.

Our rattling minibus circled the bus station and the neighbouring market while the conductor shouted the destination out the window to potential punters. It took nearly an hour to fill up before we left the city. One man got on with two huge iceboxes; another joined us lugging two car tyres.

I was never really certain what was going on. Were we actually leaving for our destination now, still filling up or just giving someone in town a lift somewhere? Actually, in general, I spent half my time in Africa unsure what was going on. I suppose it was even more so for Sam.

One passenger carried a FedEx satchel. I hoped it wasn't the video footage I had sent, as it would be going in the wrong direction. We arced north out of town. A friendly guy sitting next to Sam and me, who spoke good English but with a heavy accent, fired a thousand questions at me about Australia. He somehow knew blue gum trees came from Australia, but otherwise his knowledge was very patchy.

'Is Australia next to Germany?'

'Do you have doctors in Australia?'

'Do you have HIV in Australia?'

As Mr Friendly continued to press me, Sam, who was sitting between us, became frustrated with me repeatedly telling him to not interrupt. Increasingly cross, he squeezed my face with his hands and growled. Mr Friendly stopped asking questions.

Half an hour into the trip, the minibus pulled over in a village. A solidly built man of about forty got on and sat in front of me, while two wiry teenagers seemed to be harassing some passengers through the window. The well-built man scolded the youths in his deep voice. One of the teenagers reacted, pointing and yelling at him through the open sliding door. The man muttered at him under his breath, and the youth's behaviour intensified to real aggression. I thought the now incandescent youth was about to leap into the van and start a brawl. It would have been ill advised; Mr Solid would have easily cleaned him up. But the door slammed shut and we pulled away as the youths punched and kicked the bus.

Sam laughed. 'They are fighting!'

A very animated discussion on the bus followed. I asked Mr Friendly what the heck it was all about.

'The young guy was harassing for money,' he explained to me as the bus bounced along. 'He is always doing that. He has a nickname, "Beating Drums", because he is always making noise.'

'What did the guy say to set him off?'

'He said, "You are a stinking little thief. You should stop your ways and start a new direction in life."'

I raised my eyebrows. 'No wonder he reacted!' Mr Solid turned around to me and smiled. The bus continued to buzz with chat and laughter for the rest of the trip. Malawians are a friendly bunch.

We climbed through tanned muscular hills lined with the stubble of miombo trees. The vermiform road joined the Kasitu River. The stream was lined with banana groves and vegetables grown on terraces on the steep slopes. The majestic Nyika Plateau towered above us on the left, and then we swung around a ridgeline to the right, to see the world's third-largest freshwater lake, Lake Malawi.

Apricot beaches stretched off to the south, separating the escarpment from the sheet of sparkling blue receding to the horizon. The bus swung down the bends, dodging traffic, forest debris and screeching monkeys on the road. Down at the shore, Sam and I were deposited on the side of the road, along with our bags, at a throng of tatty shops that sat at the base of a narrow track back up into the mountains. At the track's base was a rare road sign, half-obscured by weeds: LIVINGSTONIA 15 KM.

I'd been nervous that we'd have trouble finding transport up the track, which was four-wheel drive only. But as soon as we arrived a young boy escorted us straight to a group of four-wheel drive vehicles behind the shops there exactly for that purpose. The bad news was we didn't leave for another three hours, the time it took for the car to fill up with passengers.

While we waited, I bought some pork and cassava for me, and chips for Sam, from the smoking barbecues that lined the road in front of the shops. The car was surrounded by chickens, and drowsy male teenagers who all seemed to be high on something. I encouraged Sam to do some reading. Eventually the utility filled up and we bounced up the narrow winding track with its twenty hairpin bends, numbered in descending order as we ascended. At least the numbered turns occupied Sam's attention.

It soon became apparent this was a special place. The precipice towered over the lake, and the road clawed its way back and forth across the face. It reminded me of Sani Pass in South Africa. The horizon across the lake was no longer a line but a blurred transition zone of blues, ultramarine at the lake and the faintest of cobalts at the lower sky.

We finally reached the turn-off and pitched out of the utility, backpacks hefted on shoulders, at a simple signpost pointing down a dirt track to Mushroom Farm.

CHAPTER 19

Mushroom-Farm style

The 'farm' was a scatter of huts perched on a cliff edge towering over the escarpment, centred around a terraced bar and restaurant with a seriously impressive menu and staff who were keen to please. The view was breathtaking, sweeping across vast valleys folding below, forest, terrace and fields; a patchwork quilt tossed all the way to the softly arcing lines of beaches a dozen kilometres away.

On arrival, Sam pointed at a man of European descent reading by himself at a table near reception. 'You are a white man.' I introduced ourselves to him and checked in, then Sam took off towards our hut. The 'white man' turned out to be from Poland. We were joined by four Americans and a Dane. They were all in their twenties and all fascinated by our trip, autism and, of course, Sam. As well, there was a motorbike-riding woman from London with cropped brown hair who introduced herself as Harri. I wondered what Sam would make of that.

They had well and truly picked my brains about Sam and our situation before he rocked up to the dining table for dinner and proceeded to have one of the best reciprocal conversations I've seen him have. It would be hard for any fourteen-year-old boy to have a conversation with seven older strangers, especially young women, but Sam did really well. Harry Potter, school, Australia, Africa and our trip, it went on and on; I was so impressed. *Were Sam's social skills starting to thrive?*

Sam even managed Harri's moniker without any dramas. Harri was sharp and incisive. She came across as a natural leader. Her curiosity had been kindled by the concept of our adventure, and she, Sam and I had several chats around the bar, just chilling back and taking it easy, Mushroom-Farm style. It was unplanned conversations like these I was starting to value more highly, and I began to realise my own ideas about autism, Sam and the intervention were being shaped and moulded by the people we met along the way.

The next day Sam and I planned to walk to the nearby village of Livingstonia, which had been established by a Scottish Presbyterian missionary who named the settlement after his mentor, Livingstone. We took a shortcut that started at the back of the farm, and walked up a path through a forest of brachystegia and uapaca hovering over steel-grey granite covered in pale green lichen. Upon reaching the road we turned right and hiked through hills and subsistence farms—plots on which all the food grown went to feed the family who lived there—where small children would offer to be our guides for one hundred kwacha. 'No, thanks; no, thanks.'

On the way to Livingstonia we saw the impressive Manchewe Falls. At the gate to the waterfall's national park, five young boys descended on us and attempted to guide us, no doubt for payment afterwards. Despite my attempts to shoo them away, they kept hanging around for which I eventually became grateful—the paths in the park turned out to be a bit of a warren. Africa doesn't believe in safety barriers, and after descending a jungle-covered pathway near the river I suddenly realised Sam, who was ahead of me, was standing on a large rock at the top of a hundred-metre high waterfall, only a metre from the edge. He was fine, of course, but I gripped his arm and pulled him back.

Our unsolicited guides escorted us down a steep path next to the falls to a cave which was used by locals as a place to hide from slave traders in the nineteenth century. It made me shiver to imagine what it must have been like to be so defenceless, unable to prevent your loved ones from being snatched away at any time. A dark cave for a dark time.

As we left, our guides demanded their fees. I negotiated hard, and they seemed disgruntled. As we left the park the five of them were following us at a distance. Glancing over my shoulder I wondered whether Sam and I were in danger and picked up the pace. Eventually I glanced back again and they were gone.

Livingstonia was a disappointment. I'd expected old stone buildings full of character, built by wide-eyed bearded missionaries. While there was a bit of that, it was mostly your standard African town, with wide dusty roads, ramshackle kiosks and a drowsy populace.

We had been walking for three hours and Sam was over it. Actually, so was I. I tried to negotiate a lift back to Mushroom, but the price was exorbitant. We stopped for a drink in the cafe of the technical college, which donated all profits to the local orphanage.

The Orphan Care Project was run by the David Gordon Memorial Hospital. The hospital had a catchment of ninety thousand people in the poorest area of one of the poorest countries on earth. In their catchment, they had 6,450 orphans; that is, seven per cent of the entire population were orphaned children.

I spoke to the kind woman behind the counter in the cafe. 'Is this because of HIV?'

She answered without hesitation. 'Yes.'

Walking back through the town, we passed the aforementioned hospital. One of the local four-wheel drives, which functioned as minibuses in this neck of the woods, was parked outside the gates. We climbed into the tray of the duel-cabin utility.

Over the next half hour, the tray and cabin slowly filled, and we watched loved ones saying goodbye to patients. A very sick and wasted young woman in a hospital gown, sweating, shaking and struggling to hold up her head, sat in a wheelchair pushed by one of the nurses. She had a marked bronchitic cough and was struggling to breathe. I guessed that she had end-stage HIV, complicated by pneumocystis pneumonia, but I suppose it could have been tuberculosis or cancer. She looked like she was not long for this world. Her elderly father said goodbye to her before climbing into the tray with Sam and me. Soon we were joined by others, including three breastfeeding women. Eventually there were eighteen people in the tray, eight in the cabin, a dozen or so bags and sacks, a car radiator and a chicken.

Sam didn't like the fact the chicken was being carried upside down by its bound feet. He pointed at the man holding the chicken. 'Animal cruelty!' Fortunately, the chicken holder had no idea what he was on about.

We zipped and bounced along the bumpy track through large puddles, over protruding rocks and between walls of reeds and scrubby trees, which flicked and whipped the truck and passengers. I was sitting on the rim of the tray at the passenger-side back corner, so there was a lot of ducking of branches, stems and leaves. The Africans laughed and whooped. The chicken slept through the entire trip.

Sam, wedged between a mother and infant and the old man and the radiator, seemed to be enjoying himself. So was I. It was a hoot. Albeit a bit precarious: I copped an insect in the eye, and Sam's back felt a bit sore afterwards.

I was reluctant to leave Mushroom Farm, but we'd planned to depart the next day. I could understand why a traveller we'd previously met had called it his 'highlight of Africa'.

On our final morning, I crept out of the room at dawn to watch the sunrise over the distant lake. It was absolutely silent. A front during the night had cleared the mist from the lake and you could see the faint outline of the Tanzanian mountains on the other side of the lake sixty kilometres away. The sunrise was mirrored on the lake's surface and broke through the clouds like a giant spotlight. Lake flies, which breed in huge spumes rising off the water, resembled mist coming off the lake.

Below us on the precipice an augur buzzard glided in circles searching for prey; she arced into the void and disappeared effort-lessly off towards the lake. However, it seemed the journey would not be so effortless for us. Cars heading down the hill were few and far between, and most of them were already full by the time they passed the farm. Our chance of catching a lift was slim.

We planned to take two minibus journeys that day—one to Mzuzu, and another on to our next destination, Nkhata Bay—and we needed to get to the bottom of the hill, ten kilometres of winding road, as early as we could. It seemed our best option would be to walk, but Sam had never walked that far in his life, let alone with a full backpack.

The American owner of Mushroom Farm told me that we could pay a porter to carry a pack for us. Even though I felt like a nineteenth-century colonial master, I agreed.

We waved goodbye to the other guests of Mushroom Farm and I drank in the view one last time as we turned and headed down the hill. Harri, who was also leaving that day, tooted and gave a wave as she vroomed past on her bike.

Oscar, our porter, was an amiable dad of a two-year-old daughter and had been trekking all his life. This was a gentle stroll for him. He carried Sam's pack and the camera bag and Sam carried the daypack. I struggled the most. By the end of the ten kilometres my left knee cartilage, legacy of an old football injury, was playing up badly. I realised some of the mountains in southern Malawi I'd intended to climb, particularly the famed four-thousand-metre Mount Mulanje, were now off the table, which was very disappointing.

As soon as we reached the main road, a minibus appeared and we collapsed inside, sweating and tired. As we approached Mzuzu, it occurred to me that this was probably the last place I'd be able to access an ATM for a while, which meant we had to detour from the minibus station into town and then back again. But at the minibus station we found the usual hawkers but no taxi drivers. Maybe because it was the weekend? I had all the gear, but no idea. We walked up the hill to the road. No luck—only some guys with motorbikes offering lifts. I waved them away, but after ten minutes, and Sam's complaints, I relented. With our packs strapped onto the back of two bikes, we donned helmets and doubled behind the drivers. Sam anxiously hugged his driver around his neck rather than his waist. He had doubled with a mate on a small trail bike before, but this was Africa and a whole other level.

The next minibus was run by two muscular young men who appeared to be attempting the Guinness World Record for how many people you could fit into a single vehicle. They had crammed in twenty-two people and were still refusing to leave when some of the passengers started showing rare signs of frustration. A few tense exchanges ensued between the bus guys and a businessman sitting under a big box in the back seat.

When we finally departed the driving was particularly reckless. As we hurtled into villages at one hundred kilometres per hour, pedestrians scattering, I feared if the driver made a mistake there would be a fatality, perhaps even twenty-two of them. The side panel I was jammed against bowed disconcertingly under my weight as we flew around the curves of the mountain road like the out-of-control mining cart in *Indiana Jones and the Temple of Doom*.

With a communal sigh of relief we hurtled into Nkhata Bay. While getting off the bus I cut my thigh on a sharp edge of a broken seat bracket and swore.

'Don't say that word, Dad,' Sam said. An old woman smiled approvingly at Sam's disapproval. To my embarrassment I then noticed a can of lemonade had burst and leaked through my daypack on my lap, wetting my jeans. 'Have you wet your pants?' he asked, as he spied the wet patch. He pointed at my crutch. 'You wee'd!'

It would have been understandable given the hair-raising journey we'd just endured. I was not a happy camper.

Looking like it belongs in the Caribbean, the village of Nkhata Bay is nestled around small bays punctuated with rocky outcrops and islets where figs and frangipanis spring out of the sand. The rhythm of the small surf, blown in across the vast lake, evokes a calm ambience familiar to coastal villages. Only the absence of salt in the air reminds you that this is freshwater, not the ocean.

The shopping strip was busy, bustling and bursting with colour, claptrap and customers. Women sat behind pyramids of tomatoes, trays filled with maize or peanuts, and mats containing lines of cut sweet potato, sugar cane or bananas. Trestle tables held a wide array of fish, from the large pale butterfish, a favoured delicacy from the lake, to piles of tiny silver mbuna, salted and dried. The locals chatted on corners, dodged the traffic and pushed their way through shops, sidewalks and alleys.

Sam and I did nothing. With my aching leg muscles, sore knee and cut thigh I could barely walk up the stairs to the room. My tennis elbow was still a problem too. If I'd been home in Australia, I would have seen a sports physician and had an MRI scan by now.

Lazing on the verandah, looking out across the anchored boats on the bay, lit orange by the sunset, Sam played on his DS and I read my book. We were in a pretty nice little corner of the world.

The next morning at breakfast, we gazed across the hazy lake to Tanzania. *Or was it Mozambique?* I was unsure at this latitude. Our objectives for the day were to book a boat trip to an island on the lake, complete some schoolwork and neuroplasticity exercises and try to find some wi-fi. The latter would prove to be impossible, which was immensely frustrating. But we played chess and worked on some math exercises under a frangipani near the beach in front of our hostel. This spot would be Sam's classroom during our stay.

I was feeling overwhelmed, and over it. My sister Mary-Anne had presciently warned me before we left that the greatest burden of travelling was, well, travelling. My physical ailments weren't helping. I yearned for Benison. I'd snapped unfairly at Sam, who'd actually been going well the last few days, and coping with the heavy travel schedule admirably, considering. *Better than me*, I thought.

I needed to remind myself of the positives. Overall, Sam was coping marvellously. I was convinced he was making progress he wouldn't have made at home. Certainly his resilience was improving; here he was doing ten-kilometre mountain hikes, riding on motorbikes and eating all kinds of stuff. This was the main game.

He was still saying he wanted to go back to Sydney, but not nearly as frequently or as passionately. Negotiation about the number of eight-out-of-tens in a row required to get home had stopped. His daily score now seemed more a matter of pride, or perhaps obsession, than the means to a premature return.

We had also been lucky. Apart from my twenty-four-hour gastro and scrapes and strains, we'd avoided serious illness and injury. I'd lost a lot of stuff but we hadn't been robbed. The weather had been brilliant and we'd met some amazing people, visited some amazing places and had many amazing experiences. *Yes, think positive.*

However, upon returning to our room we found an unpleasant surprise waiting for us. Ants. All over the room: in our backpacks, over our toiletries, on the computer, the phone, everywhere. Sam had spilt a Sprite on the floor the night before, which I presumed had attracted them.

My skin crawled as I discovered more and more. They crawled over our shoes and socks and up our legs. Sam shrieked and I groaned as we flicked and stomped and slapped, whopped and whacked. Eventually I screamed in exasperation and Sam laughed hysterically at me. It was the icebreaker we needed. After finishing the massacre we both flopped onto the bed and smiled at each other.

Then I found a mosquito *inside* the mosquito net over my bed and added it to the casualty list. It had blood inside it; probably mine. I remembered with some anxiety the man we'd met in Mzuzu who'd looked so ill with malaria.

That afternoon, while drawing and playing cards in our room—now littered with several thousand dead ants and one dead mosquito—Sam complained about his legs. 'They feel bendy.'

'Do you mean they're sore from the walk?' I asked.

'Yeah.'

'Yes, mine are too.'

Sam looked at me. 'I am not weak.'

'No, Sam, you're not weak.'

CHAPTER 20

The lake of stars

The waters of Lake Malawi are plied by a single fifty-year-old ferry, the *Ilala*. Every week she travels north for three days and then south for three days, with a rest day in between. Assuming that she doesn't break down. I wanted us to take the *Ilala* to Likomo Island and the ferry left the next evening, supposedly.

On the day she was due to stop in Nkhata Bay we waited with our packs in the hostel's lounge area after checking out of our room. Since the boat was leaving in the evening, I had all day for activities with Sam. We churned through maths, science, cards, drawing, chess and boxing. A full complement of neuroplasticity exercises; our first in a while. It was nice to be relatively still.

Around lunchtime I suddenly realised, to my surprise, that Sam had managed to connect the computer to the internet, which had been down in the whole town for days. We scrambled a short Skype with Benison and caught up on emails. It wasn't until later that I realised Sam had piggybacked onto someone's nearby mobile phone hotspot. Oops.

At sunset, Sam and I waddled down to the ferry on our bendy legs, backpacks hefted on one shoulder. On the wharf there was a swarm of shirtless men, shouting. Mothers carried grain sacks on their heads and babies swaddled on their backs. There were piles of wood, giant canvas-wrapped bales, hawkers, traders, fishermen, and a few *wazungu* wandering aimlessly about. It was noisy and energetic and there was a rare sense of bustle and haste in the evening shadows away from the ferry's lights.

Sam and I walked up the gangway into the second-class deck, where most of the locals travelled and filled the corridors, then up some stairs to the first-class deck occupied by businessmen, wealthier families and crew filing around the engine room, dining room and cabins. We climbed a last steep flight of steps to the upper level: an exposed deck with worn grey timber boards the colour and texture of driftwood, lifejacket bins and lifeboats.

The boat was meant to get to Likomo Island at one a.m., stopping at the smaller island of Chizumulu an hour or so prior. Under the circumstances I thought it wasn't worth paying for a cabin. We would just stay up, passing the time on the deck, and then sleep when we got to Likomo.

I got talking to three fellow travellers: Andy, a retired pig farmer from Australia, his wife, Malee, and his sister Margaret, who had joined the couple from Scotland. Andy appeared as tough as tanned pigskin, but I was to learn he had a heart of gold. He was en route to the Congo to visit a school that he'd helped build decades earlier. He was meeting up with his fellow builders to see if the school was still standing, or indeed if they were.

Out of the corner of my eye I noticed a guy hovering close to Sam, watching his DS game over his shoulder. Andy had already encountered him. 'He's fairly odd. Maybe you should go check things out,' he muttered out of the side of his mouth. I sat next to Sam and started to read my Kindle. This guy was certainly strange. He was having a one-way conversation, half in English and half in Swahili. The bits I could understand were vague religious allegories and riddles.

Sam was playing a game in which a giant white hand bounced up and down as Super Mario dodged it. The man leant even closer. 'Is that the hand of God? Is God a *mzungu*?' he said, pointing at the console.

Sam noticed him for the first time and leant away. 'Go away, you.'

'You are wholesome,' he said, with an oily smile.

I decided to step in. 'We want to be alone. We don't want your company.'

He didn't budge.

'Do I have to call the crew?' I said.

He ignored me until I stood up and leant over him, saying, 'Go away, now!' At that he smiled inscrutably, but eventually wandered away, glancing back occasionally and muttering to himself.

A crew member came around to check tickets and asked Sam for his before I stepped in to explain the situation. 'He's with me. He's my son. Here is our ticket.'

'Why is he ignoring me?' the crewman asked, nodding at Sam.

'He, ah, has special problems. He has trouble talking to people, but he's okay.'

The crewman looked at me dubiously. 'Can you just wait here a minute? I want to check with my boss.'

'Sure,' I said, smiling to mask my anxiety.

The crewman returned shortly with a white-uniformed officer and introduced him as the captain.

'Your son will be okay?' the captain asked. 'This is an open area. We must make sure everyone is safe.'

He looked unconvinced by my assurances that I'd keep a close eye on Sam, but eventually he nodded, smiled and walked away.

Then Andy told me he'd heard the arrival time at Likomo was meant to be four a.m. not one a.m. *Oh no!* It was going to be cold on the open deck at night, and we didn't have sleeping bags.

This boat trip was proving to be full of unpleasant surprises: weirdos, wary crew and wayward timetables. Still, surprise was what our trip was all about. We were after Proudhon's 'fecundity of the unexpected'.

Sure enough, after dinner the temperature dropped and the wind from the lake whipped up. I realised there and then that I'd lost Sam's padded vest somewhere along the way. It had been his only warm piece of clothing. He refused my jacket; no long sleeves. All he had for warmth was a sleeping bag liner. He lay on a bench on the deck, squirming uncomfortably, using a daypack as his pillow. I considered moving us down to the second deck out of the wind, but the corridors were now full of blanket-covered bodies, the air a thick fug of diesel and body odour.

As the *Ilala* chugged on, the lights from the distant shore disappeared entirely. The wake of the engines abaft was lit up by the soft deck lights. The lake was huge and ran a swell deserving of open ocean.

I couldn't sleep, paranoid about our bags getting fleeced, the odd guy returning from below, and Sam's discomfort. Around midnight we reached Chizumulu Island. The engines cut out as we lingered in port. I drifted asleep.

I suddenly awoke, aching from the biting cold, to a blaring fog horn. It was dawn, and we still hadn't moved! I spooned Sam to give him extra body warmth while the boat finally prepared to leave.

Finally, as the day dawned, we approached Likomo. Sam emerged from his sleeping bag liner, hair mussed into a bird's nest. I looked across to the scrappy village lining the beach. *Why was there no wharf?*

'We land on long boats on the beach,' a sleepy Andy explained as we gathered our bags. Another bloody unpleasant bloody surprise.

We bustled down the galleys to the lower deck where longboats were tethered alongside the ferry, and gingerly climbed a rope ladder into the crowded open boat as packs were thrown down on us from above. I handed my daypack, which contained valuables and the computer, down to a crewman. 'This is very fragile. Please be careful.'

He smiled. 'No problem.' A few minutes later, as I sat at the bow a few metres away, he yelled, 'Hey, *mzungu!*' and made to throw the daypack to me. The boat burst into laughter at my look of horror. I squeezed out a tepid smile as the bag was handed to me.

The overloaded boat had a mere ten centimetres of freeboard as we were rowed to shore. From the boat, we jumped into the shallows, holding our backpacks above our heads, jeans wet to mid thigh. As we flopped our packs onto the beach, Sam punched the air. 'Yes, we're here!'

A ute from the backpacker hostel Mango Drift, our destination, was there to meet us. Andy, Sam and I stood holding the rail behind the cabin as Margaret and Malee sat and bounced with the packs in the tray for the five kilometres of bumpy track to the far side of the island.

The back of my eyes ached from lack of sleep and the glare of the bleaching sunlight. We were deposited on the granular sand next to the bar-cum-reception area, which had been built around a very large old mango tree sprouting from the beach. The coarse sand of the lake, similar to river sand, invited tactile exploration; it didn't stick like beach sand but fell effortlessly off skin and clothing.

Lining the beach were huts and chalets made from thatch and wood, with mosquito nets and hammocks. Behind them willows, eucalypts, palms, mango and bougainvillea nestled under the ancient baobabs. These were a special indigenous species, dwarf baobabs, which only grew on this island.

As we settled in, I realised I was missing my computer charger, and instantly remembered where it was—sitting in the office of the hostel in Nkhata Bay. A phone call confirmed it was there. At least I hadn't lost it, and we were headed back there anyway.

It was a problem, however. The computer had no battery power left and it would be four long days until we'd be back on the mainland. Most of Sam's school material was on the computer, and I wouldn't be able to Skype. Our only hope was that I could get emails on my phone if I could buy some mobile phone data vouchers in the village.

Sam was also playing up. He was cranky that he couldn't use the computer and pestered me about it constantly. Sleep deprived and frayed around the edges, I handled it badly. Finally, I exploded: 'Just go away! Just go away and leave me alone! Go to reception!' I flailed my arms at him. 'Go!'

Sam retreated to the reception area and played his DS. I slept for ninety minutes and awoke full of guilt. Sam was tired too. I shouldn't have taken it out on him. I apologised. Sam shrugged nonchalantly.

I tried to reframe our situation: we were on a beautiful island on a beautiful lake in the middle of Africa, and I was cranky about not having a computer? *Stupido.* This would be a chance to have a break from the grind of schoolwork, writing and blogging. We could focus on neuroplasticity activities. By now he was becoming adept at most of the challenges. I was struggling to keep up with him at chess. His boxing now contained an excellent combination of punches and kicks, knocking me back on my feet at times as the mitts took his blows, and he could play handball about as well as any other fourteen-year-old boy.

It was also an opportunity to indulge in commodities we hadn't had before: space and time. To think, read, reflect, slow down.

If Nkhata Bay resembled a village in the Caribbean, Likomo looked like it belonged in the South Pacific, except with baobabs. Distant islands were serene silhouettes on the horizon while zephyrs ruffled the translucent waters into a sparkling dance. The distant shore of Malawi was sometimes visible through the haze, sometimes not.

Villagers placed racks of drying mbuna, Malawian rockfish, on the beach. Fishermen sutured nets. Women in patterned dresses and orange and blue bandanas ambled along the shore. It was like they all walked at the same slow but steady rate—an African chronometer. Firewood, fish and fruit; sack, tray and bowl, all balanced on the head.

The next day I ran into a young German woman, Sabrina, we'd met back in Cape Town. 'Hey, James,' she said, 'you know, I think Sam is talking so much better.'

I smiled. 'Really, you think?'

'Oh yes. You can really tell the difference.'

I felt like doing a jig. I had thought so myself, but couldn't convince myself I was seeing past my inherent observer bias. Observer bias, in scientific terms, occurs when a researcher knows the goals of the study and allows this knowledge to influence what they observe. I suppose Sabrina may have been susceptible to observer bias herself. You see what you want to see, and everyone wanted what we were doing to work. Still, it was uplifting to hear her impression.

The next day we attempted to walk to a cathedral. Likomo apparently boasted an impressive and disproportionally grand cathedral, which was allegedly 'just over the hill'. Forty-five minutes later, in the heat of the day, with no water, we were still scrambling up the trail, increasingly overwrought.

Halfway up the hill I realised Sam was wearing his long pants. *Great parenting, James.* Covered in sweat, he plonked himself down on the hot sand and refused to budge. I pushed, harassed, cajoled, bribed and threatened. Nope, he'd had enough. I sat ten yards away and took a few big slow breaths. What was more important: seeing a cathedral or avoiding another argument? 'Stuff this. Let's head back, find some shade and have a cold drink,' I said.

'Yay! Thanks, Dad.'

I congratulated myself on the decision as we headed back down the hill. I was learning to go with the flow, to be flexible, nimble. Sam wasn't the only one learning the art of letting go. We played some chess on the verandah and boxed on the sand as the sun set behind the distant islands.

The next day we visited the preschool in the village next to Mango Drift. Sam didn't want to get too close to the small children; I think he was worried about their snotty noses and wet coughs. They sat on the verandah of the school in apple-green uniforms, eating their morning porridge. Chickens flicked between them, trying to steal a beakful, and being shooed away.

Sam took umbrage at this. He was back on his anti-animal-cruelty crusade. He bolted around the school trying to protect the chickens. The rambunctious children were fascinated by this lanky teenager running around their school and thought it was a game. The next thing I knew, Sam was the Pied Piper with a slipstream of squealing three- and four-year-olds running after him. As he ran he shouted, 'I don't like African children, Dad!'

'Well, they seem to like you,' I yelled back, laughing.

Sometime after midnight, I awoke with a start. The night was completely silent. *Where were the waves?* Apart from the careful footsteps of a chicken on the leaves surrounding the hut and the distant faint static of crickets, there was no noise. I crunched across the forty metres of coarse sand to the lake's edge. The water was eerily still, a vast looking glass for the galaxy to gaze upon herself. Livingstone had described Lake Malawi as 'the lake of stars'. *Perfect.*

I stepped into the lake up to my ankles and had a bit of a God moment. 'And the moon and the stars and the world,' in the words of writer Charles Bukowski. I brushed the surface with my hand. After a few seconds, a few metres, the ripples vanished, absorbed again into the deep dark stillness.

Sometime before dawn, I awoke again for a much less poetic reason: the sound of a mosquito buzzing near my ear. A self-administered slap to the face gave me a minute or two of unilateral tinnitus. Then I lay awake.

A rooster crowed intermittently, setting off his competitors across the villages. I was ruminating. Round and round, like the roosters, my thoughts competed for attention. This time and space had helped. We had been active: boxing, throwing and catching, drawing, playing cards—this time the game of Five Hundred, which is similar to bridge—and then chess, checkers, snooker. I had also started teaching Sam how to draw cartoons, which he struggled with at first but eventually got into the swing of things when he realised he could draw characters associated with some of his obsessions, such as *The Simpsons* or Pokemon.

The lack of contact with the outside world, however, was messing with me. I had managed to buy some prepaid mobile phone data shortly after we arrived on Likomo, but before I realised it Sam had snuck off with my phone and tried to download a game, immediately using it all before I could even check my emails. Grr. A pilot staying at Mango Drift was flying to the mainland from the small airstrip on the other side of the island and kindly agreed to buy me some prepaid mobile phone data while he was there, so I was eventually able to check emails and let Benison know we hadn't been eaten by crocodiles, not yet.

I tried to get Sam to go snorkelling. Lake Malawi has more fish species than any other lake in the world. It's full of nearly a thousand species of cichlids—small brightly coloured fish—the majority of which are endemic to the lake. But Sam didn't like the idea of swimming with fish. (I didn't even mention the remote risk there might be hippos and crocs. I mean, it was a *remote* risk.)

'I don't want to go near the fish,' he whinged.

'Sam, they'll be scared of *you*,' I explained. 'You're much bigger than them. They'll swim away from you.'

I managed to get him to the water's edge in flippers and goggles and he sat down in the water, but that was it. His piscatorial phobia was too great. Still, it was an improvement. I gave him a 'pass', which Sam was happy with as it meant he didn't have to pursue the task any longer. He bolted up the beach to the hut.

So I went off for a snorkel alone, trying to not think about crocodiles myself. Cracks and cavities between the muddy moss-covered rocks were home to finger-sized cichlids of all colours: black, brown, green, blue, black- and white-striped, gold- and lime-striped. My favourite was an inky blue with a strip of amethyst along its spine.

Late in the afternoon fishermen from the village trawled for fish from the beach. All the men, young and old, heaved on long lines, dragging in the catch. After dozens of them had toiled for an hour, the booty was one bucket of mbuna.

The fishermen, however, weren't finished. Two long dugout canoes, four men apiece, set out as the sun danced on the horizon, lighting the tips of the waves on the windswept lake. We watched as the men, silhouetted against the sparkling sea, used nets and noise and a great deal of skill to corral their catch. They landed a sixty-centimetre kampango—a predatory catfish endemic to Lake Malawi. The fisherman in the canoes hollered and splashed their oars on the water, delighted with their catch. One hoisted the fish up to show those on shore, and the villagers on the beach echoed the celebration, singing and dancing.

As the light waned I got talking to a group of four male English medical students doing an internship at a clinic on the other side of Likomo. They had visited Mango Drift to indulge in a much-needed drink. When they found out I was a family doctor they immediately wanted to pick my brains about all of the clinical dilemmas they were facing.

They were enthusiastic, but they'd certainly been thrown into the deep end. The clinic didn't normally have a doctor but a local medic—a health worker with basic training—who was apparently very good, and did the best he could under the circumstances. The clinic was funded by a charity and was not so much short of equipment as clinical expertise and sound management. During their short stay the students had already seen multiple preventable deaths. An ultrasound machine lay idle, never used. The lads asked a nurse for a thermometer and were told the hospital didn't have any, yet they found a box of them in the pharmacy. A patient admitted for dysentery had died two days later of dehydration, despite drips and fluids being available. Their experiences were a stark reminder of Malawi's poor world ranking in health care.

Our stay in Likomo came to a close. On the return journey we jumped into the longboats on the beach that would take us out to the *Ilala*. When requested, I paid the guy standing next to the boat the five-hundred kwacha fare for the five of us. But once we'd taken off, the man in charge of the boat asked for our fares. 'We've already paid,' I replied, pointing at the guy, who was still standing on the beach, smiling.

The boat master shook his head. 'No, that guy has nothing to do with the boat.'

We'd been ripped off. Andy wanted to argue the point but I reminded him we were talking about the equivalent of thirty cents each, and it would be easy for them to accidentally-on-purpose drop one of our packs to the bottom of the lake. We paid again.

During dinner on the ferry, I couldn't help but contrast Sam's behaviour with what it had been on the ferry ride out here: he ate his meal without fuss, and then had a fantastic one-hour conversation with all of us. Andy, Malee and Margaret picked his brains about Pixar movies, computers and games, even moving on to a discussion of World War II and the Cold War. Andy was startled to find out how much Sam knew about the latter, even if he couldn't remember Khrushchev's or JFK's names.

It was Sam's best ever conversation. They were clearly entertained by him. On his own turf, he is seriously knowledgeable and often funny. Proud. As. Punch.

CHAPTER 21

Ten out of ten

Back in Nkhata Bay I pick up the greatly missed computer charger. From here we would travel for a few days back to Lilongwe. We had rushed a little through northern Malawi in order to get back to the capital to meet my twenty-one-year-old niece, Juliette, who had spontaneously decided to travel with us for a few weeks.

I was looking forward to seeing her. Even though we'd been meeting people everywhere we went, I was still feeling lonely. There's a difference between the transient contact you have with people you meet on the road and being with people you know and love. Juliette was family.

She had, however, very little experience of travelling in the developing world and had never been to Africa. She was also meeting up with us for possibly the hardest part of our journey: from southern Malawi to northern Mozambique. I knew her parents, my sister and brother-in-law, would be fretting. Still, I thought it would be good for her and good for Sam and me.

It was also great timing for another reason. On the way back from the island, the video camera suffered a stroke and died shortly thereafter. This was not good, to say the least. Apart from needing it to record documentary footage, it was also essential for the university study. But it was also not surprising. I'd been as careful as I could, but it had been lugged, thrown, dropped, knocked, exposed to moisture, sand, dust, dirt and goodness knows what else.

Juliette could now bring a camera from Australia. With only twelve hours to go before Jules left for the airport, I was able to get a message to Heiress Films asking them to deliver a new camera to her. And I could only get the message through because, although there was blackout that day, the hostel in Nkhata Bay had a back-up generator.

On our last afternoon in Nkhata Bay we passed a parked bus on a stroll around town. From the man sitting in the bus, presumably an employee, I found out that this was the bus for Lilongwe and it left at 6.30 a.m. After Sam and I had watched a local football game, we walked past the parked bus again and I thought I would double check. The man's English hadn't been the best.

'Are you sure it leaves at six-thirty?' I asked him.

'Yes, six.'

'Wait. Six or six-thirty?'

'Yes.'

'No, I mean is it six *or* six-thirty?'

'Yes.'

A woman sitting nearby stepped in to help. After what seemed like a ten-minute conversation with him, she turned to me. 'Six.'

I nodded to her. 'Thank you.'

We arrived at 5.30 a.m., just in case. The bus left at 5.45 a.m.

For breakfast we ate peanuts, boiled eggs and donuts bought through the bus windows at roadside stops. Lunch was bread rolls, bananas and hot chips. Three fish hung from a railing behind the driver. A squawking chicken took Sam by surprise as he got back onto the bus after a police check; the woman holding the chicken realised and simply compressed the bird's throat until Sam had passed by.

It was an old clapper of a bus, and a trip which should have taken five or six hours took an achingly long twelve. The engine was really struggling up the hills by the end. *I think I can, I think I can.*

We cruised into Mabuya Camp and caught up again with our friends there. I had started to delegate more responsibility to Sam for day-to-day chores. As I watched him order our lunch by himself, I chatted to an affable English rugby coach in Malawi doing voluntary work. He asked what the story was with Sam. 'That's fucking mad!' he said, when I told him what we were doing. 'In a good way, I mean. Good luck to you both.' He shook his head and smiled. 'That's fucking mad!'

The next day we picked up a jet-lagged Juliette. It was good to see someone from home. Sam was very excited that she was here. 'Juliette is in Africa!'

Jules is a charmer. A super-fit sports nut, she was up for adventure with a verve and vigour that was infectious. Her gumption would bolster Sam and me.

At the hostel, a young Englishwoman called Kiki joined us for a game of pool. She was working in a local orphanage as a volunteer, and mentioned her boss was a fellow compatriot called Harri. My ears pricked up. 'Does she have short hair and ride a motorbike?' It transpired that she was indeed talking about Harri, whom we'd met back at Mushroom Farm. We arranged to visit the orphanage. Sam was thrilled. 'We are going to meet Harriet Potter again!'

The orphanage was home to thirty-four girls, ranging in age from two to sixteen years. There was an impressive vibrancy and joy about the place. Harri was surprised and pleased to see us, and keen to show us around. She and Kiki were good eggs, doing the right stuff for the right reasons. There are so many unsung heroes in Africa. Kiki gave us, including Sam, a rundown on how the orphanage operated. As Kiki spoke Sam wandered off from the group and around the yard of the orphanage, ending up at a chicken coop near the back fence. He smiled as the chickens pecked the ground and then scattered as he approached them. He ignored the girls despite their attempts to talk to him, instead shying away and retreating to the chickens. I listened to Kiki but followed Sam around filming him with the video camera, and wondered if he was listening or not.

On Jules' first full day in Africa—and our last in Lilongwe—we visited a market down by the river. It was an ants' nest of wooden and tin stalls, all mud-grey, with dirt floors and alleyways. The market was packed to the brim with vendors, punters, dogs and chickens. Men stood in long lines at the entrances to the stalls, holding a single piece of clothing for display to the passing shoppers. That must be an achingly slow day of work: a job as a coathanger.

Jules had worn shorts, and this was causing quite a stir, provoking concerned looks from both women and men. Malawi is quite a conservative society. It's illegal for women to wear dresses that do not completely cover the knees, or to wear trousers at all. She wasn't going to make that mistake again.

The next morning we headed south to the lakeside village of Cape Maclear. We made an early start and got down to the minibus station in good time, but then we had a ninety-minute wait for the bus to fill up. As we waited, Jules bought some headphones through the bus window and I bought some mandarins.

Jules started getting twitchy, but Sam and I were used to this. In Africa, waiting is just part of the deal.

'When do we leave?' Jules asked me.

'When the bus is full.'

She looked around the bus station. 'Do you think there is a toilet here?'

'I don't know,' I said.

'How long do you think the trip will take?'

'I'm not sure,' I replied. 'A few hours, maybe?'

'You don't know much, Uncle James, do you?'

'Jules, This Is Africa.'

Once we were on the way, some excellent reggae Afro-pop helped pass the time, as the trip stretched further with multiple police and army checks, of registration, licences and whatever else they wanted. Jules noticed the slung machine guns. I hadn't, another thing I was now well used to.

As we cleared the city, the clouds also cleared from the sky. Soon the road started to climb between bulbous granite mountains, looking like giant domes tossed across the plains by some ancient giant. After passing the dusty dirty range, the bus headed back down towards Lake Malawi. Baobabs started to appear amid the sugar cane and banana. The earth became sandier, and a more tropical feel permeated the villages as our bus rolled into Cape Maclear.

The town sits on the tip of a narrow peninsula jutting into the southern reaches of mighty Lake Malawi, a shiny cap on the toe of a pointed boot. A series of eateries, hostels, dive centres and tourist shops front the lake. Standing on the coarse-sand beach, you look across shimmering waters with crayon-coloured crafts bobbing here and there, and jungle-covered islands in the distance.

There were dugout canoes and catamarans dragged up onto the sand, segmenting the beach. Skinny dogs trotted this way and that; one of them drank from the waves on the lake. Children performed acrobatics on the sand, while others washed pans. A fish eagle glided across the windswept waters. Hawkers swarmed and *wazungu* pretended to ignore them, except for Sam, who didn't need to pretend.

A man sidled up to Sam as we strolled down the beach. 'Hello, how are you?'

'Ha ha, the boy that lived!' Sam replied, smiling. The man left, baffled. He had never heard that one before.

In the village, sandy lanes barely wide enough for the occasional vehicle were lined with concrete verandahs and frangipanis. Chickens darted from small garden plots, and African dance music echoed from a cafe up a hidden laneway.

That night it became clear why the early Scottish missionaries had moved their settlement from here north to Livingstonia. Outside my blue net mosquitoes hovered like planes on approach to Heathrow, all waiting for a chance to sink their proboscises into my blood-rich epidermis. The Scots, smashed by malaria, had headed for altitude, high on the escarpment.

The next day I was able to deploy my relief teacher, Juliette, into Sam's education, neuroplasticity intervention and filming video interviews for the university. Benison had recently sent me an article outlining how 'opportunistic teaching'—grabbing the educational moment, as it were—was a useful and effective way of assisting children with autism to learn. In this way, like the pool table in Windhoek and table tennis in Livingstone, the Scrabble box in the hostel's common room was an opportunity to be grasped. A prolonged game of Scrabble, his first, ensued.

Then we did some maths, writing, throw and catch, boxing and chess. It was all underscored by the soft roll of the waves and backlit by the glistening lake. I got the impression Juliette was thinking this wasn't too hard.

After I videoed Jules talking with Sam for one of his practice conversations, she turned to me. 'Uncle James, I think Sam has definitely improved,' she said, referring particularly to his speech and social interaction.

We'll see, we'll see, I thought.

Juliette played chess with Sam. He insisted she play with the black pieces, which he'd labelled Slytherin. He was the white Gryffindor, of course. Juliette didn't mind; Slytherin were very good at Quidditch, after all. Not good enough; Gryffindor prevailed.

We booked a trip to nearby Thumbi West Island so Juliette could try an introductory scuba dive and Sam and I could go snorkelling. I offered Sam an automatic nine out of ten for the day if he managed to complete one minute of snorkelling. This already juicy offer was further sweetened when Juliette promised Sam a bonus GameCube video game of his choice from her collection back in Sydney if he managed the challenge. Boy, oh boy, the heat was on.

Our twenty-foot canopied river boat chugged across to the island. Once Juliette and the other scuba divers had tumbled backwards off the gunwale, four of us remained: a boat hand, an Englishwoman, and Sam and me. While they sat next to Sam, I lowered myself into the water. Together, the three of us worked on Sam for the next ten minutes to get him into the lake.

'Come on, Sam, you can do it,' I implored. 'Just start by sitting on the edge.'

'Just put your hand on your dad's shoulder,' the Englishwoman suggested.

'Put your foot on the ladder,' the boat hand said. 'It's okay.'

'You're doing well,' I yelled from the water. 'No, don't go back up!'

Sam was on a roller-coaster ride of determination and then fear. 'I don't want to swim with the fish. They'll bite me.'

'No, they won't, Sam,' I shouted up. 'They'll swim away from you.'

He edged closer and closer to the water, rung by rung down the ladder, as we cheered and cajoled. Finally, with a nervous flurry he leapt off the ladder and splashed into the water next to me, flinging his arms around my neck and holding on for dear life. To finish the challenge all he had to do was look through the goggles underwater for a few seconds.

'I don't want to look,' he yelled.

'That's all you have to do, then it's finished,' I replied.

With the finish line in sight, he had a surge of confidence. He unclamped one arm, tentatively held the goggles to his face and, holding his breath, popped his face down into the water, snatching a glimpse of the submarine world before scurrying back up the ladder like a monkey up a tree. I punched the air and my two assistants cheered and applauded Sam as he climbed into the boat. *Yay!*

With the pressure off, I could relax. I rewarded myself with a snorkel around the boat while we waited for the divers to return. My favourite ink blue and amethyst cichlid friends were here, but also a larger purple-striped individual with orange blush cheeks, and a luminescent little fellow coloured the hazy pale blue of a summer sky.

That afternoon we hired some bikes and headed over to a local market. Sam did pretty well with the bike riding, dodging ducks, women with babies on their backs, and a large baobab in the centre of the sandy road. But he'd had a full day and was getting tired. At dinner, we discussed what the nine out of ten meant.

'I think that counts for two eight out of tens,' he said.

'Hmm, okay, fair enough,' I said. 'Two eights it is.'

A beat. 'How do I make it a ten out of ten?'

I thought about it. 'How about you eat your entire dinner, no compromise?'

We had been served beef curry and rice, a challenging meal for Sam, and one he would normally only pick at, at best. He looked at the plate in front of him, pondering his options.

I whispered over his shoulder, 'Remember, you get a ten out of ten.'

'Ten out of ten is worth three eight out of tens,' he said, staring at the food.

'Oh, well, I suppose so.'

Juliette piped up. 'Come on, Sam, you can do it! A ten out of ten, woo-hoo!'

'Okay,' he said, eyeing the meal in front of him nervously.

He started to tuck in. It was hard work for him, and he tried to force a compromise several times throughout the meal, requesting an exclusion contract on the peas and then the sauce, but I wouldn't budge. This was for a ten.

When he finished the meal he was so happy with himself he ran out of the dining room and shouted to the world: 'I got ten out of ten!'

That night, as mosquitoes buzzed outside the net, I wondered whether I was handing Sam eights, nines and tens so readily because I secretly wanted to go home too. Fantastic an experience as Africa was proving to be, I was tiring of having to do so much, concentrate so much, try so much. It was a twenty-four-hour job, seven days a week, and we had been on the road for over three months now. Another four months seemed an awfully long time. Would we—or more specifically I—last that long?

Early the next morning, Sam rolled towards me with his mosquito net tangled around his head, a beekeeper in blue. 'Did I really get ten out of ten?'

'Yes, Sam, you did.'

He was having trouble believing it was true.

And soon I was having trouble believing how lucky we'd been in scoring a lift to our next destination of Liwonde, a small city on the banks of the Shire River, south of the lake. The serendipitous offer came from three women staying at our hostel who were heading that way, and were kindly prepared to squeeze us and our bags into their Toyota Rav. They were a Scottish psychiatrist doing a six-month stint in the southern Malawian city of Blantyre, and two American microbiologists conducting research on malaria. Their ride saved us a full day of minibus travel and hassle, and meant we had another morning to chill out on the beach of Cape Maclear. We took it easy, played some checkers and cards and did some drawing.

We left at lunchtime, chatting about malaria, mental health in Africa, autism, disability, and the impressive abdominal muscles of the African dive instructor in Cape Maclear. The psychiatrist mentioned that she'd heard that alcoholism was endemic among minibus drivers in Malawi. Not what I really wanted to hear.

Late that afternoon we arrived at our accommodation in Liwonde. Despite the fact I had booked ahead, they had no idea we were coming and seemed surprised—almost put out—that someone had actually turned up. Well, it *was* a hotel, or at least accommodation of some sort—having guests arriving should not have come as such a surprise. Eventually we figured out that the 'reception'—a boarded-up thatch hut—was normally open but the woman in charge had gone up the road for 'a while'. How long was a while? As Sam would often answer: 'Unknown.'

It turned out they had plenty of rooms available and once they'd got over the shock they were quite happy for us to stay. The reception lady returned from up the road and we organised a river tour for the next morning and a safari drive for the day after that.

The next morning, Sam knocked our water filter—a top-of-the-range, two-hundred-dollar model—off the bathroom sink, smashing its seal and rendering it useless. I had a UV wand steriliser and some chlorine tablets as back-ups, but still I wasn't happy. I added the filter to the long list of things Sam had broken: two toilet seats, a mosquito net, several plates, which had been knocked off tables, and about a dozen glass Sprite or Fanta bottles. Kids on the spectrum are frequently uncoordinated, and when you combine clumsiness with Sam's attention issues you have a disaster waiting to happen.

Zomba Plateau towered in the distance as we boarded the boat for our river cruise, a small runabout with a plywood canopy and an outboard motor with a piece of string for a starter cord. It was tied to a rickety wooden pier on the banks of the river at the back of the hotel.

The Shire River was the drainage outlet for Lake Malawi, funnelling the overflow down to the Zambezi further south, which in turn ran east to west through southern Africa into the Indian Ocean. The Shire was a conduit from a great lake to a great river.

The section of the Shire north of Liwonde was at the centre of Liwonde National Park. This would be Juliette's best chance to see some African fauna while she was with us so I hoped it would turn out well. It was also Malawi Independence Day, and so it felt appropriate to be seeing one of the country's jewels on this day of celebration.

Local fishermen dotted the river, dangling handlines out of dugout canoes or nets out of small fishing boats. The river was more than a hundred metres wide and lined with papyrus, reed grass and floating flowering hyacinths. It flowed in a steady stream. On the banks baobabs, poisonous candelabra trees and the strangling snake trees sat under the nearby Chinguni Hills, home to so many of the animals in the park. Off in the distance behind the hills, the massif of the Zomba Plateau was adorned by a necklace of white cloud.

There were birds everywhere: hamerkops, pied and malachite kingfishers and goliath herons filled the reeds and glided over the silky waters. Fish eagles circled above. A saddle-billed stork tiptoed in some shallows near a large crocodile.

Hippos bobbed up and slid down on the river edges, their pink ears flicking and nostrils snorting. Their eyes were fixed on the noisy craft invading their patch.

Sam liked the hippos. Sam always liked the hippos. 'Honk, honk.' He followed his impersonation with blowing a raspberry. Hippos probably did fart a lot. Juliette and our guides laughed.

We reached the turnaround point, as far into the park as we would venture that day, and commenced our return journey. We were running out of time to see some elephants. But to Juliette's delight, we soon spied two near the bank. As our boat approached, it became evident there was actually a herd of a dozen, which all proceeded to drink from the river right in front of us. They were decorated with cattle egrets, the birds' white feathers contrasting with their deep grey hides. Sam giggled, Juliette gawked, and I smiled and watched and videoed Sam bond with his cousin in this beautiful corner of the world.

CHAPTER 22

The Shire

We needed some cash and the nearest ATM I could use was in a town a half-hour's drive away so I left Sam and Jules at the hostel as I went in search of a minibus. I strolled up Liwonde's main road, past a bedraggled market. A collection of roadside barbecues, serving charred corn and cassava chips, spilled smoked into nearby alleyways. Kiosks sold warm bottles of soft drink and water through wire-grilled windows. There was an op shop sponsored by a telco next to a God Is Wonderful–brand hardware store next to a concrete police checkpoint, replete with boom gate and road spikes. Officious policemen in snappy blue uniforms and shiny peaked caps halted vehicles to check whatever the hell they felt like, or lounged bored inside their concrete roadside hut.

I knew that if you caught a minibus near the police you were less likely to get ripped off. But standing near the police hut, waiting in hope for a minibus and looking unsure of myself, I attracted the police's attention. They invited me in. I was quizzed about where I was from, what I thought of Malawi, how much it cost to fly to and live in Australia. They simply couldn't comprehend the figures I was telling them. Australia must have seemed like another planet.

One of the police waved his baton at me. 'You know, man started here in Africa.'

'Yes, I know.'

'Civilisation started here too,' he continued.

I nodded cautiously. I thought it had been in the Middle East, but I let that one go through to the keeper.

He stood and turned towards me. 'So how come Europe and Australia are so far ahead of Africa?'

I scrambled for a response. 'Well, because the Europeans stole from Africa when they colonised it.'

They all nodded approvingly. It was of course more complicated than that—there was this thing called the Industrial Revolution—but I was happy with my answer. My minibus arrived, emblazoned ARSENAL, and driven by someone who, reassuringly, didn't look drunk.

One of the policeman asked me for my mobile number, which I couldn't remember and I didn't have my phone on me. He gave me his number, and sternly instructed me to call him when I got my phone. Somehow this didn't feel like friendly camaraderie.

Another minibus, another chicken. This one was wrapped in green plastic as it sat on its owner's lap. I had no idea why. Halfway through the trip, we were all instructed to move onto another bus. I had no idea why.

The man holding the plastic-wrapped chicken wore a Malawi Flames jumper, formal suit pants and runners, and carried a woman's purse. His wife wore the same jumper with a traditional-print wrap skirt and a patterned bandana.

I'd noticed that across Africa, but especially in Zambia and Malawi, the dress code seemed to be: if you own it, wear it, and convention be damned. The exceptions to this sartorial anarchy were uniforms, religious garb, and the women's traditional wrap dresses and bandanas. Oh yes, and of course any garment bearing a football motif was especially highly prized.

Most other clothing items seemed to have originated from a second-hand clothing bin in a First World country—it was a continent of hand-me-downs. This led to some unconventional looks. A heavy metal t-shirt on a small boy, a tie-on knitted beanie on a petrol station attendant, a young man peddling a bicycle-taxi wearing a three-piece suit and tie.

A man on the bus, wearing what I *think* was a woollen cricket vest, held a large plate of tiny cooked birds, their bodies no bigger than that of a mouse.

'What kind of bird are they?' I asked him.

He shook his head. 'I don't know.'

Some of the other passengers bought a few of the tiny fowl. Hey, what the heck. They smelled good and I was hungry. I handed the man some kwacha. 'Can I have two, please?'

You ate them bones and all. I was worried about bone splinters sticking in my throat, but they went down okay. It tasted good. I could imagine the bones would be a fantastic source of calcium, as long as the birds weren't also a source of dysentery. The chicken stared at me accusingly as I ate its distant cousin.

The man selling the small birds had a severe convergent squint. A teenage beggar we passed had a fixed flexion deformity of his elbow, which would severely limit its function and his work options. A man selling samosas through the window had a large burn scar on his parietal scalp, and another man struggled down a dirt walkway using forearm crutches for what I thought might by some kind of peripheral myopathy. The cross-eyed, the winged, the scarred and the crippled. Broken bodies in Africa, impeded, unrepaired and manifestly conspicuous.

It was good to have a reprieve from Sam, even if only for a few hours. In the back seat of the crowded minibus I felt a pressure valve release. I was able to let my thoughts flow elsewhere. I smiled to myself to think where I was—Malawi!—and what I was looking at through my dirty cracked window. After almost falling asleep in the soporific heat I was jolted awake by the thought that my stop was coming up. I thought. I hoped.

Yep, I had guessed correctly, this was the place. I hailed a pushbike taxi to peddle me a kilometre or so across town to the ATM.

It was closed.

My juvenile stomping and swearing amused the boys sitting in front of a mosque across the road. Maybe it was closed for the public holiday. I hoped so; I would have to try again tomorrow.

On the way back, a very attractive young African woman, dressed and preened to perfection, wanted to get onto the minibus, but didn't want to sit next to the grimy-looking man sharing the back seat with me.

A heated discussion followed, as the conductor and other passengers implored her to just get on. The princess refused. Someone put a question to her containing the word *mzungu*. I think they were asking her if she would sit next to me. She refused again. Maybe I wasn't looking too good either? Eventually an old woman sat next to the two rejects and the princess got her way, securing a prized position next to the sliding door.

Back at Liwonde I was spotted by the same policemen I had spoken to earlier as I got off the bus.

One of them beckoned me over. 'Hey, you buy me a Fanta.'

'Err, okay.' He *was* a policeman.

His friend chimed in. 'Make it four.' I'd been scammed by the constabulary. I walked home, chewing on some sugar cane.

That evening, as Sam hung out in the room with his DS, I watched football with Jules, who is a terrific player and a big fan of the game. It was a match between the Malawi Flames and Uganda, held to celebrate Malawi's national day. We watched the action on the insect-covered small TV screen behind the bar, as Malawi pulled off a win in dramatic fashion, with a goal in the final minutes.

The crowd in the bar went nuts. The crowd in the stadium did likewise, but Malawian-style, swaying and dancing in unison, alternate rows swinging in opposite directions. *How did they do that?* The pitch was invaded by thousands of fans and celebratory flares were set off in the stands. It had been a good fifty-first Malawi Independence Day.

In the morning I went in search of cash once again, while Jules supervised Sam at the hostel. I waited by the road for over an hour before a minibus turned up, and then when it did arrive it wouldn't leave. Nobody on the bus spoke English, so I never found out why. The driver would stop, start, go around in circles, talk to policemen, talk to random people on the street. He was pissing me off and everyone else too; even with the language barrier I could sense a mutiny was brewing, and I would gladly have joined in if I'd had a clue what was going on.

I eventually got to the bank. Was the ATM working? Well, there was a line of people in front of it, but the ATM was closed. The guy in front of me said it would open soon. 'Soon' ended up being an hour of standing in the sun, bored out of my brain.

Finally the machine got going, albeit slowly. I inched forward in the queue, willing the old, illiterate man now at the machine to hurry up and *press the bloody buttons*. Fortunately, a young guy helped him out. I had become unpleasant.

I was third in line when a tall guy wearing a Pennsylvania State University t-shirt emerged from the bank with what looked like the manager. He was agitated, pointed to receipts in his hand. A prolonged and heated discussion ensued, with the result that the machine had to reboot. Everyone in the queue wanted to kill the guy.

Forty, yes, *forty* minutes later, the machine restarted . . . and then promptly swallowed his card. Yelling and flapping his arms he stormed back into the bank, and those behind him in the queue frantically seized the opportunity have their go.

All I wanted was to get to the machine before the guy forced a second reboot. With seconds to spare I made it to the front. I had to make six withdrawals, three with my card and three with Jules', to get all the cash we needed. Now I was the one pissing everyone off.

Ha *ha*! I didn't care anymore! The manager kept tapping me on the shoulder, to get me to step away from the machine, but I feigned *mzungu* confusion and ploughed on. I got the cash.

In the end, despite all the delays, I still got back in time to go on the safari that afternoon. Jules had managed to get Sam to play three games of chess and also do some maths. More importantly, Sam had lost two of the chess games and had accepted the losses without fuss. That was a first—losing was not a highly developed skill for Sam.

We drove up through the national park, the riverbank dotted with impalas, warthogs and waterbucks. Yellow baboons stopped beside the road, the pernickety creatures indignant at our presence. A giant ancient baobab, scarred by elephants which had feasted on its bark, spread its beams across the canopy, defying all to challenge its authority.

'What do you think of the big baobab, Sam?' I asked.

He had a faraway look as he gazed up at the giant tree. 'It's in *The Lord of The Rings*.' After a beat I realised he was referring to the Ents, the talking trees.

A forest of mopanes—with green, gold and auburn foliage rustling in a breeze off the river—gave way to a landscape brutalised by elephants, with the fractured remains of the foliage scattered on the mud. Only the baobabs survived.

Sam quizzed Jules about Super Mario Brothers; she was a new recipient of his rhetorical questions. Sam often asks questions he knows the answers to, frequently questions he has asked may times before, what I refer to as 'false questions'. I suspect they're props he uses to continue a conversation about a current obsession. When I'm motivated enough, I try to get him to turn his questions into statements. 'What is my favourite Super Mario character?' to 'Yoshi is my favourite Super Mario character.'

Speech therapists refer to this style of speech as declarative, as distinct from imperative speech. In declarative speech you make a statement or observation, you declare something. Imperative speech, such as a question or command, requires a response, such as an answer or action. Most of our speech should be declarative—this style of speech makes conversations more interactive and collegial. It was something I was trying to encourage in Sam.

'Hey, Jules,' I declared, 'I think we should throw Sam into the river with the hippos.'

Sam smiled. '*No!*'

Jules joined in. 'But, Sam, you like the hippos.'

'But I don't want to *swim* with them,' he said.

The next morning, after breakfast overlooking the river, we said goodbye to the Shire hippos and lugged our backpacks up the dirt road. The three vagabonds sang the theme to Harry Potter as we skedaddled along to our minibus, on our way to Zomba.

CHAPTER 23

Zomba

A thousand metres above sea level, the town of Zomba has a cool and calm air. High above it, disappearing into wispy clouds, is the plateau, rising up to over two thousand metres.

Zomba had been Malawi's capital under the British, and glimpses of colonial architecture poked out between African mahogany, blue gums and honeysuckles. Sam observed that the town looked like Gerringong, a beachside town on New South Wales' South Coast where his maternal grandparents had lived for many years, and I could see his point: they were both lush, green and hilly. But there is no beach in Zomba, and there are no two-thousand-metre plateaus towering over Gerringong.

Pakachere Backpackers hostel was well organised and comfortable. High mud-brick walls surrounded a sprawling garden replete with pawpaw, palm, mango and avocado trees. A friendly dog met us at the door, but she had a nasty ulcer on top of her head, the legacy of a fight with a monkey. The laidback Dutch manager kept the chaos that is Africa at bay as best he could, notwithstanding the intermittent wi-fi and electricity blackouts. It would be nice to spend our last few days in Malawi here.

After settling in, Jules and I got talking to a Dutch couple in their early twenties, Mike and Lenneke. Mike—lean, tall and crisply neat—had a razor-sharp mind and a single-minded determination to win, always. Lenneke was a placid and considerate soul who watched him wryly as he vainly tried to keep his ambition in check.

Over the next few days we staged many games of chess and cards with them as well as video interviews for the university. They were so good with Sam, engaging him constantly and involving him as much as they could. Lenneke had a brother with autism with some behavioural issues, and so she got it, and this attitude had also rubbed off on Mike.

Our first full day in Zomba was spent in neuroplasticity exercises, schoolwork and organisation: chess, cards, drawing and maths; shopping, charging electronics, writing and posting. We prepared ourselves for the next day; we had planned a long hike up on the plateau with our new Dutch friends and a guide. I hoped Sam would cope because I didn't really have a back-up plan.

In the taxi ride to the entry point for the walk to the plateau, the driver danced in his seat to reggae, while stickers on his dash advised DON'T WORRY, GOD IS IN CHARGE and LAZY MEN GET NO FOOD. The road wound up the mountain side. The hike would be twenty-four kilometres long and take approximately six hours. We'd ascend seven hundred metres in altitude from our starting point to the highest point on the plateau, then cross to the other side of the plateau and back down again.

Our guide was Isaac, a softly spoken Malawian Christian, proud of his biblical name. The six of us set off, trundling past a giant kachere, a strangler fig with significance in Malawian society. Kacheres marked traditional tribal meeting places, where people would gather together and discuss important issues. Today the beautiful sprawling fig marked the start of the path to the summit.

Shortly after we began, Sam started voicing his displeasure. 'I'm tired, I want to rest.'

Twenty seconds later, 'I want to go back.'

Soon afterwards, he held my arm as he pleaded with me. 'This is too far for me. How much further is it?'

I placated him, encouraged him, and tried to distract him. Sometimes it worked, sometimes it didn't. The complaining continued but it didn't escalate. Jules, Mike, Lenneke and even Isaac became Sam's motivational squad. He would complain for a while, and then retreat into silent protest before starting up again. 'We should get a car back.'

'There are no cars here, Sam,' I explained.

'Let's call a taxi.'

Jules turned to him. 'Taxis can't come up here, the track isn't big enough.'

He put a hand to his forehead. 'I think I'm going to faint.' I'm pretty sure he got that last line from a Harry Potter movie. Still he kept going, and we kept going. It was hard work up the steep incline.

The path cut through forests of pine, patula and cypress, intermingled with the indigenous montane and riverine vegetation. The pine timber had been planted by the Malawian government as a vital source of revenue for the local economy. Local women carted bundles of logs on their head down the path to the city below. Isaac informed us they could carry more than their body weight that way.

The view opened up as we left a stretch of pine forest. Sweeping grass plains rolled across the enormous bowl-shaped plateau, dotted with red mahogany, khaya, African juniper and jacaranda. Brightly coloured locusts and butterflies buzzed and darted over the wild-flowers. Pale flycatchers, sunbirds and blue waxbills darted for their prey. Miombo blue-eared starlings soared above, and Isaac spotted a rare pin-tailed whydah. Africa was putting on a show again.

On we plodded, and on Sam did too, whinging when he wasn't too short of breath. We negotiated an automatic score of eight if he completed the walk, which had to be upgraded to an automatic nine as the summit approached. With his low muscle tone it was harder work for him than the rest of us.

The path took us disconcertingly close to the cliff line. At times only a metre or so separated us from a drop hundreds of metres down the side of the plateau.

Finally we reached the apex, tumbling onto the soft grass, a sweaty mess. We ate the cheese and tomato sandwiches provided by the tour company as we gazed across the grassed plateau, the forests on its lower reaches, and plunging cliff lines at its edge. When the British held sway in Malawi, they described the views from Zomba Plateau across the Rift Valley as 'the best in the British Empire'.

Sam's complaints eased as we descended along the narrow walking tracks crisscrossing the top of the plateau. Some locals had set up a makeshift shop on the side of the site, selling precious stones collected from the plateau; black tourmaline, jasper, apatite and pink quartz. Jules bought a couple and I tried some gooseberries that were also on sale.

We reached Chingwe's Hole, a gap a mere ten metres' diameter but of unknown depth. Hundreds of years ago, the bodies of those who had died of smallpox or leprosy were cast in. It made for an unpleasant image. I just hoped the poor folk were actually dead at the time.

Sam didn't like it. 'Are the bodies still in there?'

'Their bones would be.'

His eyes widened. 'Are they skeletons?'

'Well, sort of,' I said. 'Do you want to join them? We could push you in.'

He jumped back from the edge, grinning. '*No!* You are *joking!*' It was good to see a smile on his face again.

We followed the rim of the bowl, skirting along cliff lines, over mounds of granite, through grassy fields. The far side of the plateau was home to a valley where potatoes were grown. Local farmers and their family members would walk the produce along a track over the plateau to Zomba, unsurprisingly called the Potato Track, carting the potatoes on their heads. Our retinue followed the track, slowly descending towards the city.

Sam called to me from the rear of the troupe. 'Hey, Dad, I'm more relaxed now.' It was an interesting choice of words. It appeared his distress had been primarily emotional rather than physical. Now that he realised the end of the walk was approaching and he was going to make it, he was feeling more comfortable. You would have thought that his complaints would have escalated by the end of a long walk, but instead they were abating.

Meanwhile my complaints were increasing. My knee was playing up again on the prolonged descent, and soon I was limping badly. I had at least twenty-five years on my trekking companions and was feeling every single one of them. We descended the steep slope from the rim, through a forest of mahogany, their trunks and limbs carpeted in moss and festooned in beard lichen. The light glinted through the canopy as we tumbled down to a series of waterfalls, our finish line. The taxi would collect us from a road near the falls.

Sam punched the air as we collapsed onto the soft grass. 'Yes, I did it!'

Yes, he did; an awesome achievement. We were all stoked on his behalf. More than anything else, I could sense Sam's self-belief rise when he overcame these obstacles, whether it be a helicopter ride, jumping in a lake or climbing over a plateau.

Sam had a well-deserved break playing his DS until dinner. But after dinner he seemed agitated, which worsened when a blackout began.

'I want an automatic ten. I ate dinner.'

'No, Sam,' I stated firmly, 'You have a nine. That is enough.'

Juliette broke out the video camera and started recording.

He hammered his fist. 'I *demand* a ten. What do I have to do for an automatic ten?'

I shook my head. 'No, Sam. I don't want to discuss this further.'

It went on and on. Sam flapped and clenched his fists and bit his lips, leaning towards me threateningly. At times he looked like he was about to grab my throat or strike me but then he backed away again.

'You are a murderer!' he yelled. 'You must give me a *ten*!'

'I'm not talking about it,' I said quietly, but through gritted teeth. 'If you want to talk then do so, but I'm not talking about it.'

I was getting more experienced at handling this sort of situation and remained calm, but I felt self-conscious as Juliette, Mike and Lenneke watched. The power came back on, and the room lit up. Finally the impasse broke and Sam agreed to calm down in our room. Jules and our Dutch friends were very sympathetic. Lenneke could relate to such behaviour, and became a little emotional. So did I.

Sam returned to the dining room soon enough, apologetic. 'Hmm, I'm sorry, Dad.'

'That's okay,' I sighed.

'Do I still get an automatic nine?'

'We'll discuss it tomorrow.'

He grabbed my forearm and looked directly at me. 'I don't want to get a six.'

'Tomorrow,' I said, avoiding eye contact in order to help kill the conversation.

'Okay, Dad. I'm sorry, Dad.' This Is Autism.

In the morning, Sam awoke early and rolled towards me through the mosquito netting. 'Nine?'

'Eight,' I replied.

He accepted the adjustment with surprising grace. 'I'm glad I got an eight.'

CHAPTER 24

Bordering on the ridiculous

We were sad to say goodbye to Mike and Lenneke as we left Pakachere. We hit the road again, lugging our backpacks to the minibus station a kilometre away. We had some daunting travel ahead of us today: we were going to try to get to Cuamba in northern Mozambique—Moz, in the local vernacular. We'd need to catch three minibuses and make a potentially difficult border crossing, where visas were required. We didn't have our visas arranged, and apparently they were either difficult to obtain at the border or a way to get ripped off, or both. *Lonely Planet* and other travellers said it was possible but might require a bribe for the border guards, so I thought we'd be okay.

The first minibus trip went well enough, complete with breakfast bought through the bus window, but transferring from the first minibus to the second proved problematic, as several drivers shouted and pulled us to their vehicle. There was a lot of pushing, shoving and pointing. I bristled.

Once we made it onto a bus, Sam started to give me some grief. 'I want a Sprite.'

'No, Sam,' I said. 'You know no fizzy drinks in the morning.'

'I'm thirsty! I want a Sprite.'

'Sam, not now! I don't need this now, I'm stressed enough.'

The driver demanded four thousand kwacha each, much more than usual. Because of all the pushing and shoving I'd made the classic mistake of not fixing the price before we got on, so he had us over a barrel and wouldn't budge. I reluctantly handed over the cash.

Despite being ripped off, the day wasn't going too badly, all things considered. After a couple of hours, the minibus parted the tumbling noisy crowds of a city I'd never heard of and came to a halt outside the central open-air market, where a sign declared Australian government foreign aid had funded the local irrigation program.

It was getting hot in the late morning sun as we exited the minibus. The driver told us to move into the rear of a utility parked nearby. 'I paid to go all the way to the border,' I reminded him.

He dismissed this with a wave. 'Yes, yes, you have to pay no more.'

We waited in the tray, exposed to the sun, for about fifteen minutes, watched by a group of men lounging on some stairs.

One of them called out to Juliette, 'What's your name?'

'Juliette.'

'How old are you?' another asked.

'Too young,' she replied, with a dash of Tabasco.

Finally, a man limped over on deformed legs, leaning on a forearm crutch. 'You will be waiting here until four p.m.,' he stated bluntly.

I jumped to my feet. 'What!' I yelled.

The man, with some of the others nodding in agreement, said that we had only paid for a group vehicle, which would take six hours to fill up.

'I paid twelve thousand kwacha! That should be enough!'

The crippled man replied for them. 'You have paid too much,' he said, with a sweep of his arm. 'It will cost fifteen thousand kwacha for a private vehicle if you want to leave straightaway.'

I lost my shit. Standing over them in the tray of the ute, I shouted, 'You think because I'm white I'm made of money? I paid twelve thousand kwacha to go to the border, and I should be taken to the border—*now!*' I pointed at the ground. 'This is *totally fucked!*'

Sam was amused. 'Dad is getting angry at the Africans!'

The crippled man and a friend conversed in Chichewa, and then the man turned to us. 'Follow me.'

He walked me back through the crowded market, found the minibus driver, and had a long conversation with him. The minibus driver extracted three thousand kwacha from his pocket and handed it to the crippled man. As we walked back, the latter explained. 'He paid six thousand out of his twelve to us to pay for a group vehicle. A private vehicle costs nine thousand more. He has given another three, so if you pay six thousand more you can go straightaway.'

'That's a lot of money,' I replied, partially mollified.

'It's a bad road,' he shrugged.

'How far is it?'

'Four to five kilometres.'

I couldn't believe it. We could have walked that distance, if not for our heavy packs and the heat. 'But that shouldn't take long!'

'That is the price.'

'Okay, okay.'

I paid the money. *Whatever, let's just get there*, I thought. I soon realised that the men I'd been speaking to were not keeping the money, that the utility in fact belonged to another man. They'd just been trying to help out and I'd shouted and sworn at them. Oops. I thanked them as we pulled away, embarrassed about my rudeness.

The utility headed off. After we had travelled what seemed to be a lot longer than five kilometres, Juliette figured it out. 'I think he might have said forty-five kilometres, not four *to* five.'

That explained the high cost. Maybe I hadn't been ripped off, well at least not by that much. We bounced along the dirt road, way too fast considering we were sitting loose in the tray. I squeezed my eyes shut as the driver dodged goats and children on the road.

Finally, we reached the Mozambique border. Dust whistled around a long concrete building that guarded the boom gate. Children from the nearby ragtag village stared at us, and hoary old men played bao, a game where pebbles are strategically moved around gouged-out positions on a wooden board—a kind of African backgammon—under the shade of the solitary nearby tree. With packs on shoulders, we trooped up the stairs of the building and into the office, where the Malawian border guards informed us, to our dismay, that the Mozambique side of the border would not issue visas at this post. We would need to a head north a hundred kilometres to the next post. *Argh!*

This meant we had to first backtrack forty-five kilometres to the main road, but by the time we realised this the car that had brought us to the crossing had long since departed.

A cross-eyed man offered to drive us back in the only car in the village. Some motorbikes were available, but I wasn't keen on the idea of Sam on the back of a motorbike without a helmet for forty-five kilometres. The border guard whispered to us that the cross-eyed man's car was very dodgy. Our options were narrowing. The guard suggested that we could wait for a car to come through the border and hitch a ride.

I looked despondently at the quiet dusty road disappearing into Moz, while Jules hung the half-dry laundry from her backpack onto the boom gate in the penetrating sun.

Just as I was about to say yes to the cross-eyed man and his dodgy car, an ambulance appeared at a small hospital station within sight of the border post. The guard beckoned the ambulance driver over and spoke to him. 'He will take you back to the main road,' he said. *What a relief.*

The ambulance driver, Prince, was a personable Chelsea fan, with a sturdy build and ready smile. 'The girl and boy can come in the front with me, but we have to pick up some patients and take them back to Liwonde, so are you okay to be in the back with them?'

'Sure, I'm a doctor,' I said.

Prince's eyes lit up. 'Oh, you are a doctor!'

Prince and a worker from the hospital laid some sheets on the bottom of the ambulance tray and then gently lifted a very unwell and wasted man straight from the doorway of the clinic onto the sheets. He was barely conscious and trembling violently. *HIV? Cancer?*

Malawian ambulances have a bench in the back down one side and that's it. There was no equipment whatsoever, not even a bandaid. The man's head lay on the floor next to my feet. He grabbed my ankle like a security blanket.

Four patients capable of walking climbed in and sat next to me on the bench. Jules and Sam anxiously stared over their shoulders at the collection of humanity surrounding me.

Prince bopped away to some tunes from The Black Missionaries, the hottest act on the Malawi music scene. We chatted about English football, my work and medicine in Australia and Malawi.

'Do people have to pay for ambulances here every time?' I enquired.

'Yes,' Prince nodded.

'There is no government assistance if people are in dire need?'

Prince's smile disappeared for the first time. 'None. It is appalling.'

Deposited back on the main road, we waited at a bus stop in a town clearly unused to seeing *wazungu*. Everybody stared at us. Sam, sitting cross-legged on the ground playing his DS, had a crowd of forty surrounding him, just watching. He ignored them all.

A bus soon arrived and we headed to the second Mozambique border crossing, further north at Chiponde. This border crossing was on the main road into northern Mozambique and much busier than the first. On the Malawi side, two problems emerged. First, unbeknownst to me, Sam and I had been issued with only fourteen-day visas for Malawi instead of the standard twenty-eight, so we had been staying in Malawi with expired visas. We were unwitting lawbreakers. Second, we were told that getting a visa on the Mozambique side would still be very problematic. The first problem was fixed with a stern look and a fifty US dollar exit visa. The second was not so easy.

'Just be flexible. Remember, this is Africa,' the guard cautioned me, as he handed back my passport.

I took this to mean that we would need to pay much more than the thirty US dollars the visa was officially meant to cost. On the back of motorbike taxis, we zoomed across the sandy road at sunset to the Mozambique immigration office seven kilometres away.

Sure enough, there was trouble, but it was worse than I thought.

It seemed it wasn't a matter of money. The machine they needed to issue the visas was broken, so they literally *couldn't* issue any. They seemed genuinely upset for us, especially once they found out about Sam's issues. It appeared we'd have to travel all the way back to Lilongwe to get the visas. Our plans for Juliette's remaining week with us were unravelling, and the overall itinerary for Sam and me was being turned on its head.

After an hour of stuffing around, of phone calls back and forth and intense discussions between the dozen or so staff in the office, they finally told us that if we came back the next morning at eight they could issue the visas then. Let heaven and angels sing!

We stole away, back on the bikes, across the seven kilometres of no-man's-land, into Malawi. The motorbike drivers didn't stop at the Malawi side of the border but instead took us straight into town, passing the closed border post. It occurred to me that we were back in Malawi without visas, but what could we do?

Take us to the nearest nice hotel! We arrived in a town shrouded in darkness—yet another blackout. Our friendly host, however, managed to organise some chicken and chips, soft drinks and bottled water.

We picked at our chicken on the floor of the room in the flickering light of a single candle stuck to the floor tiles with melted wax, and reflected on the day as we waited for the blackout to end. Jules sat cross-legged on the tiles, her elbows on her knees and chin in her hands. 'At least we don't have a tapeworm infestation, Uncle James.'

True. I nodded.

'Also, if Benison and Mum knew we'd been riding on motorbikes without helmets, on a dirt road, in the dark, in Africa, they would completely freak out.'

True! I laughed.

Sam jumped into the conversation. 'Mum would completely freak out!'

When the lights came on, we settled in for the night. A new problem was looming, which concerned me even more than our visa problems. Jules had an ache in her wisdom tooth that had worsened over the last couple of days, and now she was having trouble opening her mouth fully. She had struggled to eat her chicken.

She had an enlarged lymph node, but at least her gum line didn't look swollen. We did *not* want to try to find an emergency dentist in Mozambique, of all places. Fortunately, I had a course of broad-spectrum antibiotics in my medical kit and started her on them. Hopefully they would do the trick. I told her not to worry, that it would be fine, but secretly I was very concerned.

The next morning, half an hour before dawn, I crawled out from under the mosquito net and quickly dressed. We had to regroup. The plan was to withdraw some kwacha from the bank to change into US dollars, which we would probably need to bribe the Mozambique border guards. To do this I had to leave at six a.m. to get to the nearest ATM at Mangochi, a forty-five-minute drive away, and return in time to try to cross the border again at eight a.m.

The motorcycle rider I had booked didn't turn up. After three-quarters of an hour of frustrating messing around, I finally managed to organise a cab to Mangochi and back for probably way too much money, but time was of the essence.

We travelled up and over a mountain range in the breaking dawn. White mist in the mountain shadows mixed with blue wood smoke leaching from chimneys. Mangoes, bananas and baobabs. Villagers stirring and streets filling.

I was already nervous that we had stayed overnight in Malawi without a visa, and now I was passing directly through African roadside police checks. The police didn't usually check *wazungu*, but I still wondered what a Malawi prison would be like. I had heard stories of human faeces mixed into the *nzhima*, the cornmeal mash that was a staple of these parts. I practiced some mindfulness exercises.

At the ATM, I nervously entered the card and prayed to hear the whir of notes being dispensed. If this didn't work, we really were in the poo. I would have to travel on to yet another town, yet another ATM, until I could retrieve cash.

But it worked! Back in the cab, humming The Pretenders song 'Brass in Pocket', back to Chiponde, back to the room. Jules' tooth was already feeling better thanks to the antibiotics. This time the three motorbikes booked to take us across no-man's-land *did* turn up. We didn't stop at the Malawi immigration office. Straight on to the Mozambique border post.

They knew who we were when we arrived, but a burly officer at the army post at the front of the crossing still wanted to search our bags again. He ordered the three of us into his hut with our bags, but Sam just ran off and sat in the shade of the building.

The guard watched Sam run off. 'He is very rude.'

It was not a sentiment you want to hear an African soldier slinging a machine gun express. 'He has special needs,' I explained, nervously.

'Oh, I see. He is your son, yes?'

I nodded.

'I'm very sorry,' said the guard.

'That's okay,' I replied, 'he's a good boy.'

The officer eventually let us proceed to the immigration offices, where Jules and Sam sat on the cool tiled floor while I stood waiting at the counter. Nothing was happening in a rush, that was for sure. A junior official took umbrage at us sitting on the floor and ordered us out onto the verandah.

Waiting, waiting. We three waited, sitting on the concrete steps. The motorbike riders waited, lolling near the bikes which again had our packs strapped onto them. The enervated officials waited, sprawled on a circle of chairs at the other end of the verandah. Jules and I smiled as sweetly as possible at everyone. Eventually the chief called me into his office.

After a few concerned looks at some pieces of paper, he raised his head, took his peaked cap off his balding sweaty head and pointed a fat finger towards me. 'Why did you not get your visa at the embassy?'

I replied politely. 'I had been told you could get it at the border, and I also read this on the Mozambique government website.'

He glared at me, an eyebrow raised sceptically. 'Who told you this?'

'Some friends who had got their visa at the border, and I rang the embassy in Lilongwe the other day and they also said this to me.' The former was true, the latter was not, but I thought it would improve my chances.

He ran his hand through what remained of his hair, shaking his head. He pointed the fat finger again. 'This will cost you one hundred dollars, for each person!'

'Okay. I have this,' I said, nodding eagerly.

It was an exorbitant rip-off, but by this stage I was prepared to wear it.

'I have to check with my boss.' He shook his head again. 'This is not easy, you know.'

He made a call on his mobile, speaking in Portuguese. He mentioned the hundred dollars three times, and seemed worried. Eventually he hung up. 'The machine is broken. It is not possible. You have to go back.'

Bugger. They were not just being mulish. The broken machine, whatever it was, meant the visas really could not be issued. The only person who seemed pleased about this was Sam, who realised there was a country struck off the list, and it started with an M.

Jules and I discussed our options. If we went all the way back to Lilongwe, or south to Blantyre, to get a visa from an embassy, it would basically mean the whole of the next week Jules was with us would be spent on a bus, and it would still be difficult to get to Pemba, the town in northern Mozambique Jules was booked to fly out from, in time anyway. This was not what any of us wanted. The best course of action would be to change Jules' flight so she left from Lilongwe, abandon Mozambique altogether, and spend another week in Malawi. It was a softer option, but one I immediately felt more comfortable with. I needed to focus more on Sam, and less on travel. At least we had saved three hundred US dollars on visa fees and bribes.

We came back through Malawi customs.

The same officer met me at the window. 'Where did you spend last night?'

I sheepishly admitted we had stayed in Malawi without a visa. The officer gave me a wry smile and issued Sam and me each with a new one-month visa.

Then followed three long, bumping, bouncing trips back to Lilongwe on the roads of Malawi. The first was in an open truck with thirty people crammed in the back, an elderly woman using Sam's feet as an impromptu chair. Haggard and brutalised by bitumen, we spilled into Mabuya Camp at eight p.m. We had been travelling for twenty-eight hours of the last forty-eight, by minibus, truck, utility tray, motorbike, taxi and ambulance. Three border-crossing attempts in two days had failed. We were exhausted, hungry, dehydrated and frazzled. We ate pizza then collapsed into bed. It was only then I realised that of the three of us, Sam had handled all the hassle, the delays and the chaos best of all.

CHAPTER 25

Expect the unexpected

In the morning, I read on the front page of *The Nation*, the Malawian newspaper, that Mozambican refugees were pouring across the border as the rebel group, Renamo, threatened to take over any northern district governments not appointed by the rebels themselves. There were threats of violence breaking out. It was just as well it had proven impossible for us to get there. Maybe that had been the real reason we couldn't bribe our way through, after all.

Renamo had been a right-wing rebel movement, backed and funded by apartheid South Africa and white-ruled Rhodesia, from 1977, two years after Mozambican independence, until a ceasefire in 1992. Of Mozambique's mid-1980s population of fourteen million people, one million had died during the years of civil war, and five million were now internally displaced *deslocados*, typically living in abject poverty on the outskirts of cities and towns. Countless people had also been killed or maimed by over 170,000 landmines during the period.

I asked a co-owner of Mabuya Camp why Renamo were still fighting. 'Shouldn't they be defunct?'

'They're just a bunch of bandits now. They grew up in the war fighting, and it's all they know. They have no other skills; nothing else to do. There is no political ideology now, if there ever was. It's just about getting some money.' Moz was yet another African country still reeling from the effects of war.

While it was serendipitous that we had avoided a conflict, I was still disappointed we were not going to visit Mozambique Island, or travel on the Nampula railway that I'd been reading about for over a year. However, bearing in mind the trip's purpose, tossing the whole program up in the air was certainly in keeping with the principles of unpredictability.

So, what to do next? The next day at Mabuya Camp there was another unexpected turn: we ran into Mike and Lenneke, our Dutch friends from Zomba, who nearly fell off their chairs when they saw us walking near the pool.

'What are you guys doing here?' Mike said. 'You should be in Mozambique.'

'They didn't let us in,' Jules replied. 'We knocked and knocked but nobody opened the door.' We related our tale of woe.

'So what are you going to do now?' Lenneke asked.

'Jules has to go home in a week so we thought we'd just chill by the lake somewhere and she can fly out of Lilongwe. Sam and I might follow your suggestion and go to Uganda and then Kenya.'

Sam piped up. 'No, I don't want to have extra countries. I don't want to go to the country starting with U.'

Lenneke quickly deployed a clever strategy. 'But, Sam, there is a McDonald's in Uganda.'

Quick as a flash, Sam replied, 'I want to go to Uganda. Is it as rich as Namibia?' *Well, that was easy.*

Mike and Lenneke asked Jules if she wanted to extend her trip and leave with them in two days to travel across Zambia to Victoria Falls, and then fly out of Livingstone instead. She accepted gleefully. From her point of view things had worked out for the better. She would see some seriously good wildlife in Zambia and one of the world's great wonders in the falls, with the bonus of some nice people to escort her. I booked tickets for Sam and me to fly to Entebbe, Uganda, in a few days' time. After all, it is a bad plan that cannot be changed.

For now we got back into schoolwork and neuroplasticity, with Jules, Mike and Lenneke helping out. Back to boxing, maths, playing pool and swimming in the pool and playing cards. Speaking to strangers, ordering meals, filming for the university. I got him to talk to the hostel owner and practice ordering lunch over the counter. It took a while to set up the camera on a tripod and obtain the permission of the people being filmed, but I was becoming more used to it as the trip went on. I had a sense of relief about our changed plans. Not only did I now not have to worry about the language barrier in Moz—Portuguese is the official language and English speakers are rare—as well as the higher crime risk, but we were now avoiding some seriously long bus trips heading up to the north of Tanzania. We also had friends.

Mike and Lenneke joined a long line of travellers we'd met who had raved about Uganda. And Sam would get to eat McDonald's in Uganda's capital.

On our last day together, we were all at the poolside. Lenneke hopped in with Sam and Mike. Sam stared at her. 'Are you going to take your top off?'

'No!' Lenneke exclaimed, covering her chest with her arm.

'Why not?' Sam asked.

'Because that would not be appropriate,' she stated carefully, 'and I would be embarrassed.'

'Oh, okay,' Sam said, nonchalantly.

Yep, those hormones were definitely kicking in.

Jules, Mike and Lenneke headed off, bound for Zambia. I suddenly felt lonely again. I suspected Sam did too. Mabuya Camp was now inundated with school groups from Britain and the United States, hoards of sixteen-year-olds who kept to themselves. There was no way Sam was going to crack that social scene.

Unfortunately, our flight to Uganda was cancelled so our stay in Malawi was extended for two days until the next available flight. I planned to focus on school and neuroplasticity again, but then Sam developed a bad cold and I had to back off. For the first time on the trip, I didn't have much to do.

Paying for the flight proved to be difficult. The tickets cost around one thousand US dollars, but the maximum you could withdraw at any ATM was three hundred. You couldn't withdraw cash from bank tellers at all. In Malawian kwacha, three hundred US dollars converted to one hundred and sixty thousand-kwacha notes, the country's highest currency denomination. The travel agent's credit card machine wouldn't recognise my Visa card so over four days I had to make four separate trips to the bank and then hurry to the agent with my pockets protuberant with cash, looking like the bagman for the local mafia. It was just as well the flights were delayed.

In town one day, I saw a woman carrying a boy of about ten on her back, his body swathed to hers. He was profoundly disabled, moaning and staring into space. His body under the wrap looked way too small for his head. One could only imagine the severe challenges they both faced and limited resources they would have to meet them.

Then on the minibus I sat next to a woman in rags, with an infant strapped to her back. The infant had a squint, which I knew would very likely be resolved with simple eye patching, if properly managed. I also knew there was little chance this woman would ever get this advice.

The family doctor in me wanted to reach out to her and guide her, but I couldn't, of course. She wouldn't have spoken English, and I would have appeared a weird *mzungu* trying to pry into her affairs. The child would likely have profoundly poor vision in one eye for life, an outcome that was preventable, but not here and not by me.

Africa was full of disability. Poverty, malnutrition, threadbare health systems, poor maternal and obstetric management, high accident rates: the causes were manifest but many of them were preventable. Where disabilities existed, many of those which could be fixed, or at least managed, were simply not dealt with at all. And I saw this everywhere, particularly among the children: on the streets, on the minibuses, strapped to the backs of mothers.

Back at Mabuya Camp, I decided to use this lull to audit myself, as we were now at the halfway point of the trip.

What do you think you are doing well?

Well, as a starting point, I hadn't completely cocked up. There had been no disasters and Sam had not deteriorated, which were my two big worries before leaving. I had stuck at the task well. It had been rocky at times, but I had managed to just keep going and get things done, even on the roughest days.

I also felt I'd been alert and imaginative in seizing unexpected opportunities that had arisen. This also fit in nicely with the whole theme of unpredictability on the trip.

What do you think you could improve upon?

I'd been inconsistent with my responses to Sam, particularly when he lost his temper. I needed to keep in mind that this trip was harder for him than it was for me. I also wanted to improve the language I used with him when he was struggling with a task. More positive language, less criticism, anger or disappointment. Gently nudge.

Finally, I also needed to keep an eye on myself. I'd been really feeling emotionally fatigued at times. The recent few weeks with Juliette around had helped, but perhaps it was better we were going to Uganda rather than Mozambique for this reason too.

I left Sam to chill on the internet in our room, and allowed myself time to put my feet up in the lounge area and watch Australia beat England in the cricket. That helped replenish my emotional reserves.

It was our last day in Malawi. We'd been here nearly a month. It had fulfilled its reputation for being a country of amiable people and spectacular natural beauty, and then some. As our cab passed through the iron gates of Mabuya Camp for the last time, even Sam now begrudgingly admitted the first M country had been 'okay' after all. Then he thought for a few seconds. 'Is Kenya poorer than Uganda?'

'I'm not sure.'

'There isn't a war?'

'There's no fighting in the parts we're going to.'

'There isn't a nuclear war?'

I reassured him. 'No, there won't be a nuclear war, that's for sure.'

'I don't want to be in a nuclear war.'

'Neither do I.'

At the airport, I was slightly edgy about showing our passports to the immigration official as they showed our overstay on our initial Malawian visas, but told myself it surely wouldn't be an issue now. That is, until the Malawian immigration officer flicked a few times through my passport, and grumbled, 'Where's the receipt number?'

'What receipt number?' I replied nervously.

'For the visa.'

'I don't know.'

He looked up. 'Did you pay for the exit visa?'

'Yes.'

'How much?' he snapped.

'Twenty-five US dollars each.'

'I need the receipt.' He turned the passport around and showed it to me. 'They have not written in the receipt number.'

'I don't have it.'

He glared at me. 'Well, you will have to go back and get it.'

'*What?*' I shrieked. '*To the Mozambique border?*'

'We have a problem here. What can we do about this? You will need to help me solve it.'

Ah, he wanted a bribe. I now realised that we probably shouldn't have had to pay for an exit visa back at the Mozambique border. We'd been ripped off and hadn't even been aware of it. Now this guy saw me as a soft touch.

'How about twenty US dollars,' I said through gritted teeth.

'Make it thirty.'

Anxious to get through without fuss, I slipped him the cash. As soon as we passed the barrier, I started to get angry; I should have taken him on, refused to pay or asked to see his boss. I vowed not to let that happen so easily again.

We changed planes in Kenya's capital, Nairobi. 'This is Nai-robbery,' Sam said loudly, as we strode through the large terminal. 'Watch out for robbers!' he added, with a big grin.

'Sam, be quiet!'

I'd noticed he was in a good mood. His confidence had lifted generally over the last few days. It occurred to me that his relief at getting past the M countries, which he'd correctly anticipated would be some tough travelling, might have eased his anxiety.

It was like our descent from the Zomba plateau: he could now glimpse the finish line, with no insurmountable obstacles in his path. Sam now believed he could do this.

CHAPTER 26

Swings and roundabouts

I di Amin. He was the first thought that came to mind when I heard the word Uganda. I mean, I'd seen *The Last King of Scotland* and it had a McDonald's, but I didn't really know much more about the place. I hadn't read up on it because I hadn't known we'd be going there; until our dramas at the Mozambique border forced an abrupt itinerary change there had been only an outside chance we'd go.

As we flew into Kampala, it immediately became apparent that Uganda was significantly more sophisticated than what we'd become used to over the previous month or so. There were well-maintained gutters, and road signs, heaps of them. Sam noticed the new font on the road signs as we headed for an overnight stay at the local backpacker hostel. Not much gets past this guy.

Entebbe, a small, neat and wealthy city, was an hour on a minibus from the thumping, pumping capital, Kampala. As we got off the surprisingly clean and uncrowded minibus, we were besieged by drivers of the machine that rules Kampala, the *boda boda*, or motorbike taxi.

A curious crowd gather around Sam as he plays on his DS while we wait for a minibus back to Lilongwe from the Mozambique border.

Sam chats on film in Lilongwe, Malawi. The footage of such conversations was used by researchers at Griffith University to study Sam's speech and communication skills.

Sam and I try to talk above the roar of the rapids, Murchison Falls, Uganda.

Sam encounters a posse of warthogs at Murchison Falls National Park. 'It's Pumbaa!'

Sam up close and personal with some rhinos in Uganda. Experiences like this fired his imagination and broadened his horizons.

Sam and I riding whitewater rapids in the upper reaches of the Nile, Uganda.

Sam towers over some children in a Ugandan village. The boy with the slingshot was the same age as Sam.

Sam meets a baby in Uganda.

Sam attends a lesson in a Tanzanian special needs school.

Sam inside Ngorongoro Crater, Tanzania.

A nervous Sam smiles for the camera in Ngorongoro Crater, as a lion lies outside his minibus window.

The 'ferry' to Mafia Island, off the coast of Tanzania.

Sam reads *Animal Farm* while sitting in Stone Town, Zanzibar.

Sam studies a 192-year-old Aldabra giant sea tortoise, born before the American Civil War.

Naomi from Heiress films shoots footage of Sam aboard a dhow off Stone Town, Zanzibar. Morton, our travelling companion, chills out behind him.

A sunset dhow cruise off Zanzibar Island.

The name *boda boda* hails from a time when smuggling into Uganda was mostly by motorbikes, which were able to avoid the border crossings more easily than larger vehicles. The bikes soon became known as *boda*, a mutation of border, which evolved into *boda boda*. Tens of thousands of them swarm the city's streets or cluster on footpaths as their drivers languidly wait for customers. A couple of *wazungu* like us, looking like Tintin and the Captain, were juicy fruit waiting to be plucked.

What the heck, it was a lot cheaper than a taxi trip to our accommodation. We were staying at Red Chilli Hideaway, a large backpacker hostel on the edge of the city, some twenty minutes' drive away. The large packs balanced between the driver and the handle bar, while the two of us rode pillion, small packs on our backs, clinging tightly to the drivers' waists as we swerved and weaved, dodging trucks, minibuses and cars in the maelstrom.

As we approached Red Chilli, Sam yelled across to me, 'Where is the DS?'

Oh no! I'd asked him to put it into his pocket as we'd boarded the minibus. I knew straightaway it must have fallen out of his pocket on the bus, made even more likely because he often had his feet up on the seat to support his poor core muscle tone. There was no way we were going to get it back.

After a frantic search through pockets and bags, it was confirmed as MIA. I'd have thought Sam's head would have exploded, but he was remarkably calm. I agreed to make the futile trip back to the bus station to look for it but it was more to show Sam that I realised this was a big deal rather than from any hope we'd retrieve it. I felt partly culpable; I should have been more careful with his 'Precious'.

We caught a cab to the central bus station, which was around the corner from where we'd been dropped an hour or so earlier. From an elevated road beside the bus station, we could see around five hundred minibuses crammed into the square, honking and inching along.

Sam's face dropped. Moses, our cab driver, who was based at Red Chilli, led us through the maze of buses to the central 'office': a collection of eateries and squatteries and do-nothing-eries that looked like an island village in the sea of minibuses.

It seemed it was not the sort of place you'd normally see a tall white guy with a gangly long-haired teenager because we soon attracted a crowd, all talking in the local language, Luganda. Women and girls smirked, giggled and gossiped behind their hands, and the men peered at us with curiosity.

As Moses translated, I let the administrators of the bus station know that a reward of 100,000 shillings, about fifty US dollars, was being offered for the return of the DS. The mood changed from idle curiosity to excitement. A buzz rippled through the crowd; at least the word was getting out. It was likely the mislaid DS had been picked up by a passenger, but if a conductor or driver found it, well, you never knew. We left a contact number, just in case.

Moses led his people back to the cab, parting the minibus sea, and we returned to Red Chilli. I watched Sam closely. He seemed calm, too calm. Did he hold out false hope? Did he not fully understand the DS was in all probability gone? He had a smaller version in reserve, but it didn't have all the hours and hours of games he had played over recent months stored on it. I don't really understand Nintendo DSs, but I think that's how it works.

I took it easy on Sam that day. The Red Chilli facilities and wi-fi were impressive; Mike and Lenneke had told us that this was the place to make our base in Uganda. I let Sam binge on the internet while I spent most of the afternoon at the reception desk organising accommodation and trips into the countryside over the next few weeks. I'd been thinking that I should be getting Sam more involved in this sort of activity, but not today, not on DS Day.

As sunset approached, I found Sam hovering around the entrance to the hostel. 'Are they still looking?' he asked me.

'Yes, Sam, they probably are, but remember there is only a small chance of them finding it.'

'But they *might* find it.' I could hear the pain in his voice. He looked longingly up the driveway, hoping to see a bus approaching with his DS, a bus I knew was not going to show up. I ached on his behalf. He was like the dog listening to the gramophone in His Master's Voice, hoping and not understanding. Guilt, guilt, guilt. Shit, shit, shit.

Losing the DS was a setback for Sam, but also for myself. The next few days we didn't have much to do, and I attempted to focus on school and neuroplasticity exercises, but my motivation was waning. My carelessness had crushed my boy, and I was feeling dreadful about it. Nonetheless we pushed through. Chess was the neuroplasticity exercise I enjoyed most, and I think Sam too. Sometimes we would play several games a day, and I also enlisted other people staying at the hostel to play against him. I also took the opportunity to challenge him with some crossword puzzles from a book left behind at the hostel book exchange. We recorded more video interviews with some of our fellow travellers and staff at the hostel.

On the way into the city on the Red Chilli shuttle one day, the amiable driver struck up a conversation. I told him I was surprised how developed Uganda was compared to other African countries.

'Yes, Uganda is very organised,' he said.

The toilet seats and the door handles weren't loose, the shower heads had a smooth stream, the door frames were squared, the electrical outlets were actually attached to the walls and the mosquito nets generally didn't have holes in them. If they did, they were repaired with needle and thread, not an elastic band or a bandaid.

It was hard work talking to the driver. He and other Ugandans were having trouble with our Australian accents as we were with theirs, perhaps surprising given both Uganda and Australian are former British colonies.

As we drove, marabou storks circled above. With wingspans of two and a half metres, they expertly surfed the thermals, a posse of hang-gliders everpresent over the city.

The heat and humidity hit us as we exited the minibus to visit a shopping centre. While elevated, Uganda is still on the equator. I tried to explain this to Sam. I was surprised he didn't know what the equator was; obviously he hadn't been paying attention in that geography lesson. I gave a brief explanation.

'So it's like the x axis of the world?' he suggested.

We had been doing linear equation graphs in maths. The way that boy's brain works is so fascinating sometimes.

The shopping centre security was intense. Over thirty armed guards patrolled the centre, many of them with machine guns. All cars were searched, and many people were asked to step out of their vehicles to be frisked. All glove boxes, boots and bags were checked, and under-vehicle search mirrors were used to check under chassis. I assumed this was in response to the Westgate shopping mall terrorist attack in Nairobi in 2013. I realised we weren't far from places where some locals would love to put a few Westerners to the sword, AK-47 or grenade, and an upmarket shopping mall was an obvious target. I appreciated the machine guns.

The loss of the DS seemed to have knocked me around even more than Sam. I was having a crisis of confidence, and of momentum. I was having a lot of trouble getting going each day. *Was I just being a sook?*

A Skype with Benison went a long way to setting me right. She started organising to send a DS replacement from Australia, and I realised there were some game cards we could buy locally. Sam slowly came around to the idea that his Precious was not coming back. I gave him some space.

Over the breakfast table, Sam looked at me keenly. 'Maybe it will be found, Dad.'

'Maybe, but it's not very likely now, Sam,' I said, gently.

'But you might be wrong, Dad.'

'I might, but we're also organising a replacement.'

'But I might not need a replacement.'

I tried to frame it in a way that was more positive. 'If we get a replacement, and the old one does turn up, then you'll have two.'

Sam paused, and then smiled. 'Yeah.'

Our hostel boasted a rare luxury: hot showers in a spacious shower recess. Sam had got out of the habit of having regular showers and had started to just wash instead. And his hair, which he'd chosen not to cut while we'd been away, was now long and hanging over his eyes. Because he wasn't in school he didn't have to keep his hair short about his ears and eyebrows, a De La Salle College regulation.

Unfortunately, his newly long hair was also getting very greasy. I was determined to get him to use some shampoo but this posed a sensory challenge for him and he really kicked up a stink. I pushed back. There was a lot of shouting and threatening from me—way too much actually—and a lot of screaming and yelling from Sam.

'You are not coming out of there until you have washed your hair!'

'No, I don't want to wash my hair,' he whined. 'It gets in my eyes!'

'I'll help you and make sure it doesn't get in your eyes.'

'No! You are a hateful father!'

Eventually a compromise was reached. Sam had a (very) short shower and we shampooed his hair over a basin.

It had been a backward step for Sam and I was upset that I hadn't controlled my temper. I couldn't help but let Sam know my disappointment at his resistance. Then after breakfast I had to break the news to him that Red Chilli had no private rooms or dorm beds available the next night. We would have to sleep on mattresses in a tent. I braced myself for his reaction.

Straight up, he replied. 'I don't want to sleep in a tent.' Memories of Etosha came flooding back.

'Neither do I, Sam,' I replied, 'but there's no other option.'

I could have moved us to another hotel, I suppose, but it would have been very difficult to organise. I pushed and in the end he acquiesced with remarkable grace.

'You can stay in the reception area in the evening and play your DS,' I said. He still had the smaller DS.

He thought about it for a while. 'Hmm, oh, all right. But I will stay in the reception and play my DS.'

'Yes, that's it,' I said. 'Well done, Sam, I'm proud of you.'

Shampoo and tents; swings and roundabouts.

On a day of leaden skies and heavy air, we visited a large local mosque with two young Australian NGO workers staying at Red

Chilli, Emma and Whitney. I thought the excursion would be beneficial for Sam, some hands-on religious education.

The National Mosque of Uganda is the largest mosque in sub-Saharan Africa and can hold twenty thousand faithful. Construction started under the Amin regime but the money dried up when the economy collapsed and it remained half-finished until 2004 when Colonel Gaddafi granted funding for its completion. Before we entered, Emma and Whitney had to don a headdress and long skirt over their pants; the necessary cloth wraps were provided at the entrance.

Sam watched them garb up. 'We don't have to wear sheets.'

'No, Sam, it's only ladies,' I clarified.

'Why?' he asked.

'Because it's their culture,' I explained.

Sam wasn't happy. 'I don't want to wear a sheet.'

'Do you understand what a culture is?' I asked. 'It's what a group of people, like a country or a religion, set up as their rules.'

'Oh.' He pondered this and looked out the corner of his eyes. 'I don't want to wear a sheet. I don't want it to be my culture.' I presumed this was part of his aversion to long sleeves again.

We were shown around by a very nice guide, Ali, a father of three. The mosque itself was beautiful. A giant concrete arch spanned across the broad steps up to the mosque, while a towering minaret with three hundred and four steps up to its gallery stood to the side of the arch, like a sentry at a gate. The arch was a symbol of Uganda, and reflected the shape of the traditional thatched huts of the Bugandan nation. As we ascended the stairs the speakers suddenly crackled into life and the mullah's morning prayers boomed around us.

We ventured inside the cool and delicately lit main chamber, gazing up at vast domes covered in intricate carvings of Islamic motifs. Italian-designed stained-glass windows emitted rays of light onto a vast Libyan-made carpet, a pleasure to walk across in our socks. Over the windows were arches made of Ugandan hardwoods while the arch across the pulpit was encased in small tiles of compressed copper dust, nods to the natural resources of this central African nation.

Flecks of dust hovered in light shafts, as though time itself was held in the grasp of the mosque. It was a place where you felt compelled to whisper.

Ali sat us down in a circle on the soft carpet and told us about the formation of the Ugandan nation and the story behind the mosque. In centuries past, current day Uganda was dominated by Buganda, a sophisticated nation that had its own king, parliament and ministers. The first visitors were early Arabic slave traders from the east, either trading their goods for slaves and ivory or simply stealing them. The Arabs also brought Islam. In the late nineteenth-century British explorers also began to enter eastern and then central Africa in search of the source of the Nile, adventure, fame and fortune. As part of the 'grab for Africa' the British established Buganda and some surrounding tribal lands as a British colony under the name Uganda.

Sam liked the carpet. As he stimmed by dragging his fingertips across the tightly woven pile and the patterns contained within, he tilted his head, looked out the corner of his eye seemingly into space and seemed to ignore what Ali was saying. I wondered how much was sinking in. I tried to reinforce the principal points to Sam as Ali continued.

Sam suddenly stood up. 'I'm bored. I want to go.'

'Sam! Shh!' I hissed. I pulled him back down and explained to Ali. 'He has special needs.'

'Not a problem,' Ali said, with a gentle smile. 'He is one of God's children.' Ali was very good with Sam, not in the least fussed by his quirkiness. We continued our tour around the carpet and columns, under the domes, past the giant encased Koran.

Not only was it Sam's first experience of a mosque but his first exposure to any religion other than Christianity, as far as I knew. Maybe he had been taught about other religions at school? I peered at the Koran in its glass case. 'Sam, this is the holy book of Islam. It's like the bible of Christianity.'

'But you don't have to be an Islam,' he clarified.

'No, Sam, you don't have to,' I reassured him.

Ali led us up the long corkscrewing staircase inside the minaret. Sam thought the staircase up the minaret was like the tower at Hogwarts. We emerged, puffing and sweating, onto the gallery, buffeted by the wind coming off an inky cloud front heading our way. Sweeping views of the chaotic city rippled below us. The name Kampala is Lugandan for 'small hills with impala'. Looking at the vista stretched out before us, this made complete sense to me. There were no impala, but the city's bustling markets, crammed roads and suburbs carpeted the undulating mounds of the landscape.

Ali revealed that his youngest child was disabled. When his son was a few months old, he had developed hydrocephalus, a condition where there is build up of cerebrospinal fluid around the brain, which Ali described as a 'big head'.

Now aged eight, Ali's son could not stand or walk unaided, had impaired speech and memory and didn't go to school. A shunt to ease the pressure of the fluid in his brain had been placed just two months ago. I wondered why it had taken so long. Perhaps Uganda's health system had improved a lot in the last eight years. Ali told me they'd tried local herbal approaches early on, but his family had run out of money.

While not privy to the details of the boy's history, I wondered whether this disability might have been preventable if the clinical scenario had presented in the developed world. When he discovered I was a doctor, Ali was pleased to hear my brief assessment that there may still be hope of significant improvement, given the recent placement of the shunt. It was the best I could offer. I looked at Sam after he described his son's impairments. 'We all have our challenges to face,' I said to Ali.

'Yes, Dr James.'

As we filed out of the bottom of the minaret the storm finally arrived. Large splats of rain landed here and there before raining hard as we ran helter-skelter for shelter. The deluge of fat drops made a thundering racket on the concrete. The humidity broke, it became easier to breathe. It was the first time Sam and I had seen rain in months. As the cloudburst ran its course and faded out, we hailed some *boda bodas* and zipped through the afternoon peak hour back to Red Chilli.

The air was charged after the rainstorm. Large marabou storks swooped low over the traffic, then through the jacarandas between the low-rise buildings, their broad dirty wingspans flashing over us. As our bike drivers ducked and weaved through a hive of bikes, minibuses and cars, I looked across to see Sam's smiling face, hair swirling in the cool wind, as he gripped the driver's waist and looked around his leather-clad shoulder to the road ahead. At one stage, our bikes mounted the curb to bypass a traffic snarl, the pedestrians annoyed but not surprised as they jumped out of the way.

Over the next few days at Red Chilli we focused back on schoolwork, neuroplasticity exercises and video interviews for the university. It was also a period of consolidation and rehabilitation. We tended to our bodies, our gear and our spirits in an attempt to repair and rejuvenate.

Threadbare shoelaces that were about to snap were replaced with string. Sam's stretched and chewed t-shirts were chucked and new ones purchased. Cameras and screens and other electrical equipment were all thoroughly cleaned. I bought yet another pair of back-up reading glasses and replaced Sam's lost pencil case.

The magnetic chess board was badly scratched but, amazingly, we had managed to hold on to thirty-one of the pieces. We were only missing a single 'Slytherin' bishop. Sam postulated it was Severus Snape who'd gone walkabout.

To top things off, I'd managed to lacerate my scalp on the underside of a metal window frame while climbing some stairs. It didn't need stitching, and an Australian vet nurse conveniently staying at Red Chilli kindly irrigated the wound with some iodine antiseptic. When I was talking to Benison on Skype later that morning she was taken aback to see my hair covered in blood and iodine.

Sam's hair looked a lot better after the shampoo, but with long curls hanging over his eyes and ears, multiplying freckles and the lanky-limbed body of a teenager, he was looking rougher and tougher. My youngest child was no longer a child; an adult body was emerging, with all of the challenges that entailed. Batten down the hatches.

CHAPTER 27

Fever!

Across in Addis Ababa, Ethiopia, only 1250 kilometres to our north-east, Barack Obama delivered a speech to the African Union, the first United States president to do so. He noted that with mobile phones and increasing access to the internet, Africans were beginning to 'leapfrog old technologies into new prosperity'. Major progress was being made to allow Africa to finally utilise its massive resources, for the continent to become partners with other parts of the world instead of remaining merely a dependant. However, with the continent's population set to double to two billion in the next quarter-century, with the majority of that growth among children under eighteen, it was, the president said, also a time of great challenges. Growth in training and employment needed to match the population boom, so that young people in Africa could lead a life that had dignity.

Over lunch in the Red Chilli bar, a crowd gathered around the television, hanging on every word. They applauded at the end of the speech. From an African perspective Obama had been an important president. With a Kenyan father, he was 'proud to be the first Kenyan–American President'. The world was watching Africa, and Africa knew it.

Meanwhile, I was watching Sam, and Sam knew it. He became irritable, and so in turn did I. His maths lesson became a battle. *What was going on?* I put my palm to his forehead. He didn't have a fever, and his pulse felt normal, but I started to become concerned.

'I am sick,' he said feebly. He lay down on the couch in the foyer and didn't want to do anything.

Maybe he *was* getting sick. He was recovering from a bad cold he'd contracted a week or so earlier, but he seemed much worse than would be expected: crotchety mood, wavering concentration, a blocked nose and cough. Perhaps a new virus had piggybacked on the last?

I left him for an hour and a half to get some cash from an ATM. On my return, he was burning up. *Oh, fuck, oh, fuck! Please don't let it be malaria.*

Sam was at a high risk for malaria, of that there was no doubt. His phobia of long sleeves put him at greater risk than other travellers, although less so in Uganda where it was too hot to wear long sleeves anyway. Mosquito nets were the problem. Despite my best efforts, he would inevitably end up twisted in the netting like a shark caught in a net, often with limbs poking out, exposed to the hovering buzzing mozzies. Occasionally he'd pull the whole net from the ceiling.

I whisked Sam into a cab and we headed through the traffic to a surgery recommended by the Red Chilli staff, where an expat British doctor worked. Sam lay on the back seat, listless and lethargic. In the consultation room of the smart-looking medical practice, the doctor, who had worked in Kenya and Uganda for decades, was curious about our trip and its purpose. 'Blimey! Just the two of you, eh?'

He was very knowledgeable about tropical medicine, and not overly concerned about malaria. He was concerned about the possibility of Katayama fever, which occurs in response to a schistosomiasis infection. Schistosomes are parasitic worms that can penetrate the skin of anyone who swims in fresh water in sub-Saharan Africa and other parts of the developing world. Lake Malawi, where we had swum a month or so earlier, has been called 'Schistosomiasis Central'.

While not life-threatening, schistosomiasis can make you weak, tired and irritable and complications can occur if it remains untreated long term. Katayama fever is an immune response to an early phase in the disease, when the schistosome eggs are first deposited into the body's tissues. If this was what Sam was suffering from, it was better than malaria; schistosomiasis is usually easily treated.

The doctor felt further tests weren't necessary but advised us to return if the fever continued. Still, I continued to be anxious. Sam's temperature remained high through the night, but he didn't look dramatically unwell. In the morning he was quiet and picked at his breakfast, happy to just lie on the couch and do nothing, but he responded appropriately enough when I spoke to him. Good—no signs of delirium.

Throughout the day, however, his fever continued. I decided I needed more reassurance and bought a malaria-testing kit from a pharmacy. I required three or four drops of Sam's blood to do the test, which is to much to obtain from a finger prick. I attempted a venesection, which proved to be very difficult.

'*No!* I don't want this!' Sam squawked, as I approached the vein on the *cubital fossa*, on the inner aspect of his elbow, with a needle.

'Sam, we need to do the test to make sure you don't have malaria,' I explained.

'I don't want this, I don't want malaria. Malaria *sucks!*'

'Yes, malaria does suck, so we need to know if you have it. Malaria is very serious, Sam.'

As I stuck the needle in, he growled at me. 'Malaria is more common in Malawi. They should call it Malawia.'

I eventually got the blood, despite the syringe plunger breaking halfway through. In a hostel room, with a pillowcase as the tourniquet, dodgy equipment and an uncooperative patient, all the while being filmed by the video camera on a tripod in the corner of the room, it was not my most professional venesection. But the test was negative.

I breathed a sigh of relief and let his anxious mother know via Skype, knowing Benison would be fretting overnight in Sydney otherwise. It didn't rule out malaria altogether, but it was a reassuring indicator.

That afternoon, Sam deteriorated again. As his temperature soared, he looked worse than ever. 'I haven't got malaria,' he said, twisting and turning on the soaked sheets, his cheeks red and eyes bloodshot.

I watched him anxiously. 'I certainly hope not.'

He looked across at me. 'It's all right, Dad,' he said, 'don't worry.'

I couldn't help worrying. His skin was covered in goosebumps, but he didn't have rigors, involuntary shakes. I checked him over for unusual rashes but could find none. This was Africa, after all, and there were other worrying infectious diseases besides malaria. *Should I take him to the hospital?*

I decided to see what he looked like after a dose of paracetamol kicked in. An hour later, the medicine did its trick, and Sam improved. His energy returned, and he requested something to eat.

But I remained unconvinced. I sat on my bed, looking across at him as he tossed and turned under the mosquito net. The last fever had shaken my confidence. He'd been febrile for more than twenty-four hours—and *high* fevers too. Bugger this.

There is a principle in general practice; it's based on a driving analogy. Most of the time in my job you're hitting the brake, telling people *not* to worry, that everything's okay and nothing needs to be done. Only very occasionally it's the opposite, time to hit the accelerator, to do something, to investigate, to refer.

I hit the accelerator. I ordered a cab to the International Hospital Kampala. The hospital was significantly more down at heel than the private clinic we'd visited earlier, but moved efficiently enough. Our consultation was paid for in advance, cheap by Western standards but expensive by Ugandan, hence the empty waiting room. We were straight in to see the doctor. I was unnerved that the doctor didn't examine Sam physically, but the main thing was a blood film to look for malarial parasites, along with a blood count and other basic blood tests.

Despite the British doctor's earlier words of reassurance, the two things I was really worried about were malaria complications and a serious bacterial infection like pneumonia or meningitis. There were other investigations I would have organised if I'd been in Australia, but these tests would give us the most important pieces of information. Malaria, caused by the parasite *Plasmodium* and transmitted by mosquito, can cause liver failure, kidney failure, cerebral malaria (infection of the brain that can lead to coma and death), severe anaemia and other complications, and quickly. The World Health Organisation estimates that there were 429,000 deaths from malaria in 2015 with over ninety per cent of these deaths occurring in Africa, mainly in young children.

I desperately hoped we could sort things out; this was as good as it got in Uganda, the next step would be helicopter retrieval to Jo'burg.

Sam tolerated his second venesection of the day much better than the first; maybe now knowing what was involved in it dampened his anxiety. The formal malaria film was clear. We were processed, door to door, including pathology collection and results, in under two hours.

As soon as I had made the decision to go to the hospital, Sam started to become more congested. By the time we left the hospital he was coughing, snuffling and sneezing. We finally had a focus, doctor-speak for an explanation for the fever. The blood count also revealed a profile consistent with a viral infection and unlikely to be a bacterial infection or acute schistosomiasis. *Phew.*

The next day Sam's fever settled but I was over it all. The medical dramas of the last few days had exhausted us both. I was pining for home, for Benison, for my bed, for a half-hour hot shower, for the security of having a developed world tertiary hospital a short drive up the road.

Come on, James, I rallied myself, *pull yourself together. Regroup. We are here to help Sam.* I knew I'd have to pace it carefully though; Sam would take a while to recover. I decided to slowly reintroduce some school and neuroplasticity exercises over the next couple of days before we left on our trip to Murchison Falls National Park.

Judging him to be sufficiently recovered, I got Sam to write his second blog entry on *his* opinions of Africa. He wrote:

I would like to tell you all my opinion of Africa. I have being in Africa since 1 April 2015.

I've seen lot of things and met lots of people. It has been a tough experience.

I'd been in South Africa for nearly a whole month and I started off at Cape Town and Max the camera man had been there for filming us for the first 8 days in the whole trip and spent 6 days at Cape Town and then we went to Hermanus and stayed there for 2 days and Mossel Bay and Wilderness and Port Elizabeth and Chintza and Coffee Bay and Sarni Pass and Durban and then we travelled to Namibia.

The good bits were shops at Durban such as game shops, KFC and many more and also other things.

The bad bits were visiting and helping and saying hi to the Malawi children at preschool and African babies wah noises.

The thing that I enjoyed the most is going to the Durban shopping mall.

My blue DS is missing but they might find it eventually but Mum is going to give me another DS as a replacement or as well as the other 2.

Gabriel is a man we met in Namibia who has glasses and went to the desert in Namibia for 2 nights at a house.

I was happy about Uganda because it had McDonalds and KFC. I had a bad cough and bad sneeze for no more than 1 or 2 weeks. I got a fever for 2 days and I had being in Red Chilli for 9 days.

I met a guy named Mike who lives in Windhoek and I went to his house.

I have being in most rooms in Chameleon backpackers.

Overall, I liked South Africa the best.

On our last day at Red Chilli, before leaving for Murchison Falls, a sweet lady from the kitchen handed me the coffee I had ordered. 'How is your Sam?' she asked.

I smiled. 'He is all better now, thank you.'

'Ay-eh, he is a good boy. We are praying for him.'

It was four months to the day since we'd arrived in Africa. Cape Town seemed like years ago. It was time to get moving again.

CHAPTER 28

The greatest waterfall
of the Nile

We were on our way north, to Murchison Falls National Park. Not so long ago the north of Uganda had been a place governments issued travel warnings about. The problems had begun in the late 1980s with the rise of the Lord's Resistance Army (LRA), led by chief wing-nut Joseph Kony.

The Christian militia has the supposed *raison d'être* of establishing a state run on the principles of the Ten Commandments, but in reality the LRA is a bunch of thugs bent on rape and murder, with no identifiable political program or ideology. In the 1990s, the LRA received support from the Sudanese government, in retaliation for the Ugandan government's support of southern Sudanese rebels, who eventually prevailed and established the new country of South Sudan in 2011.

One of the more disturbing tactics of the LRA was to abduct children from schools and villages and use them as sex slaves or child soldiers. Sometimes these children would be forced to attack their own village, often in the frontline, leading to high casualties. Drug use was rife among the fighters, which encouraged risk-taking. Because the child soldiers were easily replaceable, the strategy proved to be militarily successful but brought international outrage, condemnation and, eventually, action.

In 2006, UNICEF estimated the LRA had abducted more than twenty-five thousand children since the conflict began. Millions of people had been displaced trying to flee from the terror they caused, leading to tens of thousands of deaths from disease in refugee camps.

Eventually, with dwindling support, and increasingly isolated from Sudan after the creation of the nation of South Sudan, and renewed international military support for the Ugandan forces, the LRA were driven from Uganda, only to inflict a terrible toll upon the people of the Democratic Republic of Congo. While now numbering only a few hundred fighters, they continue to wreak havoc in central Africa with their own brand of terror.

At Red Chilli, a plaque on the wall had brought the terrible conflict a little closer to home. English expat Steve Willis, who set up the original Red Chilli with his wife, Debbie, was killed by LRA rebels in 2005. He was responding to a distress call from a group of explorers in Murchison Falls National Park when he was ambushed and shot in the heart. Debbie was pregnant with their second child at the time.

Uganda was wet and green. It had rained at least once every day we'd been here. Storms bracketed periods of searing sunshine. Our van dodged the *boda bodas* and minibuses in the driving rain, until it eventually unshackled itself from the crazy Kampala chaos and we were free, on the road again. I realised that we had never actually made it to the now-legendary McDonald's of Kampala. Sam had never pushed the issue. I think he'd just liked the idea that the city was sophisticated enough to be home to the golden arches. Which was fortunate, as I found out later that Mike and Lenneke had been mistaken and there wasn't one at all.

Sam made his presence felt early on the bus trip. 'Excuse me, driver, how long is the drive?'

'About six and a half hours.'

'I don't want it to be that long. That's too long.'

The driver, Juma, looked confused.

One of the other passengers, a special-needs teacher from Liverpool, tried to help. 'How long do you want it to be?' she asked Sam. 'About two hours?'

'Let's make it unknown,' he said.

'Okay,' she agreed, 'unknown.'

Actually, the time flew. Uganda's bitumen roads were way better than those of Malawi, so Sam could read his Kindle, I could write on the computer and we could chat with new friends. It was now a familiar pattern for me: the slow dawning among our fellow travellers of what we were doing, the realisation of the challenges Sam posed, but also his innate charm and humour. Given time, people like Sam—they can't really help it.

We left the bitumen and turned onto a road of sodden paprika-coloured clay, sprinkled with puddles. By the road were baboons, vervet monkeys and warthogs. We passed small villages built of the same paprika-coloured clay as the road. Kilanyi Primary School's road sign exhorted people to SUFFER NOW, ENJOY TOMORROW. Corn, sugar cane, banana, coffee, spear grass, cassava. Pawpaw, jackfruit and mango trees. Small mosques, small churches, small communities.

Wet and green. The forest thickened and the canopy closed. As we drove through the Budongo Forest, home to the chimpanzee, we could see no more than ten metres into the East African mahogany, impenetrable and seemingly endless. The forest cleared into woodlands, still dense, still wet, still green.

We reached our second great river of the trip, the Nile. An English maths teacher on the bus turned to Sam. 'Sam, the Nile is the longest river in the world. It is 6,700 kilometres long.'

'If you were going one hundred kilometres per hour it would take you sixty-seven hours,' Sam said.

'Yes, I suppose it would,' she said, surprised.

Our minibus pulled up to a clearing next to the river above the falls. Time for a quick guided walk. The humidity was oppressive and we were soon lathered in sweat. This was the Victorian Nile, the section between its origin at Lake Victoria and Lake Albert, its waters tumbling off away from us down the valley below the falls.

At Murchison Falls, the churning white water of the Victoria Nile, a hundred or so metres across, compresses through a six-metre gap between two obdurate pillars of granite before, under intense pressure, spraying a giant upside down geyser into the river sixty metres below. In terms of pressure, Murchison is the most powerful waterfall in the world. The group peered down into the void, speculating that the force would probably tear a body apart. Sam didn't like that idea. Neither did I.

Our guide picked up that Sam needed close supervision near the cliff line; Africa doesn't usually believe in safety barriers. I gripped Sam's hand and steered him away from the edge.

We headed for camp. Sam was tired after a day of travelling and I was worried about how he would behave.

'I don't want a tent,' he declared.

I knew where *this* was going. 'There is no other option, Sam.'

Before I could explain further, he replied loudly, 'No! You fuck off! I am not going in a tent.'

That got the attention of the fifty or so people in the reception area.

Sam stomped around the tables and chairs, pointing at me. 'I want a better father. I will sleep here, in reception.'

I let him be and just followed at a distance. We missed the orientation talk but the others filled me in soon enough. Apparently warthogs frequently grazed around the tents, baboons stole anything edible that was not locked up and hippos wandered around at night.

It came time to allocate the tents, which were actually safari tents—permanent cabin-style—with two single beds in each. I managed to get Sam to have a look, and he immediately calmed down.

After Sam had chilled for a while, I called, 'Sam, come out of the tent, you'll get a surprise.'

He came out and laughed. 'It's Pumbaa!' Three warthogs were grazing just outside the tent entrance, completely indifferent to our presence.

The next morning we crossed the upper Nile at dawn so that we could reach the game drive early when the most animals were about. Because there was no power in the tent, I hadn't given Sam his medications, including his ADHD medication—it would have been too hard to organise in the dark. My headlight torch was on the long list of items lost on the trip.

The diesel-powered car ferry chugged across the smooth waters below the falls. On the other side of the river the landscape was dramatically different. The dense forest disappeared and soft waist-high grasses covered undulating hills, stippled with thornbushes, acacias and palms.

The wildlife was jumping everywhere, and so was Sam. Then we both jumped when we got bitten by tsetse flies, which inflict a nasty pinch-like sting but fortunately for us no longer carried sleeping sickness, at least not where we were. When the fly is carrying the disease, the bite erupts into a red sore and, a few weeks later, swollen lymph glands, headaches, muscle pains and irritability ensue. It can advance to the brain and cause confusion, slurred speech, seizures and difficulty walking and talking. All this can progress over years and, if not treated, it's fatal. It used to be endemic to Uganda but was now limited to other parts of Africa.

Sam announced to the bus: 'I've been bitten by a titty fly!'

I clarified. 'That's tsetse, not titty, Sam.'

Sam also wouldn't stop talking: Harry Potter, girls, impersonations of animals and different races, Malawian children, Harry Potter, girls. I hoped he wasn't going to annoy our fellow travellers, but they seemed to be taking his chatter and chaos in their stride. We continued to be blessed with such impressive groups of people on the tours we'd joined.

The game drive was pumping. There are over seven hundred species of birds in Murchison, and it seemed like we saw most of them, along with all the big game like giraffes, elephants, baboons, the list goes on. Charlie, a young Englishwoman currently employed in an orphanage in Kampala, had worked in a wild animal park in the United Kingdom for six years and was helping the guide decipher animal tracks on the dirt road. She was christened Tracker Charlie by the the other passengers.

As we all climbed out of the bus I noticed Sam pat Tracker Charlie on the bum. 'Sam, don't do that!' I yelled.

He flashed a sheepish smile. 'Sorry.'

Tracker Charlie shrugged and smiled as she walked onto the ferry.

I made sure Sam knew that was inappropriate. 'You go over to Charlie and apologise.'

He walked over and said sorry, giving her a hug. As he was hugging her, he sneaked a kiss on her cheek.

'Sam!'

Charlie laughed. 'Don't worry, that's the highlight of the day!'

That afternoon, the group was due to take a boat tour to the falls, seventeen kilometres upstream from the campsite. I wondered if I was overstretching Sam and hesitated about whether we should go. I knew Sam found these activities draining, but we were here to make a change, so I cracked on and took him.

But Sam did well. He was interested by all the wildlife on the banks, and all the travellers in the boat too. Giraffe, baboons and warthogs cautiously walked around the buffaloes and hippos on the banks. A large yellow-billed heron tiptoed her long legs through the shallows of a tributary, in the gaze of a Nile crocodile; pied kingfishers flicked and chirped in and out of their nests buried in holes in the mud of the riverside cliffs.

'Honk, honk. Mhree-ha.' Sam continued to imitate the hippos and elephants. He was getting quite good.

The open boat toiled upstream. As we approached the falls, dirty froth speckled the surface like ice on an Arctic sea, a product of the force of Murchison. The famous last line of F. Scott Fitzgerald's *The Great Gatsby* came to mind as we worked up the fast-flowing river: 'So we beat on, boats against the current, borne back ceaselessly into the past.' We rounded the same curve that, in 1864, Sir Samuel Baker and his wife had plied in two dugout canoes. He finally solved the mystery of the source of the Nile by connecting the placid river entering Lake Albert with the wild rapids of the river that left Lake Victoria above. Baker described his discovery:

> The roar of the river was extremely loud, and after sharp pulling for a couple of hours, during which time the stream increased, we arrived at a point where the river made a slight turn. Upon rounding the corner a magnificent sight burst suddenly upon us. On either side of the river were beautifully wooded cliffs rising abruptly to a height of about 300 feet; rocks were jutting out from the intensely green foliage; and rushing through a gap that cleft the rock exactly before us, the river, contracted from a grand stream, was pent up in a narrow gorge of scarcely 50 yards in width, roaring furiously through the rock-bound pass it plunged in one leap of about 120 feet perpendicular into a dark abyss below. The fall of water was snow white, which had a superb effect as it contrasted with the dark cliffs that walled the river, while the graceful palms of the tropics and wild plantains perfected the beauty of the view.
>
> This was the greatest waterfall of the Nile, and in honour of the distinguished President of the Royal Geographic Society I named it the Murchison Falls.

Now, the boat abutted a rocky outcrop on the river, as close as it was safe to go, and we took it all in, the eddies and whirls around the boat shaking our craft.

Back down the river, the current was now our ally. Quietness enveloped the boat. We were all lost in our thoughts, the jungle drifting past in the late afternoon haze. Near our landing site stood a large herd of elephants, drinking and bathing on the bank, spraying water over their backs and under their ears and sides with their trunks, babies hiding under mothers, a matriarch and a bull watching us closely.

Murchison had been an unforgettable experience, but not as unforgettable as it had been for Ernest Hemingway. In 1960, the Nobel Prize–winning writer decided to take his fourth wife on a flying holiday across Africa, which included a flight over Murchison Falls. Hemingway, an experienced pilot, clipped an old telegraph pole and crashed his plane into the jungle on the banks of the Nile. Sustaining non-life-threatening but painful injuries, they spent the night trying to avoid dangerous animals before being rescued in the morning by boat, coincidentally the same boat used in the film *The African Queen*.

While attempting to fly back to Entebbe, this time piloted by a local, the plane crashed and burned on take-off. This time Hemingway sustained more serious injuries, including a ruptured liver, a burnt scalp and a fractured skull, the last when he head-butted his way out of the plane. It was reported in the West that he had died, and he spent his convalescence reading his own obituaries.

On the way back to Kampala, our tour visited a rhino sanctuary. Rhinoceroses had been previously found throughout Murchison and other areas of Uganda but during the conflicts of the Amin era and battles with the LRA, soldiers had funded their activities by poaching rhino and elephant and hunting other animals for bush meat. The wildlife of Uganda was devastated, and rhinos were completely wiped out. The sanctuary, breeding rhinos imported from Kenya and the United States, hoped to build up its population to a level that would allow them to start reintroducing them into Murchison within ten to fifteen years.

When we arrived we had to order lunch. The easiest option for Sam was chicken and potato, a meal he would normally tolerate, but for some reason today he chucked a wobbly about it as we were being told about the walking tour of the rhino sanctuary. It was bad timing.

The owner of the sanctuary came over. 'Are you sure this is safe with your son? These are wild animals.'

I nodded and reassured him.

'He mustn't run away, you know. There are protocols to follow if the rhino's body language changes,' he said.

'Yes, I know, I'll make sure he understands,' I said. But I did wonder about it.

We were told there were three options if a rhino charged towards you: hide behind a tree, hide behind bushes or climb a tree. This didn't seem to be an encouraging set of options, but apparently rhinos have very poor vision and if they can't see you they'll stop charging. They are more likely to see a moving target. I rammed this information home to Sam repeatedly, as well as the importance of not making noise.

The group walked in single file, with a ranger at the front, a ranger at the back, and Sam behind me. Within five minutes we clapped eyes on two adult females grazing. I was amazed at how close we could get, within ten metres. It was breathtaking, exhilarating, uplifting. Sam behaved perfectly, his face lit up in awe at the beautiful creatures.

Back on the bus, the tour group was abuzz, comparing photos and teasing each other about who was most frightened. I think it was me. It sure wasn't Sam. Juma, our guide and driver, sat Sam up next to him on the three-hour drive back to Kampala.

'Hey, Sam, do you know you are a *mzungu*?' Juma said.

'What is a *mzungu?*' Sam said. He didn't know.

'A white person. I am not a *mzungu.* I am black.'

'You are Sirius Black,' Sam said smiling.

'What?'

It was difficult to explain to Juma that Sirius Black was Harry Potter's godfather. Juma persisted, repeatedly trying to start up conversations with Sam on the way back, teasing him by pointing out short-haired African children, one of Sam's phobias, or *wazungu* in the crowded streets, and various other sights and oddities.

He reminded me of Gabriel back in Namibia. This was the type of interaction I felt was perfect for Sam. A personable guy from a completely different culture trying his hardest to communicate with my boy in an unfamiliar and unpredictable environment. Gold.

CHAPTER 29

Let's get lost

We were back at our Uganda base, Red Chilli, with its wi-fi, pizza, pool, clean rooms and hot showers. We were back to schoolwork and neuroplasticity. Murchison had helped me emerge from my doldrums after losing Sam's DS, and I was now feeling more positive and less homesick. My mood seemed to be up and down a lot, but I supposed that came with hard travel, and I'd added a child with autism into the mix. It also seemed like the end of the trip was rushing up at us, like a rhino with threatening body language. I felt panicked about doing as much as I could with Sam before we had to go home.

On the evening we returned, our group from the recent tour gathered poolside for pizza and a drink. Once again, Sam blurted out an insulting remark about a woman's appearance. I was furious, and after demanding he apologise, dragged him away to read the riot act. He should have known better. He became angry, and physical, squeezing my head and then slowly butting it with his, and he refused my requests to return to the table and behave civilly. I walked away, recognising our pattern of overstretching him and then watching him lose the plot. I knew I was partially responsible given I was pushing him to his limits, but he would get a four out of ten tomorrow. This would take his tally down to two eights in a row, safely distant from the magic seven he needed to return to Australia.

I was relieved to Skype Benison the next morning, after being isolated in the boondocks for a few days. After the Murchison trip I was feeling more positive, but unfortunately she was not. Our absence, financial stresses and life in Sydney in the middle of winter were getting her down. Her mother was also unwell. But most of all I suspected, reading between the lines, that she had concluded that while Sam was making progress it was of the subtle, not profound, kind. The magic bullet outcome, while always a long shot, was not going to happen. In autism improvement is invariably incremental. Intellectually we knew that, but I guess we both still couldn't help hoping.

And then that afternoon Sam soared. He played the best game of chess of his life. His boxing, which we hadn't done for over a week because of illness and travel, was outstanding. He told me the combinations he wanted to do and then performed them with power and rhythm. Where did that come from? I couldn't wait to tell Benison.

While we were back in Kampala, Sam and I visited the Butabika National Referral Mental Hospital, which was within walking distance of Red Chilli. I was interested to see how such a facility operated in the developing world, and, if they saw children with autism, what therapy or support was offered. It would also be another experience, another unpredictable activity, for Sam. He was worried we were going to hospital because of the scratch on his arm from a cat he had been pestering, despite my reassurances. Cold calling at a medical facility is awkward, especially when you look the way we did: grubby and frayed. We walked through the large gates and up to the front office. The receptionist was dubious but referred us down the hallway to the equally dubious secretary for the director. I had pre-prepared a typed letter, explaining our backgrounds, the purpose of our trip and why I wanted to visit the children's ward of the hospital. I sat at the large polished desk across from the director while he read my letter, and Sam slumped on a nearby leather lounge chair. In the end the director was very accommodating and arranged a tour of the ward, on the proviso we didn't film the patients, of course.

Sam had his feet up on the coffee table. I scolded him. 'Sam, put your feet down!'

'It's okay, let him be,' the director said.

Sam smiled at him. 'You are an African!' And then, fortunately out of earshot of the doctor, 'He is an African wearing a tie.'

The director referred us to the child and adolescent psychiatrist for the hospital, a no-nonsense woman who showed us around the children's ward. As well as the psychiatric conditions you would expect to see in a developed world mental health facility, they also treated medical conditions that had a neurological, psychological or psychiatric overlay.

These included several patients with epilepsy, which was often poorly treated prior to their presentation here, and also cerebral malaria. Trauma victims and substance abusers might also end up here, but fortunately numbers of the former had reduced in recent years as the conflict in the north resolved. The most common substances abused were alcohol, marijuana and mairungi, or chat, a chewable stimulant widely used across eastern Africa. Domestic violence and abuse victims were also seen here. Any child in Uganda, even one living in a remote village, could be assessed and treated here for free if a referral was considered warranted. I was impressed; medical services in Africa are not all doom and gloom.

Autistic children and adults were seen here, and offered services such as psychology and occupational therapy. The place resembled an Australian hospital from a bygone era: nurses in sky-blue pinafores and caps, patients in ballooning pink gowns, the long Nightingale ward lined with metal-framed beds. Outside were elegant gardens with clipped lawns. Old school, to be sure, but clean, organised and well staffed. Walking along the road back to the gate, I peeked inside the window of a parked ambulance. It looked exactly like the inside of an ambulance should, and I thought of Prince and his barren, equipment-less vehicle back in Malawi.

Back at the Red Chilli lounge room, a young English medical student working up-country was relaying a tale of woe. 'I just nearly got robbed. A big guy standing behind me tapped me on the shoulder and then I noticed his other hand behind my back was lifting my wallet out of the front pocket of my jeans. The only reason I noticed was the corner of the wallet caught on the edge of the pocket.'

'What did you do?' I asked.

'Well, I shouted out and he just dropped the wallet and walked away.'

'Did anyone help you?' I asked.

'No, that's what I couldn't believe, everyone just laughed. In my country if someone is getting robbed people will help you out. It was like they thought it was okay to rob a *mzungu*. Even in the cab back the driver laughed when I told him about it. I mean, I was being robbed and they thought it was funny!'

I was also surprised. In my experience Ugandans were so friendly and relaxed. Maybe, in the eyes of some, the wealth Westerners have is so extreme it's okay to rob them occasionally.

With heavy hearts we left Red Chilli and Kampala for the last time. I would miss the creature comforts, and the staff, as well as the chaotic charm of the city of seven hills, as Kampala was also known. For Sam, leaving was another blow to his hope that the blue DS would still turn up. I had to reassure him that if they did find it, they had my email so that we could arrange for it to be forwarded to us.

A driver dropped us at the minibus station, giving me the three-step African handshake I was finally getting used to: a shake, a grip and a shake. To me, the prolonged handshake was a reflection of how important greeting each other and treating each other with respect seemed to be in so many African cultures.

We were out again into the Ugandan countryside, wet and green. *Let's go get lost, Sam. Let's go get lost.* Trucks bore pine-apples, melons and giant hands of green bananas. There were papyrus-lined wetlands, rainforest-covered mountains. Sam and I were deep in our own thoughts. Corn and cane, sunshine and rain.

Being the tallest person on the bus, I was moved from the back to sit up next to the driver so more children and bags could be squeezed onto more laps in the rear. While the view was better, I wasn't at all sure I wanted to see it. Our driver operated on the disconcerting rationale that overtaking while an oncoming truck was approaching was not a problem as the truck would always make room. They did, and on we went.

At a roadside stop, the bus was accosted by a gang of hagglers carrying bowls of roasted bananas, cooked chicken on skewers and soft drinks in crates. The produce was thrust through windows and waved under noses. A man seated behind me tapped me on the shoulder, babbling about Fanta.

I waved him away. 'No, I don't want any.'

He persisted. 'Your son has taken a Fanta. You need to pay.'

I spun around and eyeballed my son, who was avoiding my gaze. 'Sam, you know no fizzy drinks in the morning.'

He pretended not to hear me as he sculled the drink. He would pay in points the next day, but secretly I liked it when Sam planned a deception; it requires a certain level of social sophistication to circumvent the agenda of another person. He was thinking about how I was thinking, and using strategy to deal with it. It was un-autistic.

We cruised into Jinja, the city astride the origin of the Nile. Its streets were full of noise and traffic and bustle under decaying colonial architecture. The minibus crossed a large bridge that spanned the river above a hydro-electric dam. In the Amin era, soldiers used to throw victims off the bridge here, and elsewhere, to be eaten by crocodiles. This allegedly included four thousand disabled people whom Amin didn't feel deserved to live. Terrible images assaulted my thoughts when I heard this. I told Sam and it disturbed him as well. There was no point shielding him from the truth. If I wanted him to become worldlier I had to expose him to the truth, both good and bad. Sam was relieved to hear Amin was eventually overthrown and died in exile. Thus always to tyrants.

Jinja is billed as the adventure capital of Uganda. Our entertainment options included white-water rafting, kayaking, bungy jumping and horse-riding. The white-water rafting features some of the wildest rapids in the world as the river charges down to Murchison, eighty kilometres of rough and tumble. I thought, what the heck, and booked Sam and me to go horse-riding and then rafting over the next two days. When I mentioned this to Benison, she was okay about the horse-riding, but nearly had a fit about the white-water rafting. She was terrified Sam wouldn't cope or that he would get injured or worse, but I persisted. I wanted him to do it.

Our accommodation outside Jinja sat on a ridge with dramatic views down to the great river. We'd arrived on *boda bodas* from the minibus station relatively early in the day, and with several hours of daylight still remaining were able to fit in some schoolwork and neuroplasticity exercises.

In her 2013 book, *The Autistic Brain*, Temple Grandin explained her discovery that, contrary to what she once believed, not all people on the spectrum think in pictures like she does, that in fact there are actually three types of dominant thinking patterns. In an article in *The Smithsonian* she describes it thus:

In addition to visual thinking, there is pattern thinking and word thinking. Each of the three types of thinking is a continuum. People without autism may have some specialization, but people with autism are often on the extreme end of a continuum . . . A pattern-thinking child typically has great ability in math and difficulty reading.

In recent years it had become apparent to Benison and me that Sam was a pattern thinker. A complicated mathematical theory would be picked up quickly, yet this was combined with a below-average verbal IQ. He is also naturally adept at reading music, and has the rare and disconcerting ability of perfect pitch; if Sam hears a note played on a piano or guitar he instantly knows which it is. While listening to a piece of music, he can correctly label which chords are being played. Even a car horn or a siren can be identified as a note. It's weird but also, as his brothers would point out, kind of cool.

For a pattern thinker such as Sam, chess seemed a natural fit, and now he was rapidly improving. I allowed myself to occasionally win games, in order for him to develop the altogether more difficult skill of losing gracefully, but as his chess ability improved wins proved more difficult for me to orchestrate. That afternoon, as part of our schoolwork, I set him the task of writing about chess.

This is the description of chess.

They are 16 pawns, 4 knights, 4 bishops, 4 rooks, 2 queens and 2 kings.

Chess was invaded [sic] in the UK. A pawn can move 1 or 2 platforms straight and can take 1 piece sideways. A knight can jump of a shape of a capital L and can take 1 piece if it does that. A bishop can go any sideways but only on the certain colour and can take 1 piece. A rook can go anywhere straight and can take 1 piece. A Queen can use both the rook and the bishop's moves and can take 1 piece if it is able for the Queen to move on the platform.

A King is the most important and it is nearly impossible to be taken and can use the Queen's moves except it can only move 1 square but it can take any piece and if other that are able to take the king it is check and if it is worse and it's checkmate and game over.

Checkmate is a bad thing it is game over and you can lose when you are in checkmate.

Overall I love chess because it is fun.

And that was from a boy who had never played chess before we left Australia.

The next day we had another game. Sam was more determined and had me on the ropes. He refused to enforce the checkmate that was available to him, insisting on taking every single piece before trapping the king instead.

'You're annihilating me!' I complained.

Sam had a big grin. 'I am the enforcer.'

Playing cards was not going as well. The complexity of Five Hundred was proving too much for him, so I decided to teach him a few simpler games that still involved some strategy, like Twenty-One and poker. As had proved to be the case so many times earlier in the trip, I was constantly having to adapt and adjust my approach to Sam and the challenges I was setting him, based on how well he responded. The intervention was a work in progress.

CHAPTER 30

Playing Quidditch

S am was going to ride a horse for the first time.

   When I first mentioned our planned African adventure to a fellow parent of an autistic child back home in Australia, she joked, 'You're not going all *Horse Boy* on us, are you, James?'

The Horse Boy was a *New York Times* bestselling book in 2009, which also became a documentary. It chronicled the horse-riding journey of Rupert Isaacson, his wife, and their then five-year-old autistic son, Rowan, through Mongolia to seek the help of shamans. I think even the author now acknowledges that the benefits Rowan accrued on the journey were more due to horse-riding than any mysticism.

In her review of the book, Temple Grandin (again) explained it best:

> Children with autism need to be exposed to lots of interesting things and new experiences in order to develop. One of the reasons the trip to Mongolia was so beneficial was that Rowan could explore lots of fascinating things such as horses, streams, plants, and animals in an environment that was QUIET. The

Mongolian pastureland was a quiet environment free of the things that overload the sensory system of a child with autism . . .

Horseback riding is a great activity. Many parents have told me that their child spoke his/her first words on a horse. Activities that combine both rhythm and balancing such as horseback riding, sitting on a ball, or swinging help stabilize a disordered sensory system.

There is a small but growing body of research around hippo-therapy—the technical term for therapeutic horse-riding—and its social, emotional and physical benefits in autism. Sam had already had enough 'hippo' therapy elsewhere in Africa but here in Uganda we were offered the opportunity for our own horse-boy experience; another chance to push the boundaries of his world a little bit further.

A small group from the hostel hopped onto a small boat to cross the river, while red-tailed and vervet monkeys leapt about the acacia and umbrella trees on the steep clay banks. A Cape clawless otter launched off some nearby rocks into the turquoise water as our launch chugged to the stables. We were given a talk on safety and put on helmets. 'I look like an American footballer,' Sam observed.

As we clambered onto our mounts, the owner of the horse-riding facility, who happened to be a fellow Australian, was very particular about making sure Sam was safe. He suggested one of his instructors walk with him 'just in case'. I wasn't sure if this was necessary—sometimes the line between safety and overprotection can be a fuzzy one—but I went along with the safe option.

It turned out the walking instructor wasn't necessary, but that was easy to say in hindsight. The horses took us through the local village and farms, with subsistence plots of corn, yams, banana, coffee, jackfruit and cassava. Children ran out of mud-brick houses and yards to greet us on the side of the thin track, some naked, most not, but all smiling and waving. Girls carried babies. Teenage boys jostled each other and looked at us with half-smiles and puffed chests. A woman chopped wood. An old woman, stooped over her stick, held up her hand and said, *'Jumbo, mzungu.'* 'Hello, white people.'

Our path arced back towards the steep riverbanks before looping back up to the stables. Sam was happy with his horse. He'd been told the horse's name was Jack Daniels, but Sam had decided to rename him Bullseye. Bullseye was cowgirl Daisy's horse in the *Toy Story* movies. Fortunately, Sam didn't start riding him in the same manner as Daisy rode her steed.

Back at the stables, we lingered for a chat with the Australian owner, T.J., who'd originally been a surfer from Newcastle. I quizzed him about where he believed Africa was heading. 'Do you think they can ever break the cycle of corruption?'

'I can't see it happening soon.'

I was surprised. 'Why not?'

'It's so entrenched, and so part of their culture. In the villages, they have so little that even favours are like a currency; everyone keeps a tab on who owns what, who has done favours for who and whose tribe you are in. Those that make money or get into positions where they can corruptly obtain money are expected to get what they can out of it and pay back those they owe and favour those who they're aligned with.'

I wanted Africa's outlook to be better, more optimistic. 'But there are large parts of the continent that have come a long way. Look what has happened in Uganda over the last twenty years.'

'Sure, and long may it continue. But it's still the way that if you get power you use it to your advantage, and if you don't work or do your job properly there is no accountability, especially in government. It all comes down to education. People talk about corruption, but the corruption is there because there aren't enough educated people who can either hold those in power accountable or offer an alternative way, an alternative employee, an alternative candidate.'

Benison had been so concerned when I'd told her about our plans for white-water rafting. 'Sam and white-water rafting . . . Are you sure that's wise?'

As we drifted across the still, steel-blue waters, slowly approaching the roaring rapids, now audible but not yet visible, my eyes widened and my heart thumped and I began to wonder if my wife had been right. Fortunately, I'd opted for Sam and me to go in the safety boat. There were twenty other *wazungu* in our group, most of whom were in rafts, and a few on kayaks, either by themselves or in tandem with a guide. We'd received thorough instructions from the guide while still on shore and I was confident that Sam understood what to do if we did fall out of the boat, but still . . .

I looked at him, perched on the front rim of the raft. 'Sam, are you nervous?'

'No,' he said, without hesitation.

'I am.'

The safety boat was steered by another Moses, this one being the head guide, using two long oars fixed on each side of the large inflatable raft. A metal frame steadied the centre of the raft, adding sturdiness. Moses alternated sitting on a raised seat or standing in the middle of the frame. Sam and I, his only passengers, sat on the inflated rim at the front, but we were instructed to sit down on the floor when things got bumpy and hang onto a safety rope on the outside of the rim. On the other rafts, six passengers and one guide each had a paddle and manned the outside of the craft.

The safety boat would negotiate the softer parts of the rapids, while the other rafts would go where the action was greatest. Eight sets of rapids spread over twenty-five kilometres of the Nile River sat below us. As we approached the first edge, Moses told us to sit down on the floor and hang on.

The raft tilted over the edge of the first set of falls. A dramatic set of rapids, plunging up to two metres at a single drop but over twenty metres in length, lay below us.

'I don't want to go down there!' Sam yelled and stood up to jump over the side.

Moses and I both screamed for him to sit down. Hanging onto the rope with one hand as we fell, I lurched and grasped at the bottom of Sam's life jacket as he attempted to jump out of the plunging raft. Moses also grabbed Sam by the shoulder, abandoning one of his oar handles to do so, and we secured him just as we landed at the bottom of the first of half a dozen wrenching thumps and lurches. Walls of water loomed before us, smashing into our faces, before we'd leap up again, then tilt with ridiculous speed forward and plunge again. It was like, I imagined, riding a rodeo horse, a very wet rodeo horse.

I looked across to Sam, incredulous that he'd tried to jump out.

Sam punched the air. *'I did it!'* What? Over the course of twenty seconds he'd gone from terrified to exhilarated.

The second set of rapids was soon upon us. *Here we go again.* Plunge, thump, lurch, heave, plunge. Over the roar of the waves I heard Sam giggle. Finally we reached some still water.

He beamed. 'We are playing Quidditch!'

I burst into a fit of laughter. Moses joined in, shaking his head, before asking, 'What is Quidditch?'

'He thinks it's like riding on a broomstick,' I explained, as best I could.

A perplexed grin appeared on Moses' face. 'Heh, okay.'

We watched the others come down the rollercoaster we'd just negotiated. After all, we were the safety boat. One raft tipped, all its passengers tumbling down the rapids before being retrieved by the very impressive guides. These guys knew their stuff. I found out several of the guides were in the Ugandan kayak team and were heading to the World Championships in Canada the following month. One of the *wazungu*, an Australian, was kayaking by himself and was also incredibly skilled. He was also off to the World Championships, representing Australia, and was here to get in some practice. The rest of us were in awe of their talents, and several of the women in awe of their physiques.

On we went, gliding over the silky waters stirred by eddies and whirls and draped in the tattered remnants of lilies and reeds ripped from the shore, waiting for the rush towards the next set of rapids. The roar would build, the raft would tilt and down, down, down we'd plunge.

On smooth water once again, it was a little embarrassing just sitting in the safety boat, not having to do the paddling expected of everyone else, but I got over it and laid back and drank in the atmosphere. The Nile was magnificent, with the silver-blue currents cutting between steeply wooded banks where children would jump and wave to us from the shore. Fishermen in dugout canoes plied the waters, and cormorants and yellow-billed storks glided above and beside us. Sam thought the cormorants, with their sinewy necks ducking in and out of the water, looked like the Loch Ness monster. I could see that, but I would just never have thought of it myself.

There were no hippos or crocs above Murchison Falls so in this respect it was safe to be in the water, which was fortunate because every raft was upended at least once. The guides waiting in kayaks would haul them to safety. We approached the last set of rapids, Sam giggling and squealing in anticipation. It was a doozy, but being in the safety boat we descended a section that was calmer than the centre of the rapid.

He pointed to the wild water. 'I want to go over there.'

'No, Sam, we can't. We're in the safety boat and have to go in the easier section so we can help people if needed,' I said.

'But that's more fun over there. I want this to be an event!'

'I think it *is* an event, Sam, that you've been so brave.'

He looked at me, thinking about what had just been said. 'What does *event* mean?'

'It means something special,' I explained.

A wide grin emerged, and he looked across the river. 'Yes, this is an *event*!' The other rafts came down, two out of three capsizing but everyone safe. Sam laughed at their tumbling exits from the craft. He turned to Moses. 'I want there to be more rapids. Let's round it up to ten.'

'No, there is only eight. It is finished now,' Moses replied.

Sam wasn't content with that. 'No, let's round it up to ten. Ten is a more rounded number.'

Moses looked at me, perplexed; I waved to him to ignore it. Half of the troubadours were now in the water in their life vests, swimming or just drifting with the steady current as we approached our landing site.

Sam was watching them closely. 'I want to swim,' he suddenly said.

I was stunned. 'Really?' Was this the same boy who only a month or two earlier had needed the encouragement of three people for ten minutes to jump into Lake Malawi for a few seconds? Now he was all for it.

He jumped into the river and swam alongside our raft for a few hundred metres to the bank. I was feeling pretty damn special. It *had* been an event.

Sam was tired and crabby as we ate the late lunch provided by the raft company and changed out of our wet clothes. I let him be; it had been a big day. The troop piled into the truck that would take us back to the hostel, the group electrified by the experience. Heavy rain whipped the truck, making the deep gutters run with toffee-coloured water, distracting the small children who jumped and splashed in the water instead of giving the ubiquitous wave and 'Hello!' to the passing *wazungu*.

That evening over Skype, Benison was relieved to hear we'd survived and thrilled Sam had gone swimming in the Nile. She said it was just as well I was travelling with Sam rather than her as she just wouldn't have even considered this sort of activity, or taken this type of risk. She was guilty, in her own words, of underestimating Sam's abilities, of being overprotective. We were both aware of the ways those attitudes, however benevolent, could limit him over his life.

Much later, a friend in Australia alerted us to an NPR podcast called *Invisibilia*, and specifically an episode called 'How to become

Batman'. It recounted a famous Harvard psychology experiment from 1963, when psychology students were given rats and told they had been specifically bred for high intelligence, as measured by their ability to navigate mazes. Other students were given rats and told they had been bred for dullness in navigating mazes. The rats, however, had no such breeding; they were ordinary lab rats randomly assigned to the two groups.

The students were asked to teach the rats a range of skills including finding their way through a maze. The result? The 'bright' rats markedly outperformed the 'dull' rats, despite the fact that they shouldn't have. The students, who were unaware they were part of the experiment, were not influencing the rats' performances intentionally; it was their own expectations of the rats that caused the difference between the two groups. In subtle ways—such as how they handled the rats, eye contact, the enthusiasm of their encouragement—the 'bright' rats responded to the higher expectations of their students. It's called the experimenter expectancy effect, or, when observed outside the laboratory in the real world, the Pygmalion effect. This effect has been reproduced consistently in studies since the 1960s, including research showing that a teacher's expectations can influence a student's IQ scores.

The *Invisibilia* episode then went on to describe the experiences of the blind community where a prevailing attitude that 'blind people can't do those things' frequently limits the achievements of the blind by encouraging a sort of 'learned helplessness'.

The prevailing experience was contrasted with the story of Daniel Kish, a man about my age who lives in California. Daniel has been blind almost all his life, after his eyeballs were removed because of cancer when he was an infant, but he's able to confidently navigate the world almost as efficiently as he could if he could see, using echolocation, a self-taught technique of making clicking noises with his tongue and listening to the sound bouncing off objects surrounding him, kind of like sonar. He's like a real life Batman.

Right from the word go, Daniel's mother let her blind but adventurous little boy climb fences and trees, run around playgrounds and parks, and eventually ride a bike, all possible by using his clicking tongue. Yes, she was afraid of him getting injured or worse, and he did come to grief many times, but she was also determined to not let him be dragged down by the stultifying effect of low expectations. She banished her fears, and Daniel thrived.

So ironically, the enemy of high expectations can be love. It is understandable, of course, for parents of children, especially children with disabilities, to be fearful of the dangers of grasping a learning moment. Benison's love for Sam would have prevented her from allowing him to go white-water rafting, but she knew well enough the importance of letting him go, to have allowed the two of us to walk through that airport departure gate in Sydney. With high expectations, remarkable things can occur.

CHAPTER 31

Prayers and chickens

S am and I left the Nile behind and continued north towards Kenya. Taxi, minibus, minibus, *boda boda*; it was a full day of travel. We shared the Kindle, letting life-in-Africa-through-a-minibus-window entertain us while the other was reading. A man stood on a roundabout preaching theatrically about the coming of Jesus to indifferent motorists. A truck laden with sugar cane had tipped into a deep gutter, and twenty men with ropes were attempting to right it. A small boy waved a stick in the face of a bored donkey.

At a minibus station, as the bus was repacked yet again to maximise occupancy, Sam stood outside being gawked at by a group of giggling young girls. I wasn't sure whether it was curiosity or flirting, or both. With his long wavy hair and lanky white limbs he sure stood out from the crowd.

A young blind boy got on the bus, assisted by his father. A woman sitting in front of us carried a chicken in one hand and a small crying infant in the other. The bird was being unceremoniously held upside down by its feet and protesting wildly. It was hard to tell which was making the more noise, the squawking chicken or the bawling infant, but the woman seemed completely unfazed by either.

We had been on enough African minibuses now to understand the way they worked. There is an unspoken set of rules:

- Rule number one: there is *always* room for one more paying passenger.
- The bus never leaves until it is full.
- The minibus driver never smiles.
- The conductor never gets on until after the wheels start moving.
- The door is always closed after departure, usually as the bus changes from first to second gear and momentarily loses some momentum.
- *Mzungu* are highly prized. (We can be easily ripped off.)
- The driver's allegiances to religion and football shall be displayed on the rear-vision mirror and dashboard, and painted on the outside of the bus.
- If the horn breaks the driver shall have an existential crisis.
- Something on the bus must be broken.
- There is always a chicken, and occasionally a goat.

Our second minibus conductor for the day had agreed to an amount in advance to take us to our destination, Sipi Falls. As per usual, I didn't understand what was going on, and the bus didn't actually go to Sipi Falls, only to the *turn-off* to Sipi Falls. The conductor did, however, arrange for a *boda boda* to take us the last twelve kilometres up the hill as part of the fare. The problem was he only paid for one.

The driver jumped on, sitting as far forward as he could with a backpack on top of the handlebars. I climbed on behind him with one daypack in each hand, and Sam sat behind me, wearing another pack. The small bike struggled and spluttered with its load of three humans, two backpacks and two daypacks. It was a long twelve kilometres. Finally we arrived at Sipi.

As we dismounted the *boda boda* driver began arguing that he had only been paid for one passenger, not two. I suspected he was scamming us, and a long discussion ensued between him, me and the ubiquitous gaggle of people that forms whenever one gets on or off any form of transportation in Africa.

We compromised and I ended up paying for an extra half-person. Whatever. I was totally over another exhausting day on the road. Our accommodation had remarkable views of the falls, which sat at nearly two thousand metres altitude. It was nice to not have to worry so much about mosquitoes, which were uncommon at this elevation. Unfortunately, the remoteness of the location of our hotel meant no access to the internet and no power in the room, apart from the room light. Considering we had been planning to spend a few days here I knew Sam would not be happy.

Adding to this, Heiress Films had been trying to send me some extra equipment for the new camera and I'd arranged for it to be delivered to Sipi. Then I discovered, after a twenty-minute *boda boda* ride to the nearest internet cafe to read my emails, that it wouldn't arrive for another five days. This would not do. I found a hotel with wi-fi access in the nearby small city of Kapchorwa, and arranged for the delivery to be redirected there. I had already paid for another night in Sipi Falls, but we could transfer to Kapchorwa the day after that. Our new destination had nothing to offer a tourist apart from wi-fi, but at least we could focus on schoolwork and neuroplasticity exercises while we waited for our parcel to arrive.

This meant we now had only one day in Sipi Falls. A friendly guide, Alex, took us in the morning for a walking tour of the falls. While they were picturesque, we were becoming hard to impress after the spectacles of Victoria and Murchison.

Sam was having a bad morning. I had forgotten to give him his ADHD medication, for the third time on the trip. Given I am such a muddle-headed wombat, I thought that was pretty good going.

Fifteen minutes into our walk with Alex my mistake became evident as Sam, wired to the max, zipped along on the road in front of us, shooting the small children who greeted us with his finger. He wouldn't stop talking about 'Malawi children'. The walking tour was becoming a walking battle. My frustration boiled over. 'Sam, stop talking about the children!'

'But they are clones. They are bald clones.' For some reason he objected to the sparse curls of most of the local children.

'You've already said that five times. You don't need to keep saying it.'

'Okay,' he replied, but then two minutes later, 'I don't like the children.'

'Sam!' I yelled. And around and around it went.

This obsession had been growing ever since he'd been chased around the preschool on Likomo Island on Lake Malawi. It was now in full flower. Their 'baldness', their eagerness to engage with him and the fact he felt they looked too similar were the subjects of his incessant ruminations. This Is Autism.

We cut the tour short and returned to the hostel, where I quickly administered the forgotten medicine.

A few hours later we embarked on our second activity of the day, a tour of a local coffee farm to see how coffee is grown and processed. The farm was mainly a subsistence farm but also grew coffee and bananas as cash crops, with the produce usually exported to South Sudan.

The difference the medication made was stark; Sam was much easier to handle and also much more capable of getting something out of the afternoon. Alex showed us the plantation where the coffee beans were ripening, and then took us through the process of shucking, drying, pounding, roasting, grinding, and then brewing, pouring and tasting. Sam and I had hands-on experience of doing it all; it was a great education. After the morning I'd had, I needed the coffee too.

Sam, once again, was the centre of attention, surrounded by children. The largest of them, two fourteen-year-old boys, looked tough enough to be touting AK-47s if they'd lived in more conflict-riddled parts of Africa, but they were likely half Sam's weight. Sam's tolerance of the circle of children following him was now much greater; Gulliver surrounded by the Lilliputians.

On the way back to the hotel, we passed through a grassed schoolyard nestled among the banana trees and coffee bushes. Alex pointed to a boy sitting next to a toilet block on the edge of the yard. 'See him? He has the same problem as Sam.'

'He's autistic?'

Alex nodded. 'But he doesn't speak like Sam. He can do everything though. He helps with the farm work, he does some schoolwork. He helps out a lot.'

It brought me back to the contextual nature of disability. In this environment, social and communication deficits in an adolescent didn't stand out as profoundly as in a world of social media, selfies and texting, a world that was starting to seem a galaxy away. I'd begun to wonder whether it was the developed world that had it wrong. I thought of all the lost potential, of the untapped skills and intelligence that often comes with autism. Lacking the requisite social and communication skills to fit in, people with autism are often dismissed as 'disabled' and useless. Here a non-verbal autistic boy had found his place in society.

The language the locals used when referring to Sam's autism was also illuminating, and at times confronting. When I told them Sam had special needs, frequently the reply would be, 'Oh, I'm sorry' or, 'That's a shame'. There was no sugar coating. At home, these sorts of utterances would have been considered politically incorrect.

Yet it seemed to me to be more honest. There was a different way of thinking about people with special needs in Africa, one that seemed more accepting and inclusive. It was what it was. In the developed world, we're at best uncomfortable with disability, at worst intolerant. We're fed the myth that perfection is possible and disability is an affront to that, one that must be wallpapered over or railed against. Here, while they were 'sorry' for me, or said it was a 'shame' for Sam, I was also frequently told, especially by the women, that Sam was a 'lovely boy' and that he had 'a good heart'.

Another point of difference I was becoming aware of was the response of Westerners and Africans to what Sam and I were attempting to achieve on our trip. People from developed countries, both at home and those we met on the road in Africa, would regard our adventure as a great undertaking by Benison and me. 'Wow, that's amazing! Good on you guys,' was the invariable response. Africans were more focused on Sam: 'How is he going? What can he do? What can't he do? Would he like to come with me and do something together?'

It wasn't that the Westerners were not appreciative or supportive of Sam; it was just a different focus. I'm not sure why. Was it because disability seems so much more common, so much more in your face in Africa? And where there was disability, usually there wasn't much one could do about it but just get on with things.

The next day we transferred to the fancypants hotel in Kapchorwa. After walking down the driveway at Sipi Falls, we waited on the side of the quiet road with our packs. As usual, a group of people gathered around us. A fellow with a blinded eye asked us where we were going. 'Kapchorwa is a big town,' he said, when I told him. He scanned us as we sat on our packs. 'Are you happy to go in a truck?'

'Yeah, sure.'

'You may have trouble getting a lift today. It is market day and the road is quiet,' he explained in his lilting Ugandan accent. I would've thought market day would make the road busier, but there you go.

He held up a bulging plastic bag. 'Do you want to buy some coffee beans?'

'No, thanks. I don't want to carry more stuff in my backpack.'

A big grin crossed his face. 'No problem, ayee.' Eventually they flagged down a truck for us and waved goodbye. Sam and I flung our packs and ourselves on top of a pile of grain sacks and held onto the open frame with the other six African farm workers in the back as we barrelled up the road. The Africans sang in perfect harmony as we ascended the winding pot-holed road. The trip cost us a dollar.

Kapchorwa was a typical provincial African city of about twenty thousand people but with over a hundred thousand in the surrounding district. It boasted three sister hotels: the upmarket VIP one we were booked into, one that was middle of the range, and a motel on the main road where a sign proudly proclaimed NOAH'S ARK MOTEL—AVERAGE ACCOMODATION AND MEALS.

The tallest buildings were two stories high, and small business was the only business in town. The shops were cement-rendered recesses, mostly empty except for drowsy shop attendants and a scattering of whatever produce the owner had been able to muster. On the large cement stairs off the deep roadside gutters, young men clutched mobile phones held together with sticky tape, and the elderly and the dishevelled lolligagged with nothing to do and all day to do it. Concrete and clay; loiter and pray. Telcos and banks monopolised the hand-painted advertising, *boda bodas* and pushbike taxis dominated the roads, and machine-gun toting guards were an intimidating presence outside bank branches.

In the suburbs, the roads were dirt and the buildings mud brick, both with the same dusty maroon pigmentation. Some boys teased a frog near the reed-filled creek that dissected the town, while girls in ragtag clothing washed hessian sacks of carrots next to a small bridge over the dirty stream.

I got my hair cut and beard trimmed at Alice's Hair Salon, where they specialised in 'styling, cutting and sanity'. While I did indeed feel and look much saner after the haircut, I think they meant sanitisation. The hairdressers weren't used to cutting *mzungu* hair, so they sent out a request for a 'specialist', a fellow from another salon up the road. As he wielded his scissors, the other hairdressers stood around me and watched. Sam, of course, refused to get his hair cut.

The next day we went for a walk around town and Nancy, the manager of the hotel we were staying in, tagged along to show us around. I think she thought we shouldn't be walking unescorted, not because it was unsafe—in fact, Kapchorwa seemed very safe to me—but because we were so much of a novelty we might attract a crowd. Or maybe she just suspected we'd get lost. Sam scooted ahead as we walked along the road.

'Hey-ah, why does he walk so fast?'

'That's just the way he walks.'

'He should slow down. He will hurt himself, ai-ai.'

Nancy had a thick accent and I had to concentrate to understand her. It occurred to me that Africans talk the way they walk: slowly and methodically. Their speech has an even beat, each word and syllable expressed in a steady slow rhythm and followed by an exhaled exclamation that varied between agreement and recognition, such as 'ai', 'eh' or 'ayee'. Once I learnt to listen with the slow chronometer in mind their speech became easier to follow for me. You didn't hear raised voices; no one pressed a point. Their speech was calm and easygoing, for the most part like the people who spoke it.

We walked through the small market, children peering at us from behind windows and doors, past the second-hand clothes laid out on mats; past stalls selling pineapples, avocados, passionfruit and dodo—not the bird, but a spinach-like indigenous African vegetable.

On the way back to the hotel, it occurred to me that not only were we the only *mzungu* in the hotel, as far as I could tell we were the only white people in the city. No wonder everybody stared at us. Later I heard a rumour there was another *mzungu* staying in the mid-range sister hotel. Really? It almost seemed surprising.

On the back streets, hens and chicks flitted through the doorways of tin-roofed houses while goats and cows gnawed the roadside grass within the radius of their rope tether. I told Nancy that you didn't see these animals in the streets of a town in Australia.

She was surprised. 'Why not?'

'They're on farms, not in the towns and cities,' I explained.

She cocked her head in a typically Ugandan way and looked at me. 'But where do you get a chicken if you need to cook one?'

'You go to the supermarket.'

'The big ones with all the bright lights?'

'Yes.' It occurred to me she probably hadn't been in one, or possibly even seen one.

She looked confused. 'They have chickens in there?'

I thought for a moment. 'Dead chickens, not live.'

'Ai-ai,' she said, as she pondered this strange revelation.

I smiled to myself as I imagined my local Woolworths with live chickens running around.

The next day I had organised a trip up to the nearby 4,300-metre Mount Elgon. Simba, the ebullient owner of our hotel who was both pleased and proud that we were staying in his establishment, offered to personally drive us up to the mountain. It was a crisp Sunday morning and church bells and hymns drifted over the city. Nancy and some of the other staff watched me talking to Benison on Skype, fascinated with the technology and that it was evening in Australia. However, nothing was as perplexing as the fact Sam and I were not going to church.

'So you are not going to prayers?' Nancy asked.

Another woman joined in the conversation. 'You are not going to church?'

'Ah, no.' I felt a little awkward.

'The mosque?' Nancy suggested.

I shook my head.

'Then you are a pagan?' the other woman asked.

'No, pagans have gods. I am not very religious.'

Nancy was curious. 'Do you know how to pray?'

'I think I could do it if I wanted to. I prayed when I was young.'

'But not since then.'

'Correct.'

'Ai-ai . . .' Nancy clicked her tongue, smiled and half tilted her braid-covered head as she walked away.

Perhaps we should have gone to church, as the gods were not kind to us that day. As Simba drove us up the hills in his schmick people mover, of which he was immensely proud, weather closed in. He reluctantly closed the sunroof.

The sodden and verdant countryside was prime farmland. The rich red loam soil of the declivitous fields supported a treasure trove of crops. Laterite brick huts spotted the hills. The vehicle bounced along the potholed road, dodging apathetic cows.

Adults and children alike waved to us as we passed. Simba was clearly a local celebrity and his car easily recognised, and added to that, *wazungu* were clearly just not seen in these parts. Their smiles on recognising the vehicle were replaced by expressions of surprise as they spied our two white faces inside. As we reached the gates to the national park surrounding the mighty mountain, the heavens opened up. A walk was out of the question.

Simba invoked plan B. He drove us down to another of his hotels—it was becoming apparent he owned half of the district—and we ordered lunch. Back home in Sydney, if restaurant food took a particularly long time to come, we'd often wryly comment that they must have had to slaughter the cow/chicken/fish before they cooked it.

Well, in Uganda this was true. Two hours after we arrived we were feasting on a poor chicken that had been running around the garden when we'd arrived. I'm not generally used to making eye contact with my lunch, as she was carried into the kitchen past us, wearing a deservedly nervous expression. She did taste good though.

During our long wait for the recently deceased to be plucked, prepared and roasted, I talked history with Sam, given there was nothing else to do. History, geography and art are my go-to school subjects when we have no access to resources other than my own education. We discussed ancient Rome, the Dark Ages (ruled, according to Sam, by Lord Voldemort), the Renaissance, the Industrial Revolution and the British Empire.

When we got back I ran into the other *mzungu* in the city, a Dutchman who was conducting research in sports science and talent identification here. He told me the Kalenjin tribe, whose homelands straddle the Uganda–Kenya border, have a genetic makeup that makes them incredibly good long-distance runners. An Olympic and world champion marathon runner, Stephen Kiprotich, lived just up the hill and knew Simba well, and another runner just outside of the city was a junior world 10,000-metre champion. The genetics combined with the altitude, which allows the body to produce extra red blood cells, bred champions.

That evening, as Sam and I played cards on the verandah, the sounds of the city echoed across the shadowy streets. Bovine groans gave way to shrill insect static, an aural curtain over the chatter and laughter of the shanty-lined lanes. Music and singing soothed the suburbs. I spied Sam drifting off from time to time, sensing the sprinkle of magic emanating from the town. Such a perfect evening.

The next day was our last in Kapchorwa but we were still awaiting our package. An email arrived from FedEx informing me it had reached Entebbe airport but Ugandan customs were demanding to see my passport as proof I had been in Uganda long enough and wasn't using FedEx to smuggle expensive electronic equipment to myself, or something like that; I didn't really understand. I suspected it was about money; that is, they wanted a bribe. Anyway, if I wanted it I had to go all the way back to Entebbe to show customs my passport—and probably slip them twenty US dollars. This would entail three days of hard travel. I told FedEx to send the parcel back to Australia; we would have to do without it.

It was a frustrating day. There was a fourteen-hour-long blackout at the hotel so I had to make four *boda boda* trips to the shops to read my emails at the post office; four because the internet wasn't working there the first three times. We even lost the trusty rubber ball we used for throw and catch when Sam threw it over my head into some thorny bushes.

Worst of all, though, was the drama at the ATM. I'd left Australia with two travel cards and one Visa card. Over the months a travel card and the Visa card had gone missing in action. The stash of US dollars I'd hidden in various places had been depleted. I was down to my last card, with no other way to get money. This was serious.

And then, like a malevolent monster, the ATM in Kapchorwa swallowed my last remaining card. Panic swept over me as I rushed inside to the bank. The bank tellers refused to take me seriously.

This called for drastic action.

I stood in front of the only open teller with my back to the counter and arms out wide, and shouted, 'Nobody gets served until I get my card back!'

The locals looked at me dumbfounded. One of the customers in the queue decided he'd had enough of the crazy *mzungu* and tried to get around me. I blocked his path and yelled, 'I mean it! This is my life we're talking about here. I have to get that card back.'

The guard, him with the gun, looked at the teller and then to another staff member nearby, trying to figure out what to do. After a protracted discussion in Lugandan, they powered down the machine, and finally my precious card was regurgitated.

We had now spent four days in an obscure provincial city for no reason. Yet for me, and also I suspect for Sam, Kapchorwa became a real and entirely unexpected highlight, an unpretentious place with folks who greeted you with open arms and took you for who and what you were and were just, well, genuinely nice.

Still, the shenanigans over the parcel had further diminished my attenuated emotional reserves. It was becoming harder to resist Sam's pleas to return to Australia earlier. We'd also spent a lot more money on the trip than I'd thought we would, and discovered that airfares home to Australia were a lot more expensive in October than September. Benison and I talked it over on Skype and we decided: she booked us to fly out of Dar es Salaam in Tanzania on 30 September, in seven weeks' time, six months to the day since we'd left Sydney. Sam would like that, I knew: six was much more rounded.

I didn't let him know the departure was definite just yet, but hinted it was possible if he tried really hard. He promised he would. You could see his spirits lift, and mine too, I suspect. The revised finishing date now put us over three-quarters of the way through the trip. The flip side was that I had to make the most of the diminishing opportunity for intensive intervention.

CHAPTER 32

The Africa of dreams

We left Noah's Ark VIP Hotel and headed north-east to Kenya. I was sad to leave Uganda, which, despite setbacks with illness, a lost DS and a never-to-arrive parcel, had delivered on its promise—a magical country with wonderful people. In 1907, a young traveller by the name of Winston Churchill had described Uganda as 'the pearl of Africa', a phrase that Ugandans often repeat with deserved pride.

Another big day of travel lay before us. What I had anticipated would be an epic day of three minibus trips and one border crossing was made a little easier at breakfast when Simba kindly offered to drive us an hour or so to the regional capital, saving us a minibus trip. As he manoeuvred his people mover around potholes and traffic, Simba and I chatted about Australia and Uganda, the relative economic state of the countries, and also the relative state of the roads.

Simba explained the complex communication system that exists between the drivers—lights, horns and hand signals can send dozens of different messages, such as traffic ahead, move over, pass me or watch out.

Sam piped up from the back seat. 'They aren't going to find my DS, are they.'

I felt for him. 'I don't think so, Sam.'

'That's all right,' he sighed, 'the black DS can take over from the blue DS.' I think it was the fact that we were leaving Uganda—he was finally ready to let go.

After a second minibus, a *boda boda* to the border and a relatively painless border crossing we were in Kenya, our ninth and second last country. We obtained some local currency from one of the money-changing hawkers and hustled to board a coach that was conveniently leaving for our next destination, Kisumu, in 'half an hour'.

Two hours later, the bus left. At least the three-hour coach trip was more comfortable and safer than in a minibus, and we could read. Through the dusty windows a woman boiled peanuts in a hub cap over a roadside fire. A boy skipped with a vine. In the fields, charcoal smoked in kilns resembling mini-ziggurats of mud brick, and the roadside rattled and hummed with horns, engine noise, yelling and laughter. The road flattened, the temperature rose, the dirt yellowed from paprika-coloured to peach-coloured, the countryside dried out and dust returned. We had crossed a political border and a geographical one: from wet central Africa to the dry east.

Sam had obviously been pondering the practicalities. 'Does Kenya have a McDonald's?'

'Yes,' I said, 'there would be one in Nairobi.' Well, I *thought* there would be.

'I don't want to go to Nai-robbery,' he quickly replied.

'Stop calling it that, Sam. We'll get into trouble.' I hoped the passengers around us weren't from Nairobi.

We finally reached Kisumu, Kenya's third largest city, at six p.m. and took a *tut-tut* to the hotel. We had only travelled around two hundred kilometres, but it had taken ten hours and involved a car, a minibus, a *boda boda*, a coach and a *tut-tut*.

Kisumu was a bustling place on the shore of Lake Victoria, the largest lake in Africa. The city was reminiscent of India, where I'd travelled in my twenties, and had many residents of Indian descent. But it also had the tension inherent in a larger African city. You needed to be careful on the streets here.

The next day we caught a *tut-tut* to the shore of the murky and crocodile-infested Lake Victoria. We stopped for lunch at a restaurant by the lake; its waters were the shade of blue metal. Sam ordered his lunch. He was now ordering meals with such ease I didn't really pay attention anymore. I sometimes had to remind myself what he'd been unable to do at the beginning of the trip.

We had planned to play chess and cards by the lake before a spot of boxing, but a storm hit and we scuttled back to the hotel. Our insalubrious accommodation was accessed by a stairwell from the street up to a solid wrought-iron gate. It had wi-fi, ceiling fans and street noise. The reception desk bore a sign saying DO NOT LEAVE VALUABLES IN YOUR ROOM, WE WILL NOT BE HELD RESPONSIBLE IF THEY ARE STOLEN.

Up on the rooftop terrace, we could see across the groaning city to the great lake. As night tightened its grip, the dim glow of a streetlight below revealed *boda boda* drivers sitting astride their bikes on a corner and harassing a young woman walking past with a bowl balanced atop her head. She ignored them. A security company car zoomed down the narrow street. Music blared out of a dark bar with flashing neon signs in the shape of beer bottles. Dogs barked and car horns blared. I contrasted the sights and sounds with those on the verandah in Kapchorwa.

I wondered what to do next, where to go. This wasn't a backpacker hostel but rather a one-star holding bay for travellers who kept to themselves, low-key business folk and desperadoes.

Sam didn't like it. 'I don't want to stay here.'

I agreed, but we couldn't do anything about it. 'It's the best we can manage.'

I let him chill on the DS while I read on my Kindle, both of us quiet and alone with our thoughts under our mosquito nets, in the prison cell of a hotel room. Our backpacks and belongings were strewn on the concrete floor, there was a broken toilet seat with a bucket for flushing, the blank bleached walls were lit by a single naked bulb and mosquitoes droned relentlessly.

The next day we got organised. I tried to get Sam involved in planning where we should go as we scanned the tatty map of southern Kenya in the reception area of the hotel. We found a local Indian travel agent who efficiently organised a four-day tour, which took in the Maasai Mara and Devil's Gate national parks before finishing in Nairobi. Maybe Sam would get to McDonald's after all.

When we'd arrived in Kenya I'd had no idea this was the time for the annual wildebeest migration, which only lasts for a few weeks in the period from August to October—the exact time varying from year to year. We discovered the Great Migration was now starting in the fabled Maasai Mara. We were incredibly lucky. I was excited, and I hoped Sam was too. He just seemed very spacey.

The day our tour began the overnight rain had cleared to a fresh clear morning. Joseph our Maasai guide steered the small van south towards the Tanzanian border, Sam and I the only passengers. After a few hours the traffic thinned and we hit a corrugated dirt road which wound down a precipice. Stretching out to the horizon were the vast grass plains of the Maasai Mara.

As we descended, wildlife started to emerge. Zebras scattered off the road, pods of elephants roamed through the zephyr-tousled grasslands, a family of giraffe grazed nearby. Thomson's gazelles, Grant's gazelles, waterbucks, topis, impalas and elands. There were the vibrant colours of lilac birds, yellow-billed storks and ground hornbills, the majesty of secretary birds, marabou storks, vultures and ostriches.

This was the Africa of dreams. The flat horizon was broken only by the occasional flat-topped Vachellia tree. Thousands of wildebeest stood in vast herds. A huge sky arced above, laced with wispy strands and ringlets of cirrus cloud. Buffalo glared at us, baboons darted up trees and warthogs marched across the plains. A hippo splashed away, startled by our van. A massive crocodile sat immobile on a muddy bank. All this just on the drive to our hotel, which was located in the centre of the park.

When we arrived at the hotel I realised why the trip had cost so much. This place was way better than anywhere else we had stayed on the entire trip. The hotel was seriously up-market.

Sam clearly had his mother's 'champagne' taste in accommodation. 'I want to stay here longer,' he said a microsecond after we entered our room. Before us lay two immaculate queen-sized beds, a marble bathroom, a writing desk and a panoramic view from the verandah doors to the animals milling on the Maasai Mara plains below the precipice on which the hotel was situated.

'We are only here for two nights,' I cautioned.

'I want longer.'

I fully sympathised. 'So do I, really, but we can't afford it.'

'Oh . . .' he moaned, as some giraffes wandered by the window.

I was glad for his sake that he was getting some luxury. We had been roughing it for so long; it was nice that he could enjoy some comforts. With five-star hotels, though, come five-star wankers. This became all-too evident during the afternoon game drive, as fellow guests boarded the line of safari vehicles outside the hotel. Men toted camera lenses the length of a wildebeest's leg, probably compensating for something. One man, who, of course, was also loud and opinionated, had a drone camera. Seriously? I secretly hoped the camera would crash amid a pride of lions and he'd try to retrieve it. Now *that* would make for an interesting photo.

On the game drive, the van passed teeming herds of wildebeest, numbering in the tens of thousands, all heading for the Mara River. They formed long columns of bovine nomads stretching out in meandering lines to the horizon. Their silver bodies were banded with black slashes, and their black faces and manes were festooned with white beards; the clowns of the plains.

Sam watched them pass. 'They are like *The Lord of the Rings*. They are an army.'

'Yes, I suppose they are,' I replied with a wry smile.

'They are buffalo soldiers!' Sam said, and started to sing the song that we had heard about a thousand times since arriving in Cape Town. Bob Marley is huge in Africa. Technically they were wildebeests and not buffaloes, but I still liked his joke.

Each year nearly two million wildebeests and hundreds of thousands of Thomson's gazelles, zebras and other ungulates make a three-hundred-kilometre trek which circles the Serengeti ecosystem of northern Tanzania and southern Kenya. The Maasai Mara is the northernmost point of the arc. The migration never stops, and as African wildlife expert Jonathan Scott puts it, 'The only beginning is the moment of birth.'

Then, way down south in the Serengeti, eight and a half months after the rut, more than 300,000 calves are synchronously dropped over a short few weeks to reduce the window of opportunity for predators. The wobbly-legged calves can outrun a lioness within five minutes of being born.

From there the great herds continue clockwise around the plains, stalked by lions, leopards and hyenas, crossing crocodile-filled waterways but always marching on, driven by instinct and rain patterns. When they reach the Maasai Mara, for unknown reasons, the wildebeest feel compelled to ford the Mara River, their greatest challenge, before heading south to cross the river again, often only a few days later. The river crossing is dangerous, with dozens being taken by crocodiles, but still every one of them does it. It is usually the old, the young and the weak that are taken. The wildebeests' defence is their vast numbers; as a species they can afford to take a few hits at the river.

The line of cars stood beside the river, lingering to see if the herd would make the dash across the shallows. As they often do, the herd threatened to but didn't cross; not this time.

We woke early in the morning, keen to see the lions when they're most active. It paid off, as we soon spotted a pride. They were feasting on a few wildebeests they'd killed overnight. This was the happy hunting season for the lions. At this time of year, they fattened up before the herds disappeared south. Then they would need to feed on more difficult to catch game such as zebra, antelope, and even giraffe or hippos.

Sam was wrapped in a red and blue Maasai rug, kindly supplied by Joseph. It was Joseph's coat of many colours. Well, two. Even though we were on the equator, the plains were sixteen hundred metres above sea level so it got chilly. Joseph was being very patient with Sam, who was continuing to make way too many references to black- and white-skinned people. I explained about the documentary and why I was using a video camera. I didn't want him thinking I was another Western wanker.

We could hear the ripping of tendon and muscle as a female lion tore apart a dead wildebeest's legs. Jackals hovered nearby, aware she would eventually have had her fill and then it would be their turn. A male lion was also hooking into a carcass. He then marked the territory with a piss before strutting across the road right in front of our parked van.

Sam was transfixed. 'He has big balls.'

During the quiet time in the middle of the day I tried to get some schoolwork done. We attempted some maths. It soon deteriorated.

'I don't want to do the pi questions. It's too hard,' he complained.

'Sam, you're very capable of doing this. You're not trying.'

'No, I am not capable. I am disabled. I have a disability.' That was a new one.

I wasn't going to back off. 'Not in maths you don't.'

'Yes I *do*. You are a *mean* father. You should be kinder to me.'

I was getting angry. 'Just do question four *now!*'

He punched me, tight and hard, with a hook to the side of the head. I was shocked by how hard he could punch. It was one of the best punches he had ever thrown; he had kept his body steady and balanced. Perversely, as I recoiled, I thought of congratulating him on his technique.

He immediately knew he had gone too far. I frankly felt like punching him back, and nearly did. Instead I stormed out of the room with the DS in hand, and Sam at my heels.

'Don't take my DS!' he screamed.

With a set jaw, I snapped, 'I am not taking it. You are just banned from using it for an hour.'

'Oh. Okay.'

I turned to face him. 'Go back to the room and leave me alone. *Now!*'

I took my bruised feelings—and head—to reception to calm down. Where had that come from? Sam is normally fine with maths. And as for the punch, I hoped that wouldn't set a precedent for future tantrums. As a seasoned father of three boys, I reckoned a lot of this behaviour was in the typical range of other fourteen-year-old boys. Still, there had to be a consequence. This was an extremely bad behaviour, which couldn't go unacknowledged.

Parenting experts tell you that enforcing 'consequences' for more extreme 'unwanted behaviours' is appropriate, as long as you don't overdo it. There are certain commonly accepted rules for doing this: only occasionally implement consequences, try to have the indiscretion and related consequence clarified beforehand to both parties, and implement the consequence calmly. I took a few deep breaths.

When we'd both calmed down, Sam apologised, sincerely. I knew I'd have to be careful the next time we had a maths lesson about π, the symbol which Sam referred to as 'two Js'.

Late that afternoon, Joseph took us out in the van again. We descended onto the plain below the resort. Joseph suddenly pulled over, stood up through the pop-top roof and peered through his binoculars. 'Hold on!' He leapt down, thrashed the gears and hit the accelerator, soon overtaking other trucks and vans. At the river, we came to a sudden skidding halt right at the edge on the raised bank. We all stood and looked back out of the pop-top roof towards the herd. Hundreds of beasts were charging straight towards us. The herd was at full gallop and the ground began to shake.

My heart was racing. 'Bloody hell!'

'They're coming straight at us!' Sam yelled.

The thundering herd hurtled around our stationary vehicle and plunged into the wild river directly below us. Occasionally a beast would thump the side of the truck in the pandemonium. Hundreds of them catapulted down the two-metre drop before splashing into the water, without hesitation or care for their safety, their legs splayed and tangled, smashing into each other and slipping on rocks and goodness knows what else as they leapt and bounded across the shallows.

'Fuck!' I couldn't help it; it slipped out.

'What are they doing?' Sam was wide-eyed at the window.

'They're trying to cross the river!' I yelled above the roar of hooves and bellows. Dust filled the air.

Crocs materialised from everywhere. There was a violent splash near the far bank. A croc had grabbed a youngster. The crowd in the quickly gathering vehicles gasped in unison. A woman in a truck near us mouthed, 'Oh no.' The young calf struggled and kicked but it was of no use, he was dragged under the water and disappeared under the torrent of the crossing herd. Both he and the croc were trampled to death, and the carcasses were feasted on by the other crocodiles. It was real, it was intense, it was life and death on the high plains of Kenya.

Several hundred had crossed when a new threat suddenly emerged from the scrub on the far bank. A lioness flashed through the exhausted wildebeest, which scattered in every direction to escape her. It was chaos. There were gasps and screams from the trucks. A few seconds later the great tan beast made a second run through the animals but with no kill. Well, not one we could see.

The herd stopped crossing; they'd had enough for now. I didn't blame them one little bit.

'Wow, Sam. First the crocs and then they have to deal with a lion!' I said. His eyes were like saucers.

Joseph drove us around the park. We spotted some rhinos in a swamp. A hyena feasted on a carcass, watched by jackals and vultures. Another carload had spied a leopard lounging in some thickets, but was now hidden from view.

We crept back to the river. There had just been another crossing, zebras this time. We saw the tail-end of the group: five zebras trotting through the water in single file. I smiled to myself: this was a real zebra crossing. As we parked on the bank, the aftermath of another kill was revealed in the waters below and I stopped smiling.

The body of a young zebra was being torn apart by thirty massive crocodiles. The black and white stripes of his coat were still perversely clear in the violently splashing bloodied water, with the four-metre crocs radiating outwards from the poor victim like writhing spokes on a wheel. They thrashed around each other, jostling for position and a chance to rip off some flesh, before devouring it in large gulps with their huge gaping mouths pointed to the sky. Occasionally the fat white belly of one of the crocodiles would flash at us as they rolled their bodies to twist a piece of zebra meat off the rapidly shrinking carcass. It was enthralling but grotesque.

I was later to learn, from some traumatised English newlyweds, that the zebra had taken a long time to die. Pinned by a croc biting one leg, he had managed to free himself repeatedly before being retaken, struggling and screaming in fear and pain the entire time. It was all too gladiatorial for me. I knew it was nature, and that's the way it had always been, but I was still relieved Sam and I hadn't seen it.

CHAPTER 33

When September ends

We left the park the next day. Maasai Mara had been seriously intense in several ways.

Outside the park Joseph took us to a traditional Maasai village, where you paid some money to be shown around. Given I had set Sam the school task of researching and writing about the culture only a few days earlier, this was perfect.

We learnt a man could have several wives, if he owned enough cattle to buy them with, but that each wife would have to live in a mud hut she built and maintained herself. The village would move holus-bolus every few years because that was the lifespan of the huts they built. If a man had no cattle he was expected to try to steal some from another village. There was a lot of fighting in Maasai culture, hence their fierce reputation.

The men all wore red cloaks. At the coming of age at fifteen, the Maasai youths were required to go out and kill a lion while wearing their cloak. The theory was that the lions learnt that humans wearing red were a threat and left them alone to tend their cattle. I tried to imagine Sam, who would be turning fifteen in a few months—or indeed any pampered teen from the West—hunting a lion with spears and arrows.

Sam and I joined in the jumping dance with the warriors. In Maasai culture being able to jump high is considered a sign of virility. Sam was, of course, a skilled jumper because he jumps up and down so much anyway. Maybe he could find himself a Maasai bride if I could just rustle up a few head of cattle.

We headed north towards Nairobi and stayed near the Hell's Gate National Park. At dinner, Sam had yet another meltdown when I insisted he eat more of his meal. Embarrassed by his yelling and screaming, I got cross with him. These tantrums were becoming altogether too frequent. We returned to our room where I told him he would only be allowed to use his DS if he watched an hour of a movie of his choice. He chose *Toy Story*, and ended up watching the whole thing, which was fine by me; the more narrative he is exposed to the better.

Once again I reassessed my plans and objectives for Sam. I needed to draw a halt to this increasingly obstructionist and defiant behaviour, but getting him on board would require both a carrot and a stick.

I sat down with him for a talk. 'Sam, you are getting in too much of a habit of saying no or negotiating, and not just saying yes to things sometimes.'

He looked sheepish. 'Yeah.'

'We need to change this,' I said firmly.

'Yeah.'

'How about, if you start saying yes when I ask you to do something, that is, yes without arguing or negotiating, I'll let you know you have done it, and if you do it a few times I'll give you a secret reward.'

'What's the reward?'

I didn't have one figured out. 'It's a secret.'

'Hmm, okay.'

'Also, if you argue or negotiate, especially over silly things, I'll let you know, and you'll receive negative points.'

He looked down at his feet. I gently raised his chin with my finger to make eye contact. 'So, are you going to try really hard?'

'Yes, I promise,' he mumbled.

I'd planned for us to do a walking tour of Hell's Gate National Park, which Mike and Lenneke back in Malawi had highly recommended. It sounded interesting but it was three hours long, and I felt I didn't want to stress the two of us out anymore. We'd already seen such amazing wildlife in Maasai Mara. I decided to pull the plug.

Instead we took a one-hour boat tour of nearby Lake Naivasha, part of the Rift Valley system of lakes. It was a soft option but that was okay. We saw some interesting birds, a few hippos, and our guide threw a fish to a fish eagle, which scooped it out of the water with exquisite style and grace. An added advantage of our abbreviated sightseeing was that we would now arrive in Nairobi at lunchtime, allowing us extra hours to fit in some schoolwork and neuroplasticity exercises, and get back on track.

We climbed out of the Rift Valley for the last time, and inched our way further east across Africa.

Nairobi. Nai-robbery. Nai-Hermione Granger. I didn't quite get the last of Sam's mash-ups, as he called them, except that Sam continued to be obsessed with Hermione Granger, and her alter ego, Emma Watson.

But Sam was right: Nairobi had a reputation as a dangerous city, especially at night, and everyone we'd met who had visited there said it was the sort of place you stay in for as little time as possible. Get in, get out.

I actually didn't think it was that bad, and Sam loved it. The crime rate apparently rivals that of Johannesburg, so maybe we were just lucky. The hostel we were staying at was basic but functional. There weren't mosquito nets but the wi-fi was the fastest we'd seen.

However, there was one serious issue. McDonald's. I'd just assumed that Nairobi would have several, but it turned out there were none, only three KFCs set away from the city centre. At first Sam wasn't happy, but then he thought about it for a few seconds. 'I can have McDonald's when we get back to Sydney.'

Despite the thousand or so conversations we'd had about going to McDonald's in Nairobi, when he discovered there wasn't one it was dismissed with a shrug of the shoulders. It seemed he was measuring the sophistication of cities by what takeaway chains were present, and when he saw that Nairobi had big modern buildings and other trappings of a major city, McDonald's didn't really matter to him anymore.

We had a few days of school, shopping, neuroplasticity, restocking and recharging. Pythagoras, a PowerPoint on the Congo, public-speaking practice, chess (minus the missing bishop), boxing. Kick, kick, uppercut, uppercut, cross. Meeting people, talking to staff, ordering meals, playing pool. Riding pillion on motorbikes, walking down broken sidewalks, ignoring hawkers, discomforted by disabled beggars rattling coins in plastic cups. A blind ten-year-old boy, a woman with cerebral palsy propelling herself with her arms while her twisted legs trailed behind, a pre-school-aged girl thrusting her severely deformed wrist at us as we passed by.

For our third and final day in Nairobi, I'd organised for us to visit a school on the outskirts of the city where a cousin of mine, Denise, had worked as a volunteer. The school, funded by the Australian consulate and donations from Australian sponsors, taught children from Kibera, the largest slum in Africa.

Home to one and half million people, the tin and mud-brick shacks of Kibera latched onto the rolling hills; a chronic rash on a scarred surface. Denise's close friend Sister Leonida was there to greet us. A vibrant and kindly soul, her sharp eyes examined us from behind her thick-rimmed glasses. She outlined the tremendous work the school did and introduced us to her staff members, who were all fascinated, of course, by Sam and what we were doing. We were well used to that.

The head teacher, Jeremiah, took us for a walking tour of Kibera, which he had called home for all of his life. Smartly dressed in a pressed white business shirt and tie, Jeremiah had a gentle and tilted smile. He rolled up his sleeves and loosened his tie when we walked out into the searing sunlight. As a child, he had been bright enough to earn a scholarship to complete his schooling and, subsequently, an education degree at university. As a teacher for the most disadvantaged, he was now giving back to his community in spades.

We walked down narrow winding alleyways, where rubbish lined the open drains, children tumbled through doorways and chatter filled the air. Rusting tin roofs covered tiny mud-brick houses, doors open, but their dark interiors impenetrable as we squinted in the sunlight. Overhead was a spider web of tilting electricity poles, thick black powerlines and fuse boxes.

Jeremiah apprised us of life in Kibera. 'A typical house is about six square metres, and somewhere between six and twenty people live in that space. During the day there is a table, but this is packed up at night and people sleep together on the floor.'

I was astonished. 'Is there a lot of crime here?' I asked.

'In some areas, but not this one. I was brought up here. If someone came up now and stole your camera, they would chase him, catch him, and beat him to death.'

He smiled as I replied, 'Well, I certainly hope that doesn't happen!'

Despite the poverty, people were smiling and laughing. Jeremiah told us about the sense of community spirit. 'You know, you see people who live in big fancy houses in other areas of Nairobi, and they don't even know their neighbours. Here, everyone knows each other and looks after each other.'

I suspected Jeremiah, intelligent and articulate, was a local hero. People smiled and nodded at him. We were welcomed because we were in his company. I looked at the communal water pump, funded by the World Bank, where women and children filled their yellow plastic containers, at the local medical clinic where apparently some doctors and nurses stole medications to sell to private clinics, at the garbage, the chaos, the confinement, and was in awe that he had come from this to be where he was today.

Sam was cool. This sort of experience didn't faze him at all these days. I thought back to Cape Town, where the sights and smells of the township had distressed him so much. We had come a long way in a geographical sense, but he had come a long way in many ways.

Back at the hostel, Sam jumped onto the bed to settle for the night, and several of the wooden slats under the mattress snapped, leaving the mattress tilting at a thirty-degree slope.

He was worried. 'I'm sorry, Dad.'

'Don't worry,' I reassured him. I took one for the team and swapped beds with him, spending an uncomfortable night sliding off the mattress.

Early the next morning we left the creaking city and drove south to Tanzania. Along the way our altitude descended and the temperature ascended. It was flat and dry. Sam remarked that the landscape resembled Namibia, but the occasional flashing red robes of the Maasai driving the cattle on the side of the road revealed we were in east Africa.

Our penultimate African border crossing into Tanzania was the usual slow-motion affair, but then the flat straight road started to undulate as we approached a massive conical volcanic mountain and swung around its foothills.

On the southern side of Mount Meru we cruised into Arusha. The tourist town served the Northern Circuit, a collection of spectacular national parks that dot northern Tanzania. Arusha was full of tour guides, hawkers and more tour guides. Outside the front door of the hostel, people standing nearby would suddenly gather, like moths to the flame, with a patter of questions.

'Hey, where you from?'

'My friend, my friend, what do you want to see?'

'Do you recognise me?'

Whatever it took to start a conversation. Unfortunately, it was just about impossible to finish one without getting confrontational.

Apart from this hassle, the town oozed charm. The mystical, smooth upper slopes of Mount Meru peered through breaks in the cloud hovering around its waist, like a shy lady aware of her beauty. Flashes of mauve jacaranda blooms decorated the bustling city streets, where red-cloaked Maasai strutted, veiled Islamic women travelled in groups and *boda bodas* and minivans honked and weaved. It was a town small enough to be digestible to the newcomer, but large enough to have vibrancy and vitality. Arusha was a liveable city.

We sorted out money and SIM cards for Tanzania, our last African country, accompanied by Morton, a Danish tourist we'd met in the hostel in Nairobi, who'd joined us on the bus. Despite his youthful appearance, Morton had a master's degree in international relations and was a seasoned traveller. He was a rolling stone, trundling his way around Africa, trying to figure out what to do next with his life. He was also a thinker, enjoying chess challenges with Sam and philosophical discussions with me. Morton had a brother with Down syndrome and was evangelically enthusiastic about the purpose of our trip: improving outcomes for a disabled loved one. Another welcome support, another companion for both Sam and me. We weren't to know then how great a role he'd come to play to our future travels.

Even though I now had a SIM card, my phone was out of battery and we'd arrived in what we'd soon learn was a daily blackout, usually ending towards sunset.

That evening, with the power finally back on, Sam and I discussed going home to Australia and I confirmed what I'd previously only hinted at: we were going home sooner than planned.

He looked me in the eye. 'For sure?'

'For sure.'

'So I don't have to get seven eights in a row.'

'No, you don't, but I think you deserve to go home. You've tried very hard. You should be proud of what you've achieved in Africa.'

Sam sat back, exhaled, and beamed. 'Yes, I am.'

He starting singing the Green Day song, 'When September Ends'. While the song lyrics actually explore American paranoia after the September 11 terrorist attacks, they also summed up Sam's point of view perfectly.

CHAPTER 34

Rolling with the punches

We awoke to a sparkling blue sky day in Arusha. Mount Meru rested peacefully above. My sister-in-law had lived in Arusha for two years, working as a teacher, so she'd teed us up to meet her very good friend Onesmo, a Maasai businessman.

I called Onesmo, who picked us up with his nine-year-old daughter, Siyana, and took us to lunch in a very flash Lebanese restaurant he part-owned. The restaurant was in the upmarket part of town where the British colonialists had erected their grand estates and institutions. The elegant piles, with their broad verandahs and contorted ancient trees in sweeping gardens, were where 'matters of state' had once been discussed by district commissioners and officers of the Empire wearing crisply starched uniforms. Many of these buildings were now home to a range of restaurants, offering cuisines from all over the world to the well-to-do of the city, many of whom were expats.

Onesmo, Sam and I chatted while we were served mixed mezze plates, pita bread and lamb kebabs on white linen draped over an outdoor table. The sunlight dappled the lawn and an excellent jazz band played near the bar. *This is not too bad at all*, I thought to myself. Sam, however, was being autistic, speaking little, drawing his legs up onto the chair and ignoring Onesmo's attempts to engage him in conversation.

I explained what was going on to Onesmo. 'He always does this. In a new environment with new people, he goes into his shell. With time he will start to open up to you and you will start to see more of the real Sam.'

Onesmo, who was astute and good with children, didn't need much convincing and kept trying to engage Sam. And sure enough, Sam soon started to open up. We discussed African political history, including apartheid, Mugabe and Idi Amin, Sam's school and, of course, our trip and the concepts behind it.

Sam fired question after question at me, while Onesmo looked on bemused. 'What would happen if you mashed up the leader of Zimbabwe who starts with an M with Idi Amin?'

'I think you would have a very bad person,' I replied.

Sam leant forward. 'As bad as Stalin?'

'I don't know, Sam.' It wasn't a comparison I'd thought a lot about.

'I don't think he would be as bad as Stalin. Stalin was the *worst*. Do you think Idi Amin would throw me out of a helicopter to the crocodiles if I tried to punch him in the nose?'

'I'm not sure, Sam. Probably, er, I really don't know. But you don't have to worry about that because Idi Amin is dead,' I said, trying to find an answer that would satisfy him.

Sam pumped his fist near his shoulder. 'Yes, he died in *disgrace*.'

Onesmo drove us back to the hostel where I then filmed Morton and Sam playing chess; the score was one all. Sam was a good winner but a sore loser. Morton smiled and shrugged. We all headed out with some other backpackers to a Chinese restaurant two doors up that had a good reputation. It was our second big meal of the day and the second challenging cuisine for Sam, but he did all right, apart from talking incessantly and asking the same questions over and over. We left earlier than the others and headed back to the hostel, both sleeping well that night.

The next day Benison had organised for us to meet up with Kerri, an American special-needs teacher now living in Moshi, a one-hour drive from Arusha. Kerri was the director of programs for Connects Autism Tanzania, the peak autism NGO in the country. Kerri worked with Mama Grace, an inspiring Tanzanian woman and mother of a twenty-three-year-old man with autism called Erick. As a child, Erick's erratic behaviour and lack of speech meant he hardly got any education at all, despite Grace's best efforts, and he remains largely non-verbal. Her advocacy largely fell on deaf ears, despite her strong belief that Erick did have skills and intelligence that were not being developed.

Although he was placed in a special-education unit, it was a kilometre from the bus stop in front of the mainstream school; he walked the kilometre alone every day. After a few years, the parents of other children on the bus became concerned that hanging around a disabled child somehow put their own children at risk and encouraged their kids to kick Erick off the bus every day. Mama Grace had to figure out a way to get him to school so she bought a bicycle for him, and worked hard to teach him how to ride it alone, a massive expense and inconvenience that none of the other parents had to face.

As a young adult, Erick faced an uncertain future in a country where there was no vocational training for young people with disabilities. Stuck in a education facility that was just re-teaching him the basic academic skills he already possessed, Erick was floundering, and Grace knew it.

Erick was in the habit of scavenging precious glimpses of television shows he liked by peering through the windows of shops, but he didn't like football and in 2010, when the football World Cup came to South Africa, every television set in the city was constantly tuned to it. Frustrated and confused when the shopkeepers ignored his pleas to change the channel, he threw some rocks through a store window. There was a furious reaction: a vigilante group was organised and paid for, with the express intention of killing Erick. Grace, alerted to the danger by an informant, hastily convened a community meeting with the police and successfully prevented a disaster.

Still, Erick struggled. Grace refused to give up. When she met Kerri, things started to fall into place. With her new ally, they developed not only the beginnings of a vocational training program for young adults with a disability, with Erick as their first graduate, but also continued to fight for awareness, opportunities and basic human rights for children with special needs in Arusha and surrounding districts.

In Africa, people with special needs and their families face hurdles that go way beyond those that exist in developed countries. Foremost of these is the assumption that children with special needs can't learn. Why place such a child in a school when they'll be taking up scarce resources that another child could benefit from?

Second, it is commonly believed that the disability is caused by the family themselves, a result of a sin, a misdemeanour, some piece of black magic or a curse. I thought back to Manga's village in Zambia. In *Unstrange Minds*, Roy Richard Grinker describes encountering similar beliefs in black populations in South Africa, where children who seemed physically normal but behaved abnormally were often thought to be 'possessed by an evil spirit'.

Finally, and bizarrely, many believe disability is contagious. This was a large part of why Erick was kicked off the bus. The other parents didn't want their children to catch what Erick had.

These barriers, unfair and infuriating, all had to be overcome before people like Grace and Erick could even begin to think about the objectives and hopes that autism-affected families in the developed world aspired to.

We visited the school Erick had attended. It was on a dirt road in the verdant foothills of Mount Meru. As we entered the school gates, curious children in the playground peered at our car. The teachers welcomed us and showed us around the school. There were a few classrooms and a large hall, which also served as a dining area, with bare floorboards and tall barred windows.

As the lunch of rice stew was served, Sam watched the children eat, laugh, play and squabble. I explained that this was an African version of the special-education primary school that Sam had attended back in Sydney.

'It's a bit like it, but it's not the same,' he observed.

'No, Sam, it's not the same,' I agreed, thinking of the sparsely furnished and dimly lit rooms we had just seen.

'They don't have white children. All the teachers are black, too,' he continued. Fortunately, no one else was in earshot.

A more pertinent difference was that the school catered for a wider age range of children and a diverse range of disabilities. Anyone who didn't fit in elsewhere ended up here. One of the students was eighteen. Another small boy had cerebral palsy, and a winning smile. He was being fed on the lap of one of the older girls. He couldn't walk and I noticed his lower leg contractures, which I would have loved to get a physiotherapist working on. In class he sat on a mattress. Children with Down syndrome were mixed in with those with developmental delay, learning disorders and, of course, autism.

Mama Grace remained head of the parents' association at the school, although Erick had now moved on. She explained the significantly different aetiology of the disabilities compared with what you would see in Australia: disability resulting from cerebral malaria and other infectious diseases was common, as well as from poorly managed epilepsy, which we had also witnessed among the patients of Butabika hospital in Uganda.

The school faced an uphill battle on several fronts. They constantly had to fight for classroom space with the mainstream primary school next door where Erik had previously exited the bus. That pervasive belief that disabled children can't learn helped keep this battle alive, as well as their chronic underfunding. It seemed no one not directly involved with the school placed any value on it or the students who went there. It was confronting and disturbing.

After our tour we visited the furniture workshop where Erick had started his apprenticeship. Erick was a tall thin young man with a beaming grin who twitched and jumped around, but it soon became apparent he got things done around the workshop.

He also had some smarts. He was fascinated by my camera and, after grabbing it from me, figured out what all the buttons did and how to navigate the menu in seconds. Considering I still didn't know half of the functions of the camera myself, I was impressed.

I was also impressed that a young man with autism was able to cope in this environment. The shed was filled with sensory challenges that would stress most people: ear-piercing screeches from lathes, drills and industrial saws echoed through the sawdust-filled air.

Erick was very excited to see his mum. He was tired from his morning's work and he knew her arrival meant it was time to leave. We went to a burger joint in town as a special treat for both Erick and Sam. Erick communicated in his unique way, Sam talked incessantly about Harry Potter, and we all had a nice lunch.

Grace wondered what Erick would be like now if he'd had the sort of early intervention that children like Sam had benefited from. As she watched Sam and heard his odd but fluent speech her expression spoke less of envy than regret. My heart ached for them both: Grace, with her humanism and sheer energy, and Erick, a good guy who should have been given a better chance in life, but was caught in the reality of disability in Africa.

We said goodbye outside the burger joint. Sam shook Mama Grace's hand and said thank you in Swahili: 'Asante, Mama Dis-Grace!' She was taken aback for a second, and then flashed a broad smile. Sometimes Sam could do with a touch less speech.

At six o'clock the next morning, Sam and I headed off from Arusha on what was planned to be our final animal nature trip in Africa: a day tour to the World Heritage–listed Ngorongoro Crater. Our car headed west through Maasai country, past roadside villages with circular stick fences surrounding mud huts and cattle yards. Locals waited at bus stops in their traditional coloured robes: purples and blues in this area of Tanzania, as well as the reds. After such a confronting experience of nature in Maasai Mara, I wondered whether we really needed another safari, but apparently the crater itself was something to behold.

It was. The steep rim, 2,500 metres above sea level and six hundred metres above the floor of the caldera, was all that remained of a volcanic mountain that had once reached higher than Kilimanjaro. It had erupted and collapsed in upon itself three million years ago, which was a blink of an eye in geological terms.

Our guide drove us up through the misty and wild montane forest on the outer slope, over the crest of the rim, and then down into the caldera. As we descended beneath the clouds the crater opened up before us in a grand reveal.

The thirty-kilometre wide giant cup was verdant and dotted with trees and wildlife. The still air inside the crater was aglow from light that pierced the cloud cover hovering at the level of the rim. It looked like a giant roofed stadium. The lakes shimmered, vapour rising off them as the waters warmed as the day unfolded.

Thorn trees and umbrella acacias, their underside adorned with weaverbird nests hanging like baubles, gave way on the lower slopes to spiky sisal plants that dominated the crater floor. The whole gang of animals was here. Among them, the giant kori bustard strutted in the grass, yellow-billed storks stood guard on the muddy banks and marabou storks and black kites spied from above. A mating pair of ostriches circled each other like Spanish dancers, the female nonchalantly assessing the male's ruffles and flourishes. We had our first sighting of the magnificent crowned crane, the national bird of Uganda, their outrageous golden mohawks dipping high and low as the gadabout and his mate watched for predators while grazing the fields.

As well as over a hundred thousand animals, a quarter of them large mammals, the crater was also home to fifty thousand Maasai, who grazed their cattle and goat herds.

The Ngorongoro Crater is an ecosystem in which man has existed in harmony with the environment for millions of years, as paleoanthropologist Mary Leakey discovered in 1959. In nearby Oldevai Gorge she found the skull of a *Paranthropus boisei*, a hominid species that had lived in east Africa roughly two to four million years ago, the first of many significant nearby findings unveiling the origins of man. He was dubbed Nutcracker Man for his large molars.

Halfway through the drive three older lionesses, thin and tired, sauntered towards us. They were indifferent to our presence. One plonked herself under our car, presumably for the warmth of the engine. She was half visible as we carefully looked over the edge of the pop-top roof of the four-wheel drive, her head resting on her paws near the back tyre. *How high can a lion reach?* She didn't look too menacing. Sam was excited, if a little nervous. After ten minutes our driver scared her off by starting the engine and gently moving the wheels.

The crater had exceeded my expectations. Sam enjoyed it too, and told me so. Ngorongoro was another phenomenal place in Africa that I'd only vaguely heard of prior to coming here.

The days ebbed and flowed in Arusha. Sam and I got into a rhythm. It was the sort of place we felt comfortable just hanging around, not doing much at all except schoolwork, neuroplasticity exercises, and filming video interviews, including a bizarre interview with the Masai guard dressed in his red robes at the front door, where Sam asked him why he carried a large knife. The guard just laughed. But I knew there would come a time where our feet would start to itch and then we'd move on.

As we sat on the rooftop verandah of the hostel one afternoon, the ever-present noise from the street below started to become very loud. We peered over the railing to see an open truck coming down the road. It was trimmed with the banners and flags of the main opposition political party in Tanzania, and packed with large audio-speakers and men holding megaphones. Music blared while they shouted into the megaphones as loud and as fast as they could.

Within seconds a sizable crowd had gathered and started to chant, some people raising their fists. Suddenly two police trucks, their canvas-covered trays full of policemen, came hurtling down the road and screeched to a halt. The police jumped out, some of them holding up their rifles and automatic weapons. The crowd fled in every direction, dissipating as quickly as it had materialised. The hostel staff were relieved the police hadn't used tear gas.

This was politics in Tanzania. The five-yearly general election was in two months. While Tanzania was a democracy, it worked very differently here than what I was used to back home in Australia. Nearly all of the advertising was for the government party. A taxi driver told me if the opposition had the temerity to hold a rally, the police (or somebody) would simply cut the power. The spontaneous rally we'd seen, presumably announced on social media or mobile phones seconds before occurring, was a tactic to try to get their message out.

We had been glad to see Morton again at the hostel after our trip to the crater. One evening I chatted with him after Sam had gone to bed. I reflected that the end of our trip now seemed to be rapidly approaching.

He thought for a second. 'So, what in particular do you want to get out of the weeks you have left?' he asked.

I considered my answer. 'I want to maximise his independence.'

'Then put him in charge,' he said. 'In charge of the trip, I mean.'

It would be a leap—a departure from the way we'd operated to date—but I immediately liked it. I'd been theoretically aiming for this throughout the trip, but it had been hard to stick to in such a challenging environment as Africa. *Yes.* I would push myself to take more risks, and hand decisions over to Sam. From now on the default needed to be that Sam would decide.

'Yes, from now on Sam is in charge,' I said.

Morton grinned and nodded. He was also going to travel with us towards Dar es Salaam and his company and travel experience would be welcome.

The next day Sam seemed to take to his new leadership role. There were more firsts, including eating cereal with milk, a major leap forward on the food front. One morning he spontaneously untied and then re-tied his shoelaces without any prompting from me, after only the briefest of lessons the day before. I was seriously impressed.

He was also in a terrific mood. He knew the end of the trip was close, and would tell me every day how many days we had left. The need to allocate a score for the day had disappeared completely, though we did still talk vaguely about positive and negative points at times. I think his mood went beyond happiness at being close to the end of the trip. I sensed he knew he had accomplished something special.

But nothing was ever uncomplicated. One night, in the midst of yet another evening blackout, Sam accidentally upended my beer onto the nearby computer keyboard as he picked up his DS.

Sam, distracted by his game, failed to tell me as I lay on my bed reading my Kindle, blissfully unaware. I didn't discover the truth until several hours later and by that time the motherboard was coagulated with sugar crystals.

Keep calm, keep calm. Don't lose it, James. There was no point in getting angry, but it was very frustrating. Most of Sam's schoolwork was not going to be accessible for the remaining three weeks, and I didn't know how I'd be able to blog and record our journey.

In the morning, with Morton's help, we found what seemed to be a good computer-repair service in the city and dropped the laptop off. Over the next thirty-six hours the technicians tried to fix it, but to no avail. They said I should be able to recover all the data when I got home to Australia, but still.

Sam was also upset about the death of the laptop. I think he thought my head would explode. 'You're not angry, Dad?'

I sighed. 'No, I'm okay.'

'I didn't mean to break your computer.'

'I know.'

He put his hand on my forearm. 'You can get a new one when we get back to Sydney.' I smiled at his concern.

My cobbled-together plan was to use my phone for internet, and to borrow Morton's laptop to write and blog, keeping all the files on a portable hard drive. We were limping to the finishing line.

But I was buoyed by two pieces of news. My best mate, Matt Rickard, a colorectal surgeon back home in Sydney, was going to be able to meet up with us in Dar es Salaam for six days, and would be arriving in only three days' time.

I had known Matt since we'd started medical school together at the age of seventeen. After the first two years of university, Matt and I had decided to take a year off—what you'd now call a gap year—and after earning some money for a few months, travel the world. That trip, all those years ago—nine months through India, Europe and the Middle East—had been a large part of the inspiration for what Benison and I had designed for Sam. I strongly felt that this experience had greatly benefited my own development, social skills and worldliness at the time. It seemed right that Matt was going to join Sam and me.

The second development was that Heiress Films had decided to send another cinematographer out for the end of the trip. The cinematographer was going to join us just before Matt left, and stay until a few days before the end of the trip. Much to Sam's disappointment, it was not to be Max, our first companion in South Africa, as he was now tied up with another project, but that was okay.

I'd have someone to give me a hand, and access to a computer, for most of the time we had left. Even when significant setbacks happened, like losing a DS or wrecking a laptop, you just had to roll with the punches. I was learning this skill along with Sam.

CHAPTER 35

Life lessons

We had spent over a week in Arusha, hanging out on the verandah overlooking busy Sokoine Road, where Sam struggled through his Pythagoras or played chess with Morton or cards with me, having juggling lessons or boxing on the small enclosed verandah near our room, filming Sam talking to the Maasai security guy downstairs. Things just *happened* in Arusha, and it was a fun place to be. Still, the computer drama had artificially extended our stay, and it was time to move on. There's a German word—*Fernweh*—which means a desire to travel, and it was what I, and I suspect Sam too, was feeling. We were now accustomed to moving on. I was meant to be meeting Matt in two days, so we had to high-tail it. Next stop Moshi, an hour away at the foot of Kilimanjaro.

On the road again, cloud hovered over the lower reaches of ominous-looking mountains, thrusting up from the acacia-studded plains until they disappeared into the vapour. Wisps and chunks of the cotton veil would break away and descend before evaporating over the granite drops. Grass and scrub was lit sparkling lime where the sun broke through the canopy.

Moshi was a small, quaint town situated at the base of the world's largest free-standing mountain, Mount Kilimanjaro, or Kili for short. Eateries and hotels on tree-lined boulevards maximised their views of Kili from rooftop verandahs. On the dusty streets, hawkers lined up to greet us as soon we left our hotel. Morton and I were experienced enough to mostly strike the right balance between completely ignoring them—and risking an escalation into aggression—and minimising engagement to the simplest of answers, thus avoiding conversation. As we strolled along the volley of questions would start. 'Hey, sir, where are you from? Do you want safari? I am a mountain guide. Here, take my card.'

Avoiding eye contact, never stopping, we would reply: 'Australia. Yes, kangaroos. No, thanks. It's okay, we're fine. *Asante asante.*'

Sam was the master though. He either genuinely didn't notice the hawkers or, smiling constantly, would talk in non sequiturs about something totally off-topic. It completely threw them. Morton and I tried to emulate his approach but we just couldn't get the hang of it.

We landed in a hotel where there was a kind of a view of the mountain, but it was mainly obscured by the cityscape. I wanted to get out of town to take a photo and maybe some video footage of Kili without a bunch of electrical wires and rooftops in the way.

I asked at reception, but I just seemed to confuse them. 'So you want to see Kili?'

'Yes,' I said.

The girl at reception looked at me blankly. 'You can see it from the verandah upstairs.'

I took a deep breath. 'Yes, I know, but I want to see it without all the electrical wires and stuff. Is there somewhere out of town with a good view of the mountain?'

'So you want to *go* to the mountain?' I had really confused her.

'No, just to *see* the mountain.'

'You can see it from upstairs.' Around and around the conversation went. I'm sure they thought I was quite stupid. They eventually organised a taxi to a place that was meant to be half an hour away. We headed off in the cab, zipping through the trucks and buses of the traffic surrounding Moshi, dust and fumes swirling in the dying light, the three of us with not a clue where we were going.

Our taxi driver spoke little English. I just hoped he understood what we were after. I just wanted to take a bloody photo of the mountain! As far as I could tell we were going the wrong direction, skirting the mountain base. It was also taking a lot longer than half an hour. Eventually we headed in towards Kili. He was taking us to the park entrance.

Given the language barrier, there was no way we could explain to him what we actually wanted, and we had a lot of trouble convincing him to turn around as the sun disappeared behind the canopy of cloud surrounding the mountain. We couldn't see Kili at all. Morton and I shrugged. It wasn't a big deal. To Sam it mattered even less—just another long drive on the crazy roads of Africa.

We were meeting Kerri and Mama Grace for dinner in their home town. They knew the best place to go: a local steak restaurant run by British expats. The food was excellent and Sam was stoked he could have real ice cream. In between stuffing his face, he talked and talked and our hosts got to know his quirky personality a little better. Sam has a knack, for all his social inappropriateness, of winning people over. Throughout the trip this aspect of him, previously only known to people close to him, was increasingly apparent to those he'd only met once or twice. Due to his frequent exposure to strangers, the time between a first introduction and a prolonged reciprocal conversation was shortening. It also made him a lot more fun.

It had been a good night, despite Sam insisting on patting the head of a small baby on a table of *wazungu* women sitting nearby. Fortunately, the mother didn't mind.

The next day was a big one of travel, as we journeyed east across northern Tanzania to Dar es Salaam. It would be our last long bus trip in Africa. There was the walk to the bus station with Sam whinging constantly, a crappy roadside coffee with me whinging constantly, and then nine and a half hours on a crowded bus.

The Jurassic landscape of northern Tanzania, with its mountains soaring up from the flat plains, gave way to a more stereotypical Africa: acacia and thorn bush scrub scattered with roadside stalls selling mobile phone data cards, warm soda bottles and a cornucopia of Chinese-made just-about-anything. Piles of burning rubbish smoked the air, young men filled their *boda boda* tanks with petrol from Coca-Cola bottles and brightly swathed women, shrouded and veiled, swayed along, their cargo motionless atop their heads and infants on their backs poking out from their robes. When we slowed, children waved at the bus and shouted 'Jumbo' (Hello) and 'Mumbo?' (How are you?).

Our progress, as always, seemed to falter as we neared our destination. As the bus crept along, I was having trouble deciding which was moving more slowly, the bus or the plot of the melo-dramatic Swahili movie flickering on the television suspended from its ceiling. There was no escaping it; you had to look at the screen. One-dimensional characters (with baddies inevitably getting their comeuppance), hilarious special effects (devils and spirits invading the souls of the protagonists), and a music score that made spaghetti westerns look understated were interspersed with more modern African elements. Mobile phones were omnipresent, money meant everything and HIV was a common theme. Sam was mesmerised, Morton and I were anaesthetised.

We crawled into the Dar es Salaam bus station. While a city of three million people, Dar had a reputation for being, well, boring. Several years earlier, Morton had lived in the city for six months, so it was good to have a knowledgeable guide handy. He organised a cab and we ducked and dodged our way across town in the ridiculous traffic, past embassies and shopping malls, through shanty suburbs and roadworks, until we finally reached our hotel, one that Morton was familiar with, on the north shore of the city.

A familiar ritual followed: unloading packs, organising laundry, sort out wi-fi access, deciding on dinner, checking emails and just lying down for a spell. I tried to get Sam to help me in such situations, but sometimes I was just too knackered to bother.

Matt arrived at our hotel after spending two hours crossing the city from the airport in the peak-hour traffic. It was great to see him.

He looked at Sam and did a double take. 'Sam, you're so tall! And what's going on with your hair?'

Sam flapped, bounced up and down, and smiled at Matt, peering at him through the greasy long hair covering his eyes. 'Matt Rickard is in Africa!'

We headed to a beach-side restaurant nearby. Sam devoured a pizza and we got devoured by mosquitoes; I had forgotten the insect spray. Matt and I had a big catch-up, and Matt got to know Morton, although he kept mistaking his name and nationality: Morton the Dane became Milton the Norwegian.

We tried to figure out what to do in our time together. Go to Zanzibar? Travel up the coast? How long should we stay in Dar? Sam, what do you think? Sam talked and talked but it wasn't quite on-topic: Harry Potter, *The Incredibles*, *The Simpsons*, Mugabe, 'Idiot' Amin, Hermione Granger.

Matt turned to me. 'Er, Sam talks a lot now!'

The next day we cruised around the city with Morton as our guide. I tried to get Sam to take the lead but it was difficult with the four of us, and it was also a challenging environment. The roads were, like in all African cities, quite dangerous, and the footpaths were obstacle courses: impromptu shops, parked cars, *tut-tuts*, motorbikes, boxes, crates, displays of CDs, clothing or electrical equipment on racks. Anything, everything, and then some.

On a corner a man was making a racket, somewhere between singing, rapping and just being a pain in the arse. He was surrounded by a crowd of thirty or so people, some of whom were taking pictures on their phones, their interest perhaps piqued by his oddness.

As we skirted the small crowd I accidentally stepped on a man's foot. I immediately apologised, but he grabbed my upper arm and squeezed, *hard*. I winced in pain as I continued to profusely apologise. But then with his other hand he grabbed Sam. At this point I got seriously worried.

It was now a scuffle. Sam cried, 'Hey, Dad, he is hurting me!'

'*Let him go!*' I yelled. I pushed the man, who let go of Sam but continued to squeeze my arm. His eyes were bloodshot and hazy, and I realised he was stoned. I managed to hit his hand away from my arm. People were jostling and yelling all around us. In the middle of the melee, the man suddenly smiled, put his hands up in the air and retreated. *He's up to something*, I thought to myself.

Matt sidled up beside me. 'Check your bag. Some people were close to it.' I checked the daypack I had been carrying; it was closed and intact and the stills and video camera were both inside.

Morton took the lead. 'Let's get out of here.'

We headed for the nearest taxi stand and tumbled into a cab, out of the glare, dust, noise, heat and chaos. As I hit the tatty vinyl back seat, the penny dropped. 'My wallet is missing.'

'Fuck, really? What was in it?' Matt said.

I checked my money belt as I replied. 'Only about thirty bucks. All the big stuff and credit cards are in my money belt.' I felt cross. 'Damn, I knew he was up to something . . . But I trod on his foot . . .' I was turning the events over in my head.

Morton joined in. 'He probably stuck it under yours on purpose.'

'Bastard!' My anger was rising, as was my embarrassment. I examined my arm. Some bruises were coming up.

Sam wasn't happy. 'The police should arrest them. They should apologise for stealing your wallet.'

'I don't think that's going to happen anytime soon, Sam,' I replied, reminding myself that, unpleasant as it was, this was probably another of life's valuable lessons for him.

CHAPTER 36

Sam in charge

The next day, Matt, Sam and I flew to Mafia Island, while Morton stayed in Dar to sort out his upcoming trip down to Zimbabwe. We had selected Mafia, an island south-east of Dar off the Tanzanian coast, more on a whim than anything else: it sounded good in *Lonely Planet* and we could make endless jokes about Italian gangsters. We could have gone to Zanzibar, but we knew we were visiting there later when Heiress Film's camerawoman, Naomi, arrived, and Sam didn't want to go twice. He was now in charge, after all.

It had been over a week since I made my commitment to Morton to put Sam in charge. I had certainly increased the level of responsibility I was giving him, but still wasn't able to do it perfectly. Sometimes, for safety reasons, or even time management reasons, I just had to do things myself.

It was my natural inclination in this uncertain environment that I had purposefully placed the two of us in to be protective. Consciously I knew this, and I had to actively resist the urge. Since the new commitment, I'd become more focused on letting go. I also think it helped that I'd overtly made that commitment to Morton, and also to Matt, who'd been informed. I felt like I was being watched in how well I performed my role, which was a good thing.

Sam was making more decisions: what to eat, when to go, when to stop, how to get there, what to buy. I had to keep handing over the reins.

So, with Sam involved, we decided to go to Mafia. The ten-seater plane was the smallest Sam had ever been in. We flew over the tropical waters and landed on the island's tiny airstrip. Mafia, home to forty-five thousand people of mixed African, Arab and Indian descent, had been fought over for centuries due to its strategic position. The Arabs, Portuguese and various African tribes and kingdoms had held sway at different times, with vicious battles for supremacy and atrocities committed.

We found the single budget accommodation on the island and settled in. We were the only guests, and the first in over a week, despite the hostel's spectacular position on a beach-side precipice, with sweeping views across the Indian Ocean back towards the African mainland. The hostel manager said tourists were staying away because of the upcoming general election in Tanzania; people were spooked about potential political violence. Looking through the palm trees to the deserted beach below, it was hard to imagine significant activity here at all, let alone violence.

The three of us took a stroll down the beach. With the tide out, fishing boats were marooned by the receding waters, lying tilted on the sodden salty flats stretching away from the beach nearly to the horizon.

On the beach, fishermen mended their nets, children played with crab shells and old anchor chains, and women carted sacks of grain and buckets of fish on their heads. It felt like we were the only *wazungu* on the island.

We walked into Kilindoni, the capital, for lunch. We sat down in a dodgy and dimly lit bar, near empty, with white plastic tables and chairs on a concrete floor under a broad conical thatched roof. *Mayai na chippi* (eggs and chips) was the *plat du jour*. We ate our lunch while Matt tolerated the slurred rants of a local alcoholic on the scotch at midday, and I tried to decipher the persistent requests from a woman who clearly had some intellectual impairment. It appeared to me she probably had foetal alcohol syndrome. I eventually figured out she wanted me to take a photo of her so she could request some money from me for doing so. I relented.

I unsuccessfully looked for a wallet in the threadbare shops, to replace the one stolen in Dar, before we grabbed a *tut-tut* back to the hostel. The afternoon was idled away in chess, games of Five Hundred and reading. We watched the massive tide sweep in from the sea and pluck up the fishing boats from their resting positions, our footsteps from our midday stroll down the beach now three metres underwater.

The sun dived, dissolving into the mauve haze before reaching the horizon. We ate some decidedly good Indian seafood and slept well despite the echoes of village life outside the hostel walls: dogs barking, roosters crowing, the call to prayer through crackling speakers at dawn and laughter on the sand-lined streets.

Our second mellow day in Mafia began with some much-appreciated free time for me. While Matt and Sam played chess at the hostel, I headed down to a pier shooting off from Kilindoni and strolled the two-kilometre stretch of sun-bleached grey boards, out to an open and unfenced twenty-metre-wide platform at the end.

I was the only person on the entire length of the pier.

A fishing boat, its hull painted in red, yellow and black stripes, with SURE BOYS in large white letters on the free board, rounded the pier and headed towards the village. It was packed to overflowing with men, ropes, boxes and plastic crates. The crew waved to the *mzungu* sitting alone on the platform in the wind, probably thinking I was very odd, even for a *mzungu*.

Thirty metres below me, a one-armed man snorkelled with a spear gun in the deep waters around the great pylons of the pier, which were cloaked in orange kelp below the waterline. I could see no way he could climb up onto the pier, so I guessed he had a long swim back into town when he was finished. I was worried just watching him, but he probably did this every day.

Buffeted by strong winds, I sat in the centre of the platform and looked out to the endless Indian Ocean. An eerie feeling swept over me. I reminded myself it would be very foolish to plummet off the platform. I didn't know why I would ever fall off, but I reminded myself just the same.

When I returned, batteries recharged and thankful to Matt for my ticket-of-leave, the three of us walked along the beach to Kilindoni again, with the intention of catching a local minibus across the island to the ferry to Chole, the ancient capital, which sat on a tiny island off the south coast of Mafia and was now home to all the ritzy resorts.

The bus was filled with Islamic women and children, adorned in colourful robes highlighted with sparkling jewellery and metal threads. After a one-hour drive to the 'ferry'—a four-metre runabout with an outboard motor—we were on our way across the emerald waters to Chole.

As we chugged along, the sea breeze buffeting us, Matt turned to me. 'Sam is pretty chilled. I don't know how my kids would go if I got them to do this sort of stuff.'

I smiled. 'Oh yes, travel doesn't faze him at all these days.'

We jumped into the warm shallows and waded ashore, shoes in hand. We walked around ruins of nineteenth-century gaols and administrative headquarters, the stone buildings now only held together by the strangler figs growing in their courtyards. I pretended I was stuck behind the bars of a derelict gaol.

Sam pointed and grinned. 'It is Azkaban!' The prison in Harry Potter was probably much more secure than this one.

We looped back through a cute village with no roads, only walking tracks. In the primary school, a baobab dominated the grassed playground, and children in white shirts and emerald-coloured pants and skirts gazed and giggled at the *wazungu*.

That evening, on the hostel verandah, we once again watched the tide come in while we played chess and practised juggling and catching.

'I've never learnt to juggle,' Matt observed.

'It's not a skill that's normally required in surgery,' I reflected.

It was another spectacular sunset, the sky lit high in crimsons and pinks, reflecting on the water like a Turner seascape. We all just looked. Nobody spoke. My heart rate was possibly the slowest it had been the entire trip. Perhaps, as the journey drew to a close, I was finally adapting to the African pace.

Perhaps. That night my heart rate was not so slow. Booming reggae and African dance music thumped across the village all night. We would later learn that it was a wedding, which I suppose made us feel a little more conciliatory It stopped at four a.m. but then restarted, much to my and Sam's annoyance, twenty minutes later. It wasn't like you could call the police to complain. Just before dawn, the music competed with the call to prayers from the mosque. It made for an interesting contrast in vocals. At least I couldn't hear the mosquitoes hovering inside my net.

We reluctantly left Mafia and flew back to Dar. Matt took a second flight to Zanzibar, where we would meet him in a couple of days. I met Naomi, the new camerawoman from Heiress, at the airport and we caught a cab together back to our hotel, where Naomi struggled with her jetlag and Sam got used to the fact that she wasn't Max.

The next morning Naomi, feeling human again after a decent sleep, got to work. I'd forgotten what it was like to be under the microscope. Probing interviews, retakes and waiting for shots to be set up became part of our day once more. Like Max, Naomi did what she needed to do while remaining respectful of Sam, cognisant that it was indeed a burden but an unavoidable one.

We vanished into the crowds of the market area again, the site of the theft of my wallet. I was still nursing the bruises from that visit but we thought it might provide some interesting footage. The streets were lined with mats and sheets covered in shoes, belts, books and jewellery. Motorbikes and *tut-tuts* slipped through the maze of people and wares. Bowls and bales were carried on bobbing heads. And a thousand colours exploded everywhere we looked: in the spices, the haberdashery on display and the hijabs and buibuis women wore.

Shopkeepers sang to the streets, music blared from speakers, megaphones competed to send out messages from politicians atop political party trucks and from mullahs atop mosques. Corn roasted on coal fires, and peanuts boiled in gas-fired pots. And we didn't get robbed.

The next day an American woman sat next to us at breakfast and Sam spontaneously started up a conversation with her. 'How old are you?'

Taken aback, she smiled. 'How old do you think I am?'

He thought about it. 'Twenty?'

She was happy with his estimation. 'Hah! Unfortunately, I'm a fair bit older that that!'

Sam replied quickly. 'Forty?'

There was no way she was forty. I jumped in. 'Sam! It's rude to talk about women's ages.'

Sam paused and looked at her again. 'She's not wearing a bra.'

Oh crap. '*Sam!*' I yelled.

'Well, she's not,' he protested.

'Sam, I think you've finished breakfast.' I bundled him out of the dining room, Naomi and her camera in tow.

We were finally going to Zanzibar. I was looking forward to visiting the fabled island, and Sam was looking forward to getting to our last destination. We packed our bags, and Morton, who'd been staying with friends up the road, decided to rejoin us for a few days in Zanzibar. At the time of independence in 1961, the old British protectorates of Tanganyika and Zanzibar were independent countries. A few years later they formed a union, leading to the name Tanzania, but Zanzibar has long been considered to have different cultural and political characteristics to the mainland.

The modern ferry, carting hundreds of passengers, a mixture of *wazungu* tourists, local business folk and families, skipped across the Zanzibar Channel in ninety minutes. We trundled up the gangway to the chaotic customs area. Sam and I approached the counter.

'Passports,' the official barked. I handed them over.

'Yellow fever certificates.'

'I don't have them here,' I explained. 'They're back at the hotel we were staying at in Dar, in storage. I didn't think we would need them given you have to present them to get into Tanzania.'

The official frowned. 'This is a problem.' He spoke to a nearby female official in Swahili and she approached us. 'You must follow me.' She marched us through the crowd and we entered a quiet glass-enclosed room, sectioned off from the chaos of the crowd outside the windows.

'You must understand you have only two options,' she said. 'By WHO regulations, if you do not have physical evidence of a yellow fever vaccination, we cannot let you into the country. Zanzibar is an independent country. Your other option is we take you to the department of health and you both receive another vaccination, which is not harmful even if you have had a previous vaccination. This will cost you seventy US dollars each.'

'Can I telephone the hotel and get them to find the certificates, take a photo and send it to my phone? That is physical evidence,' I said.

She responded curtly. 'No, I do not have time for that. I am going home soon.'

I thought to myself that that was an odd thing to say.

Sam wasn't happy. 'I don't want another needle. I don't want to go back.'

The official looked at me. 'You must help me solve this problem.'
The penny dropped. I'd heard *that* phrase before.

'Will money help?' I reluctantly asked.

'How much money?'

I thought about it. 'How about twenty US dollars for both of us.'

'I can't hear you.'

The hide! I carefully replied, 'Thirty US dollars, and I'm now speaking very loudly.'

She opened the top drawer of the desk she was sitting behind. I now noticed she had strategically positioned my chair so that I was sitting near the drawer. This was a well-practised routine. I slipped the money into the drawer and she closed it. She leant forward and looked me in the eye. 'You must not tell anybody about this. I like my job.'

'No problem.' I said. But what I thought was, *Well, you are ripping me off.*

Meanwhile and unbeknownst to me, Naomi had been filming through the window the entire time. I was also wearing a microphone, which I'd completely forgotten about in the kerfuffle, so the entire interaction had been recorded.

We got through customs, as did Morton, who went through the same process in the glass-enclosed room and slammed his twenty US dollars on the woman's desk. We rejoined Matt as we left the building and entered the glare, dust and archaic beauty of Stone Town, the capital of Zanzibar.

Matt had organised our hotel room for us and we settled in before heading out for dinner in Forodhani Gardens. The gardens were a short stroll from our hotel, through narrow winding alleyways lined with stone buildings. Large, dark wooden doors were capped with elaborate carved motifs in squared or semicircular friezes, reflecting Omani Arabic and Indian influences respectively. Many of the doors dated back hundreds of years, and some had large wooden or copper spikes protruding from the panels, designed to stop elephants knocking them down. Not something you usually have to worry about in Sydney.

We arrived at the gardens before sunset. Stone Town is set on a rounded protrusion from the island, and the gardens sat at the furthest point. From the sea-wall perimeter African teenagers took flying leaps into the water.

Sam was laughing at each jump. 'I want to go in.'

'No, Sam, you'll get your clothes wet and we don't have any others with us,' I replied.

Matt nodded his head sideways towards the water. 'You should let him go in.'

I thought about it. But it was dangerous, what with the boys landing on top of each other in the water. Sam might also attract some unwanted competitive attention from them given he was the only *mzungu*. He took some convincing but eventually relented. It was, however, pleasing that he *wanted* to do it, reflecting his growing confidence in grabbing new experiences.

As Naomi was filming Sam and me, she was approached by a plain-clothes police officer, who showed us his ID and promptly marched her off to a mobile police station at the edge of the park. We followed to give moral support.

At the police station, Naomi received a stern lecture about not filming in the park without a permit, and she dutifully acted chastened, telling them it was for personal use and she had only been filming for five minutes. Eventually the policeman let her leave with a caution, feeling he had done his duty.

'Why do you need a permit?' I asked Naomi.

'Oh, it's all about money. Maybe you don't even need a permit, and he was just trying to scam some money out of me. It might be a per hour thing, that's why I said I'd only filmed five minutes.'

'This has happened to you before, hasn't it?'

Naomi, who had spent many months in Africa on an earlier assignment, nodded. 'Ooh yes, many times.'

Sam was excited. 'Naomi got arrested!'

'No, Sam, she wasn't arrested,' I clarified, but it was sometimes hard to explain the difference.

After sunset, we grabbed some pizzas and seafood kebabs from the trestle tables surrounding barbecues in the centre of the park. Locals and tourists shared the space, which had a vibrant and relaxed feel. We sat on the sea wall with our paper plates and watched the world go by as a quiet moon rose over the strait.

CHAPTER 37

Zanzibar

The next day, our first full one in Stone Town, was a relaxed affair. Sam and I took off on our own, wandering the narrow labyrinthine streets where grapevines and bougainvillea canopies gave relief from the heat, moss- and lichen-covered plaster crumbled off the red-coral-rock walls, and conversations echoed from dark entrances and shuttered windows, while phone and electrical wires tangled around gutters and across roofs. In one place entire walls had collapsed into an empty building. As Matt would comment later, it seemed like the whole place was slowly and gracefully falling down.

We purposefully got lost in the old city. Each corner could reveal a sun-bleached small square, where a gathering of men discussed politics while sipping coffee sitting on *baraza*, the long stone benches outside of the buildings, wearing *kufis* (small white caps) and traditional long white robes. Young men sat astride their red Vespas chatting on mobiles, and clusters of schoolchildren scattered off to school or prayers, the girls with colourful *kangas* wrapped over their heads.

There were cats in doorways, latticed verandahs, horseshoe archways, carved wooden balustrades, and stairwells disappearing into shadows. Stone Town oozed mystery. It also promised excitement. As Major F.B. Pearce exclaimed in 1919, 'Over all there is the din of barter, of shouts from the harbour; the glamour of the sun, the magic of the sea and the rich savour of Eastern spice. This is Zanzibar!'

It seemed not much had changed, beyond the mobiles and the tourists.

We strolled the streets, drank coffee on cafe balconies, browsed the tourist shops and ducked and weaved to avoid the incessant hawkers, known as *papasi* (ticks), who were relentless in their attempts to winkle some shillings out of the *wazungu*. Sam and I played chess and cards, did some reading, writing and drawing, juggled and boxed. Sam read the whole of *Animal Farm*, his first non-Harry Potter book, while sitting in the stone amphitheatre in the centre of town. It was a good day in Africa for both of us.

In the evening, the five of us headed out to dinner in an upmarket restaurant, taking our seats on a balcony overlooking the narrow winding stone alley below. It was our last evening with Matt who was heading home early the next morning. An attractive African woman came over to take our order. Matt, Morton and Naomi placed their orders. The waitress turned to Sam. 'I'll have an African woman, please,' he stated, clearly and firmly. Matt shaded his eyes with his hand, Morton's head hit the table and Naomi burst out laughing. I jumped in to rescue the situation. 'He'll have a burger and chips, and so will I.' The woman just smiled and gently shook her head as she walked away.

The next morning Matt headed off to fly back to Australia. It had been great to have him around, and for Sam to encounter another familiar face. It was also good to have someone who had known Sam all his life observe his progress and participate in his adventure.

Sam, Morton, Naomi and I then got to work over breakfast, planning our time on Zanzibar, maps and the *Lonely Planet* guide sitting beside our coffee and toast. We allocated another day in Stone Town and three days travelling around the island. We thought hiring a car was probably the best option after leaving the city. Minibuses were possible, but accommodation in the rural areas was often hard to get to in places, especially with packs.

The rest of the day was more organised. Morton, Naomi, Sam and I booked a boat trip out to Prison Island, five kilometres offshore, and then a dhow cruise at sunset. With events piling up I reminded myself not to push Sam too hard in the middle of the day; it would be a lot for him to cope with.

The Arabs had isolated recalcitrant slaves on Prison Island. Later the British had erected a prison there but the buildings were never used for their intended purpose. Instead those on ships suspected of having yellow fever or cholera were quarantined there for a week or two, to protect Stone Town, then the busiest port in east Africa, from epidemics. More recently, its isolation has provided protection for another species, the Aldabra giant sea tortoises of the Indian Ocean.

Previously widespread but then nearly hunted into extinction in the nineteenth century, the tortoises are now only found naturally in the wild on one atoll in the Seychelles. In 1919, four specimens were gifted to Zanzibar by the British governor of the Seychelles, and they were kept on Prison Island. Isolated and protected, their numbers quickly increased. In the late twentieth century, however, poaching dramatically reduced the population, nearly wiping out the colony, before a secure enclosure allowed the tortoises to thrive once again.

Sam was fascinated by the huge beasts, which can weigh more than two hundred and fifty kilograms and have amazing longevity. One specimen on Prison Island was 192 years old.

'What do you think of that, Sam?' Naomi asked.

'That means he was born in 1823,' he replied. 'He was born before the American Civil War.' Naomi was impressed with Sam's history knowledge. All those conversations we'd had at the back of buses were paying off.

We had unfettered access to the animals, and Sam was brave enough to gently stroke one old timer's head, which apparently they liked. Unfortunately, an idiotic tourist stood astride one of the tortoises, which we'd been unambiguously instructed not to do as it distresses them. I thought the South African curator was going to explode. 'Get off that tortoise now!' He told us he'd had to put a tortoise down a few years earlier when some clown stood on its shell and broke it.

The dhow cruise was a much more laidback affair. The elegant sailing ships are masterpieces of simple design. A single triangular sail was rolled and tied to a long yard, mounted at an angle on the mast. By adjusting the angle of the yard and the sail with two simple ropes on each end of the yard, the sailor can easily adjust direction and speed, including being able to tack into the wind. It was like a giant windsurfer, or more correctly, a windsurfer was like a mini dhow; dhows have been around the coastlines of eastern Africa, Arabia and India for thousands of years.

Sam chilled as we glided along in the waters beside Stone Town, our taut and trim sail a cream obtuse triangle floating on the jade waters. He draped his fingers over the gunwale, trailing a white V in the sea water. His floppy hat, which we had bought way back at Guma Lagoon Camp on the Okavango Delta, blew off his head and landed in the water, beyond my reach in a flash. Another item to add to the list of the lost, broken and missing in action. Well, at least our packs were getting lighter.

That evening, Morton, Naomi, Sam and I went to an Indian restaurant where the food was excellent, the electricity supply intermittent, and Sam's behaviour, to put it in his words, 'disappointing'. I think he'd picked up that adjective from his mother. The source of the dispute was that Sam wanted all of the garlic naans and none of the curries, a point on which he proved inflexible. I finally had to pull the plug and leave early so the rest of the restaurant could eat in peace. I think the heavily scheduled day had knocked him around: three boat rides, lots of sun and too much novelty. Maybe a curry was a bridge too far.

In the morning we bade goodbye to Morton, after nearly a month travelling together. He had been a terrific ally and good friend to both Sam and me. Coming into our lives when he did was perfect timing, as I was really flagging at that time. After he departed, it was down to Naomi, Sam and me. We were on the road again, but for the first time in almost six months I was doing the driving. We hired a small Suzuki four-wheel drive and drove north out of Stone Town. But finding a petrol station immediately proved to be a challenge, given the African penchant for vague directions.

'Yes, turn left down there,' we were told, followed by a sweeping wave off into the distance.

'It is some kilometres,' was another response.

'Yes, we have one. It is close around here.'

The driving also proved challenging. I warned Naomi my plan was to give way to everybody.

Leaving urbane Stone Town, we headed north through plantings of coconuts, bananas, avocados and jackfruits, the latter's bulbous forms heavy on the branches. Rainstorms and glaring sun reminded us how close we were to the equator. Young schoolgirls walked past in matching veils, drenched but unfazed.

We were approaching the northern tip of the island when a turn-off to a beach appeared on our left. I pulled up to have a look around.

On the beach stood a young lad, probably close to Sam's age but half his weight, standing tall in a high-buttoned shirt. He stepped forward. 'Sir, I am Ishmael. I would like to act as your guide, if you would like. There are some nearby historical ruins.'

'How much?' I replied.

'Two dollars,' Ishmael said, carefully, 'but if you don't want to pay, that is all right.'

I was stumped by Ishmael's honesty. Meanwhile his friends were mocking and imitating Sam, who was excited and jumping around. I became irritated until I realised they were imitating all three of us. I guess we were novelties, after all.

Ishmael walked us down the beach and then across to a nearby decaying coral-stone building. Ishmael told us that the house had been built by Portuguese traders in the fifteenth or sixteenth century. 'They lived here for a few hundred years. They traded metal materials for spices and ivory.' His account was backed up by some official signs around the site. I was not only impressed by Ishmael's English and his knowledge but his delivery. He was a bright spark all right.

I was also impressed by the ruins, and tried to convey a historical picture to Sam. 'Imagine, Sam, living back here in the sixteen hundreds, where the only people you would know would be in this house, and it would be years and years before you would see any of your own people.'

Sam looked out the corner of his eye in his enigmatic way. 'Yeah.'

On the way back to the car Ishmael told me he wanted to be a doctor. 'I want to help people. I want to help women and babies who are dying when they shouldn't be dying.'

'I'm a doctor,' I said.

'Oh, really?' Ishmael's eyes lit up. 'You have studied mathematics, and physics, and chemistry? These things?'

I smiled at his enthusiasm. 'Yes, sure.'

'Oh, I want to study these things,' he lamented.

'I really hope you get to do this. I think you would make a good doctor,' I said, meaning it.

In Africa, however, so much talent goes untapped.

As we arrived at the tip and headed down the east coast, surf beaches stretched out before us, lined with five-star resorts. This was the other major tourist attraction in Zanzibar besides the history and culture of Stone Town: the natural beauty of the beaches on the east coast. However, as we hit the intersection to the road heading down the coast, our trip hit a snag.

We had already gone through three police checks since leaving Stone Town. In general, African police and army checkpoints are uncertain affairs; you never know whether you are going to be met with a smile or a scowl. Many officials seem overly fond of their uniforms and the authority that comes with them.

Here a single soldier stood at the intersection, holding his machine gun. He stood in the middle of the road as I drove up and signalled for us to stop. He approached Naomi on the passenger side of the car and she rolled down the window.

'Put your seatbelt up over your shoulder,' he snapped. 'You are not wearing your seatbelt correctly.'

We had a scowler.

Naomi nodded and adjusted her seatbelt, which she'd had under her arm to allow her to manoeuvre the camera more effectively. He checked the insurance stickers on the windscreen. Then he walked towards my open window and thrust out his hand. 'Papers!' I handed him my international driving licence and car registration papers.

He looked at the papers with a frown. 'Are you a good driver?'

'Yes,' I replied, my voice rising a few octaves.

'No, you're not. You're a bad driver,' he snapped.

Sam piped up from the back seat. 'No, Dad! You're a good driver.'

'Sam, be quiet!' I hissed out of the corner of my mouth.

The soldier glared at Sam before turning back to me. 'You did not indicate when pulling off the road, and your passenger was not wearing her seatbelt correctly. You are a bad driver.'

'Yes, sir,' I agreed, willing Sam to keep quiet.

He stood for a long time reading our papers, which really didn't have much information on them to read. Finally he looked at me. 'Why did you not indicate?'

'We don't use indicators in Australia,' I lied, although it did seem overkill to indicate when you'd been specifically directed by an official to the side of the road in the middle of nowhere.

He shook his finger at me. 'This will cost you one hundred and fifty dollars. You understand?'

'Yes, sir.'

He pulled his ticket book out of his pocket and pushed it towards me. 'So you will have to go to court and pay this money. When do you fly home?'

'In a week,' I said.

'Hmm.' He didn't seem happy with that. A pause, then, 'What are we going to do about this?'

Naomi and I both recognised the language; this was a set-up for another bribe. I was getting heartily sick of this and was reluctant to cave in too quickly. He repeated again. 'Well, what can *you* do to help me solve this problem?'

Looking back and forward to Naomi, I pretended to be confused. 'I'm not sure. What are you suggesting? Do you want me to apologise? If I have to pay a fine, I have to pay a fine.'

Naomi joined in. 'I'm not sure either. I can't think of anything that will help.'

His frustration was rising at our apparent stupidity. If it wasn't for the fact that I didn't want to land Sam in a potentially dangerous situation I'd have been tempted to call his bluff. But not today. As he reached for his pen and started to write on the ticket pad, I pulled out my wallet. 'Will some money help?'

'How much?' I opened my wallet, where the equivalent of twenty US dollars was visible. I'd learnt this was the amount you should always have in your fake wallet: enough to satisfy most extorters, but only just enough.

He nodded. 'That will do.'

'What a dick!' Naomi said, as soon as we had pulled away and were out of earshot.

Sam was unhappy. 'You're not a bad driver. The police officer is wrong.'

I smiled. 'He was just trying to get money out of me, Sam. He's a corrupt policeman.' Sam was familiar with the word corrupt from computer programs. It's not often a boy Sam's age gets to witness official corruption firsthand. He talked about it for days.

CHAPTER 38

A boy to a person

The next day we cruised further down the east coast. The beaches were magnificent, picture-postcard perfect. Lagoons were reticulated with swirls of seaweed that was being harvested by local women. Distant reefs were marked by breaking surf, coconut palms swayed in the breeze and time slowed, defined merely by the inclination of the sun.

Further south the lagoons disappeared and the gentle surf splashed onto the beach. After stopping for a coffee for me and a Sprite for Sam at a particularly nice five-star hotel perched on a giant coral rock hanging over the creamed-honey shallows, Sam decided he liked Zanzibar. So did I, despite being ripped off twice.

Sam glanced around the hotel. 'Let's stay here.'

'No, Sam,' I said, 'we can't afford to stay here.'

Sam thought about it for a second. 'Let's go to the bank and get some money.'

'No, it doesn't work that way,' I explained. 'We only have so much money left, and it's got to last until we get home.'

'Hmm, okay,' he grumbled.

We looped south on our final full day on Zanzibar. After a quick tour through a monkey sanctuary in a red mahogany forest we were back to the crazy streets of the capital. The driving became challenging again. Increasingly narrow streets sometimes ran unexpectedly into dead ends, or we came face to face with another vehicle. In a tiny lane we encountered a cart piled with thirteen mattresses pulled by a lean and wiry local. I had no choice but to reverse the Suzuki.

Sam seemed a bit off-colour through the day and hardly ate any food. I took him to Mercury's, a pizza restaurant on the foreshore named after Freddie Mercury, the lead singer of Queen, who was born in Zanzibar before emigrating to the United Kingdom in his teens. Sam only ate half a pizza, way below par for him, and then sat for ten minutes in the toilet deciding whether he would vomit or not. Fortunately, the nausea passed and we headed for the hotel. I wondered if he was getting sick again but it didn't return.

The return to Dar on the ferry was uneventful and we headed for our hotel. There would be no more travel until we left.

Naomi headed off to the airport the next day. Sam and I would be here three more days. For the first time in the heaving city we were alone. Sometimes solitude seems more profound the more people you have around you; we were surrounded by three million souls but connected to none of them. Like so often before in the trip, it was just Sam and me, lonely as two clouds. After constant probing questions from Naomi on interviews to camera, I was a kaleidoscope of emotions.

Sam sensed the solitude too, but also the significance of the moment; the realisation we had arrived at the point where there was nothing more to do than go home. I began to again look at Africa with the eyes of an outsider. At some time during the preceding six months it had become so familiar that I'd stopped noticing it; I, and perhaps also Sam, had become immune to its chaos.

Outside the hotel, a group of young men, all dressed in red, were jogging in time while chanting in deep sonorous tones. A political rally or a religious ceremony? No, they were just exercising. A shirtless middle-aged man stood on a street corner, furiously drumming with his neck extended and eyes closed in concentration, sweating in the equatorial sun while the rest of the street ignored him. Conductors shouted out of the open sliding doors of minibuses as they neared a bus station, crackling political slogans echoed through the streets, swirling in the auditory soup of engine noise, horns and chatter.

Sam and I walked down the footpath, sweating and on alert in the glare, watching our feet to avoid puddles, rubbish, mud and the occasional beggar. The latter would thrust out a bored hand and mumble 'Friend', or '*Mumbo*', as I scanned their body to assess their particular tragic circumstance. Deformity, amputation, paralysis or perhaps just being very old or very young—the more visible the tragedy, the more effective the plea.

I focused on Sam. Chess, cards, writing, reading, drawing and talking.

I was also looking at him a lot, which annoyed him. 'Why are you looking at me?' he asked.

I smiled. 'I'm just wondering if you're different to how you were before the trip.'

'Yes, I am,' he stated forthrightly.

'How?' I asked.

He paused for a moment. 'I've changed from a boy to a person.'

Interesting. I pushed him, but he couldn't elaborate. It suggested to me his insight into the purpose of what we were doing was profound. I was proud of my young man.

I continued to try to step outside myself and observe him as objectively as I could, while trying to remember what he'd been like in Cape Town, in Hermanus, in Durban. Yes, he was more self-reliant, more confident, more independent. As he crossed the road, ordered a meal, ate the meal, chatted with me, I could see he had progressed. I started to look forward to Sydney. What would Benison notice? Our family and friends? His school?

Would he go back into his shell? A shiver went down my spine at the thought.

We packed our bags for the last time. Given we had lost or broken half our possessions, we had plenty of room for souvenirs bought at nearby markets: Tingatinga paintings, carved ebony statues of Maasai heads, and handcrafted jewellery.

We walked around the dirt-floored market. Sam was quiet and reflective, but then would suddenly smile to himself. 'Stop looking at me,' he said again.

'What are you smiling about?' I asked.

'Home,' he said, beaming.

I smiled too.

It was time. I had given it my all, and Sam had done brilliantly. As I packed our bags, I was also packing away my emotions. My mind was swirling with anxiety, pride, regret, relief, fear, but mostly joy.

A series of lasts: our last night, our last meal, our last walk on an African street, and finally our last cab. I was on the verge of tears as we piled into the taxi for the trip to the airport. The cabbie, oblivious, nattered about Tanzanian politics, food and the bloody Dar traffic. Thanks to a delayed flight we missed our connection to Perth and Sam kipped for a few hours of the floor of Jo'burg airport. Then, after thirty hours of travel and two nights in the air, six months to the day since we'd left, we were home.

We spied the familiar skyline of Sydney as we arced over the emerald city, shimmering in the dawn light, and finally the exhausted ragtag travellers fell into the arms of Benison . . . and the Heiress film crew.

'Can we just film that reunion scene again?' the cameraman asked. Ah yes, nothing about this trip had been ordinary.

CHAPTER 39

Life skills

As we emerged from our jetlag over the next couple of days, there were three occasions where Sam's progress was evident.

First, Benison, Sam and I went shopping. We sat down for a coffee in the local shopping centre, the glare of the artificial lights reminding me of Nancy, the lovely Ugandan in Kapchorwa; there were no live chickens for sale in Norton Plaza, Leichhardt. It seemed somewhat the poorer for it.

Sam piped up. 'I want a Sprite.'

Benison rose to buy him one, but I grabbed her arm to stop her. Sam headed off to the shop by himself after requesting some money from me. She watched him as he stood at the shop counter waiting to be served.

'Yep, it's there, he's changed,' she said. 'And his speech is different.'

'I just hope it doesn't go away,' I replied.

She frowned. 'We just have to keep pushing.'

The following day my mother and sisters hosted a welcome home. Sam did his usual trick of hanging out in the bedroom with my nephew's electronic games, but he emerged when the barbecue meal was served, sat at the table and chatted about Africa. And chatted, and chatted, and chatted. I was now used to this, but my family wasn't. My sister, Mary-Anne, turned to me and smiled; I knew what she was thinking.

A few days later we rocked up to the school to meet the principal and Sam's learning support teacher, to sort out Sam's re-entry into year eight. The whole experience contrasted with previous school orientations prior to our trip. Sitting in the front office waiting for the meeting, greeting the teachers and chatting about his trip, observing the other children in the playground, waiting while Benison and I discussed some of the practicalities of his return to the school; he was, well, just *different*. Easier, calmer, more regulated, more of a 'person' perhaps.

There were other little snippets of progress. One afternoon after school, I sent him into a local butcher shop to buy some meat for dinner while I stood back and observed. The woman behind the counter was very offhand with him. When we left the shop, he turned to me and said, 'They weren't very friendly, were they?' When someone with autism comments on your lack of social skills, you know you have a problem!

Yet for all that, Sam is still 'autistic'—still too obsessional and lacking social graces. The thing is, I no longer mind. Benison and I have grown fond of his quirkiness, his oddity, his difference. I never want Sam to be anything or anybody other than Sam, and autism is a central part of his makeup. I don't hate or resent autism, and I never will.

We still need to wait to see what the Griffith University researchers will find, whether they will observe, in a clinical sense, that the intervention has 'worked'.

Yet in a wider context, what does it all mean? What does it mean for others? We haven't found a cure for autism. Sam and I have, however, *contributed*. We were two foot soldiers in the great unremitting army of science, marching along—sometimes stumbling—but doing our bit. I feel what we have done will, in an unorthodox way, expand understanding of autism in adolescence. There will need to be further study, further exploration of these concepts, but we had made the first tentative start.

Personally, and in a completely unscientific fashion, I believe that his experiences in Africa reduced Sam's disability in ways that will translate to life in Australia and the developed world. We owe the continent a big whopping thank you.

Africa, oh mother Africa. Sam's alma mater. It had started in my mind as a mysterious, magical place and finished even more so. Six months on the road and I felt like we had barely scratched the surface of a full understanding of its quirks, its oddities and charms. Endless in scope and depth, it seemed so much more interesting than normal life. Maybe that was just because we were travelling, not working or studying, but I think it was more than that.

As I said to Benison, staring out a bus window in Africa was the best reality TV show you could ever watch. See a bus being pulled out of a ditch by a herd of cattle roped together, a group of Maasai warriors playing bao at a bus stop, people on the sidewalks dancing and clapping in rhythm for no apparent reason.

I was struck by reverse culture shock; I found myself continually stunned at how 'developed world' Australia was. Everything worked, everything was clean, everything was efficient, and everyone was just so *tense*. At Perth airport, I found the terminal too clean; it looked sterile. On leaving, I stepped back in surprise as the automated doors opened on my approach. While crossing the road, a car actually stopped for me as I approached the pedestrian crossing, but the driver frowned in irritation that I'd halted his progress for a few measly seconds. I would miss the smiles, the long handshakes, the ongoing greetings and blessings, the jokes, the back slaps, the laughter and the banter, the bonhomie; just the sheer *craziness* of the place. I wouldn't miss the constant anxiety of not knowing what was going on, the gut-wrenching worry about Sam, the pressure of keeping everything going, the roads, the filth, the mosquitoes. Yes, it had been tough all right, but we had come through unscathed, and both Sam and I had been significantly moulded by the experience, and for the better.

Over the first few weeks after our return, some of Sam's old undesirable habits returned straightaway, but then seemed to evaporate again, as if he'd realised that they were not a necessary part of him anymore. Lying on the floor in a school classroom, letting someone else escort him across a road, passively waiting for the world to come to him rather than actively turning it the other way around: he had left these things behind. He had changed; I really had no doubts now.

I will leave the last hoorah to Sam, who is now, in his parlance, more of a person.

Hi, this is Sam and I'll tell you about my African trip.
The big fact of my African trip is I've been to ten countries
in six months and I have just ended the trip. The reason
that I had to go to Africa is to learn about Africa and lots
of other things like talking to people and organising things.
I have met a lot of people such as tourists and locals but
unfortunately some places only had locals which is not fair.

I was very unhappy when the Malawi preschool children try to scare the chicken away. I think this is animal cruelty so the Malawi woman and children are sometimes cruel to animals.

I only had been to McDonald's two times in the whole African trip. Dad and I have been robbed once in Dar es Salaam which was very nasty. I have seen all of the animals except for gorillas. I have done white-water rafting which was crazy fun and on a helicopter which was cool.

Bad things included getting sick in Uganda (I had to go to the hospital) and scary stuff like bad places like Zimbabwe.

I am now a smart person because I learnt lots of stuff such as the actual noise of the hippopotamus. I've used the million number dollar notes in Zimbabwe. We went to the biggest African airport which is in Johannesburg which is in South Africa and it is also the last place of Africa we have seen before going back to Australia. I met lots of people and I am now a famous boy. I am now home at Sydney but we have to go to Perth first then back to Sydney so it took thirty hours to get back to Sydney.

Overall the trip helped me because it taught me life skills. I like this.
Cheers Sam xx

P.S. Next time I might learn some life skills in Japan. Maybe or maybe not.

Epilogue

As I write this, eighteen months have elapsed since Sam and I stepped off the plane at Sydney's Kingsford Smith Airport as travel-hardened Africa veterans, and less than a week since we returned from our second trip to Africa, this time with Benison accompanying us for the first time.

The recent trip was just a family holiday—two weeks in South Africa and Namibia, rather than ten countries and six months on the road.

In some ways, however, it presented as a microcosm of the first, Sam initially anxious and counting down the days until our return to Australia, then relaxing into the vibe of Africa and becoming open again to new experiences.

However, the anxiety and stress that he had endured in 2015, particularly in South Africa and Namibia, was far, far less evident this trip.

Familiar folk we encountered remarked on the difference in Sam. Lee, the manager of The Backpacker in Cape Town, sat down with Sam for an interview in front of the video camera. Sam fired off question after question for minutes, until I had to stop him and tell him to wind it up.

I thought back to the interviews we'd struggled over in the early months of 2015. The thirty-second pauses, Sam scrambling to think of ten questions to ask, his inability to follow a lead in the conversation.

Lee was stunned. 'He couldn't talk anything like that before. He couldn't even keep still.'

A week later, at breakfast on our first morning at Chameleon Backpackers in Windhoek, we ran into one of their drivers, Fernando, the same one who'd picked Sam and me up from the airport on our first visit to Windhoek in 2015.

'He is much better now,' Fernando said without prompting. 'He is much calmer than the last time.'

Benison and I shared a look of satisfaction. 'Yes,' I replied, 'he seems to be enjoying this trip much more.'

We were worried, you see, that much of the hard work of that earlier trip had been undone by the realities of life back in Sydney. The year 2016 was a difficult one for our family, and as Benison and I dived back into our workaday lives we just didn't have the time and energy to focus so totally on Sam.

Fortunately for us, we stumbled across an amazing teacher's aide, Virginia, who we employed privately two days a week to support Sam at school. Virginia had worked as a behavioural therapist with children with autism previously but, more importantly, just *got* Sam and his needs.

Throughout the past year, Virginia has built on the hard work Sam and I put in during our first African trip, extending him further and encouraging independence. She has engineered conversations between Sam and all his teachers, coordinated movie dates with his peers and supervised his work experience placement at Target. In short, she's been a life saver.

⁂

On the final afternoon of last week's holiday, we visited an animal sanctuary an hour's drive from Windhoek. Sam, who'd been whinging all morning about going, ended up loving it. 'Things go fast when you enjoy yourself,' he said.

'Yes,' Benison explained. 'There's an expression for that: Time flies when you're having fun.'

As we were preparing to leave the next morning for the airport, I filmed Sam having one last conversation with Rosa, a staff member at Chameleon. Sam had spoken to Rosa on our first visit, once again in front of the camera. She was astonished at the difference as he casually chatted with her about her family and work. She asked whether we had been doing a lot of therapy of some sort. Well, yes, we had, of course.

On arriving back home in Sydney, I checked my emails, and was stoked to receive one that Benison and I had been sweating on for a while. It was from David Trembath, the Griffith University researcher, outlining the preliminary results from his research on the video interviews recorded with Sam during 2015.

A comparison of the videos taken early and late in the trip demonstrated that speech skills critical to good conversations— such as staying on topic, body position and eye contact—all increased in Sam over the course of the six months, while abrupt changes in topic reduced. One key parameter, 'cues from Dad', dropped from twenty per cent of conversations early in the trip to zero later in the trip. The research's conclusion was that 'the journey was associated with positive changes in social-communication skills.'

That is, it worked.

For all that, Sam remains Sam. He still talks way too loud, and way too much about his obsessions (currently Tintin and 1980s children's videos, but no doubt that will change). He still doesn't get that it's not a great idea to comment on all the 'black people' in South Africa! While he's holding his own in maths, school work presents an increasing challenge. And while we've been teaching him about sarcasm and idioms, he can still be delightfully literal.

One night in Stellenbosch, the picture-postcard perfect university town in the wine region near Cape Town, Sam scanned our dinner menu, then looked up at us with a slightly pained expression on his face. 'There is nothing here I want to eat.'

'Yes, there is,' I said. 'What about the Monster Burger?'

Then it dawned on Benison and me. 'Sam, it's not a burger made from monsters. "Monster" just means it's big.'

'Oh,' said Sam, with visible relief. When his monster-sized beef burger arrived he happily chowed it down.

Africa was good for Sam, good for me. Part of me wants us to remain there forever, but we have two other sons in Australia who need us, aging parents and work commitments. The challenge will be to sustain the good work, to somehow recreate our own Africa at home, to challenge Sam to embrace independence and to get the most possible out of life.

He remains a work in progress.

Acknowledgements

This book only exists because of the astute judgement of my literary agent, Jane Burridge, who saw its potential when she first heard of our planned adventure. My publisher, Jane Palfreyman of Allen & Unwin, has been unwavering in her support, and her editorial colleagues Christa Munns and Aziza Kuypers have done a magnificent job in realising its potential.

It should be acknowledged that this adventure was more than a book. Sam's progress was recorded and analysed by leading autism researcher Dr David Trembath, from Griffith University, and we are very grateful for his experience, knowledge and patience in guiding this research project to completion.

A special and heartfelt acknowledgement goes out to Jennifer Cummins and her team at Heiress Films, whose dedication to documenting this journey on film has been outstanding. The two producers who travelled to Africa with Sam and I, Max Bourke and Naomi Elkin-Jones, will always hold a special place in our hearts.

Also, a thank you is needed for hundreds of people who allowed themselves to be filmed with Sam. We were not refused on a single occasion.

On the road we met countless friendly fellow travellers, but I want to especially acknowledge Anka, Ed and Lana, Andy, Harri, my darling niece Juliette, Mike and Lenneke, Morton and Professor Matthew Rickard. We also stayed at many wonderful establishments, and our gratitude goes out to the staff of The Backpacker (Cape Town), Chameleon (Windhoek), Jollyboys (Livingstone), Jungle Junction (Zambezi River), Mabuya Camp (Lilongwe), Mushroom Farm (Livingstonia), Red Chilli (Kampala) and Noah's Arc (Kapchowra), as well as the many other places we stayed.

Throughout Africa, Sam and I were blown away by the relaxed and welcoming manner of the local people. A special mention goes out to Etienne, Petra and Michael, Godfrey and Manga, Onesmo, Mama Grace and Erick, Kerri, Sr Leonida and Jerimiah. Our travel guides made time to connect with Sam and I acknowledge the wonderful efforts of all of them, but in particular Gabriel, Milner, Tuhafeni, Juma, Joseph and Ian.

Thanks to the teaching and support staff at Sam's school, De La Salle College, Ashfield. They have been so supportive of Sam, before, during and after the trip.

Special thank you to my extended family for supporting Benison and my other sons while Sam and I were away. Particular gratitude goes to Roslyn and John Driscoll, without whom this trip would not have taken place, and Linda and Brendon Gregor, who backed us every step of the way. A big thanks also to Matthew and Nicholas, my older two boys, who also had to make many sacrifices for this 'mad' undertaking to occur, but never (or perhaps only rarely) complained, knowing of the importance of helping out Sam.

Finally, and most importantly, I would like to thank my wife, Benison O'Reilly. She is quite amazing, really. Her dedication and mother-love to Sam led to this quite extraordinary gift, and her superhuman resilience, intellect and compassion is what got us all through the process. She also gave me unending advice on the writing of this book; she is almost a co-author. Sam and I owe her so much, and we acknowledge her for the amazing person she is.

Resources

Temple Grandin, *Thinking in Pictures: And other reports from my life with autism*, Doubleday, New York, 1995.

Temple Grandin and Richard Panek, *The Autistic Brain: Thinking across the spectrum*, Houghton Mifflin Harcourt, Boston, 2013.

Roy Richard Grinker, *Unstrange Minds: Remapping the world of autism*, Basic Books, New York, 2007.

Lynn Kern Koegel and Clare LaZebnik, *Growing Up on the Spectrum: A guide to life, love and learning for teens and young adults with autism and Asperger's*, Penguin Books, New York, 2009.

Anthony Macris, *When Horse Became Saw: A family's journey through autism*, Penguin Books, Camberwell, Vic., 2012.

Kamran Nazeer, *Send in the Idiots: Stories from the other side of autism*, Bloomsbury Publishing, London, 2009.

Benison O'Reilly and Kathryn Wicks, *The Complete Autism Handbook (3rd edition)*, Ventura Press, Sydney, 2016.

John Elder Robison, *Look Me in the Eye: My life with Asperger's*, Crown Publishers, New York, 2007.

Steve Silberman, *Neurotribes: The legacy of autism and how to think smarter about people who think differently*, Allen & Unwin, London, 2016.

Andrew Solomon, *Far From the Tree: Parents, children and the search for identity*, Scribner, New York, 2012.

Barbara Strauch, *The Primal Teen: What the new discoveries about the teenage brain tell us about our kids*, Doubleday, New York, 2003.

Daniel Tammet, *Born on A Blue Day: Inside the extraordinary mind of an autistic savant*, Free Press, New York, 2007.

Michael Whelan, *The Other Country: A father's journey with autism*, Macmillan Australia, Melbourne, 2013.